Between Washington and Jerusalem

Between Washington and Jerusalem

A Reporter's Notebook

WOLF BLITZER

New York   Oxford
OXFORD UNIVERSITY PRESS
1985

Oxford University Press

Oxford   New York   Toronto
Delhi   Bombay   Calcutta   Madras   Karachi
Petaling   Jaya   Singapore   Hong Kong   Tokyo
Nairobi   Dar es Salaam   Cape Town
Melbourne   Auckland

and associated companies in
Beirut   Berlin   Ibadan   Nicosia

Library of Congress Cataloging in Publication Data
Blitzer, Wolf.
Between Washington and Jerusalem.
Includes index.
1. United States—Foreign relations—Israel.
2. Israel—Foreign relations—United States.
3. United States—Foreign relations—1945–
4. Jews—United States—Politics and government.
5. Blitzer, Wolf.   6. Foreign correspondents—
Washington (D.C.)—Biography.   7. United States—
Ethnic relations.   I. Title.
E183.8.I7B44   1985   327.7305694   85-15243
ISBN 0-19-503708-1

Printing (last digit): 9 8 7 6 5 4 3 2 1

Printed in the United States of America

To the Blitzers

Cesia and David
Lynn and Ilana

Preface

It was Wednesday, April 6, 1977. The Egyptian president, Anwar Sadat, had just wrapped up two days of talks with the new U.S. president, Jimmy Carter. In keeping with the custom in Washington, the Egyptian leader agreed to host a news conference at Blair House, the official residence for foreign guests located directly across Pennsylvania Avenue from the White House.

That day, Sadat was more impressive in person than he had been on television. He seemed taller and more handsome. He was dressed immaculately in a dark pinstriped suit. Though he started to sweat under the heat of the camera lights, he kept his cool in response to the questioning. He insisted that he was eager to make peace with Israel, if only Israel would agree to the establishment of a Palestinian state on the West Bank and Gaza. "Everything will be normalized after that," he said.

That one minor gesture suggested to some of us that perhaps a bit of a change was about to take place. Some fifty reporters had crowded into the relatively small living room at Blair House. In the past, the Egyptian embassy (as did other Arab embassies in Washington) restricted admission to press conferences to invited guests only, to avoid having to permit representatives of the Israeli news media to attend. Today, to its credit, the Egyptian embassy opened the news conference to the entire accredited White House press corps.

Before the question-and-answer period began, the Egyptian ambassador, Ashraf Ghorbal, asked reporters to identify themselves and their news organizations before they posed their questions to the president. When a well-known American journalist from one of the major television networks stood up and announced his name and affiliation, Sadat nodded his head in acknowledgment, puffing on his ever-present pipe. "Go ahead," he said, clearly pleased by all the attention.

Near the end of the news conference, I raised my hand. To my surprise, Ghorbal called on me right away. At that time, he may not have known who I was—although he does now.

"Wolf Blitzer, *The Jerusalem Post*," I said, looking directly into Sadat's eyes. He showed no emotion, and I went on. "Mr. President, you seem so sincere in your quest for peace. Why don't you do something to demonstrate that to Israel? Perhaps you could open some direct human contact with Israel. Why not allow an exchange of journalists or athletes or scholars?" I asked, thinking of the novel ping-pong diplomacy of a few years earlier which had been the precursor of normalization between the United States and China. With such direct contact, I believed, perceptions all around might change, and concessions that seemed impossible might become obtainable.

"Part of the Arab–Israeli conflict is a psychological one," Sadat replied. "I myself have no objection to this. But, believe me, our people are not yet ready for this after twenty-nine years of hatred, and four wars, and bitterness. All that has happened . . . we must take it gradually. Whenever we end the state of belligerency in the peace agreement that is supposed to be signed in Geneva by all of us, I think all this will be very easy."

Later, I walked back to the National Press Building, thinking that Sadat's answer was actually quite reasonable given the years of conflict between the two nations. I filed my story on the news conference. It was the lead item on page one of *The Jerusalem Post* the next morning. The headline read: "Sadat: Normalcy After Statehood for Territories."

Seven months later, in November 1977, despite the fact that there still was not an Israeli–Egyptian agreement ending the state of belligerency, let alone the creation of a Palestinian state, Sadat stunned the world by announcing his readiness to visit Jerusalem and to address the Knesset. He was even reported to have given my question some of the credit for having triggered the chain of events that led to his decision. Two weeks later, in early December, I visited Cairo with the first-ever invited group of journalists from the Israeli news media. I had a lengthy meeting with the director of Egypt's semi-official *Middle East News Agency*, Mohammed Abdul-Gawad. Along with other senior Egyptian editors and publishers, Abdul-Gawad had accompanied Sadat to Washington that past April. Indeed, Abdul-Gawad now told me that after Sadat's news conference, he and the other editors had been invited to dine that evening with the Egyptian leader at Blair House. Abdul-Gawad recalled that my question to Sadat had struck a sensitive chord. "At dinner," Abdul-Gawad said, "the president asked me whether my reporter had filed his remarks at the news conference back home. 'Yes,' I told Sadat, 'he sent back every word— with the exception of what you told the reporter from *The Jerusalem Post*.' "

"Why didn't he send that?" Abdul-Gawad quoted Sadat as having asked.

"Because, Mr. President, I thought that your answer was too sensitive. You were saying that you personally were ready to open direct contact with Israel but that your people were not. I wasn't sure if we should send that back home."

Sadat, according to Abdul-Gawad, had been clearly upset. The Egyptian leader directed him to leave the table, call the reporter immediately, and instruct him to send a separate story on that one question and answer. "I want my people to know everything that I say to the outside world," Sadat said. Abdul-Gawad, of course, did as the president asked.

Looking back, I now see that one incident with Sadat as an important highlight in my journalistic career, which started in 1972 when I became a foreign correspondent in the Tel Aviv bureau of the British-based *Reuters* news agency and continued when I moved up to the position of Washington correspondent for *The Jerusalem Post*. I have learned throughout this period that being at the right place at the right time, and asking the right question, can make a big difference.

The Jerusalem Post has a first-class reputation in the United States and around the world. Because it is written in English, it is without a doubt the best-known Israeli newspaper among Americans, although it is by no means Israel's largest. Its weekly international edition has a sizable circulation in the United States, especially within the Jewish community. Many non-Jews read it, including congressmen, senators, and key U.S. officials at the State Department, the White House, and the Pentagon. Because *The Jerusalem Post* is regarded as a serious and important newspaper, and because it is in English, diplomatic sources in the U.S. capital— who are the staple source for all foreign correspondents—have usually been willing to answer at least some of my questions. These sources generally like to be able to read what they've said, even if they are not identified by name.

I have also represented other Israeli newspapers in Washington during the past several years. Under the name Zev Blitzer, I have written for *Al Hamishmar*, a small morning daily. (*Zev* means "wolf" in Hebrew.) And under the name Zev Barak, I have served as the correspondent of *Yediot Ahronot*, Israel's largest newspaper. (*Barak* means "lightning," or "blitz.") *The Jerusalem Post*, *Al Hamishmar*, and *Yediot Ahronot* all have different perspectives and editorial biases, ranging across virtually the entire political spectrum of the country. In my dispatches to them, however, I have always tried to be fair and objective and to separate those stories in which I simply reported the news from those in which I analyzed it. They have generally published my stories without significant editorial changes, although the headlines, which they write, usually reflect their own particular slants. I have taken it as a compliment that I have been both criticized and praised over the years by Israeli editors, politicians, and readers who come from both the right and the left wings of Israeli politics.

Beyond the Israeli press, I have written for many other Jewish publications, including the London *Jewish Chronicle*, several weekly American Jewish newspapers, and such magazines as *Hadassah* and *Present Tense*. In addition, I have had articles published in *The New York Times*, *The Washington Post*, *The Los Angeles Times*, *The New Republic*, *The Wall Street Journal*, and many other newspapers and magazines. Naturally, my specialty has been the Middle East.

Representing Israeli newspapers in Washington has meant focusing primarily on U.S. policy toward the Middle East, with a special emphasis on the latest twists and turns in American–Israeli relations. That, in turn, has meant establishing good contacts with the Israeli embassy in Washington— with the ambassador, the minister, and other diplomats and attachés there, all of whom must stay closely in touch with anything going on in Washington that may be of concern to their government. Cross-checking reports has meant developing good ties with American sources as well, especially at the State Department, the White House, the Pentagon, Congress, and elsewhere in the U.S. government's enormous foreign policy bureaucracy. It also has meant cultivating relationships with Middle Eastern experts in the academic community. Many times they will have access to information that is generally unavailable to journalists. In addition, activists in the American Jewish community can be quite useful at times in providing tips and directions on certain stories, since they, too, are spending a lot of their time worrying about American–Israeli relations.

One of the best fringe benefits of covering Washington for Israeli newspapers has been crossing the paths of so many fascinating people. When I first arrived in Washington, for example, Joseph Sisco was still the assistant secretary of state for Near Eastern and South Asian affairs, the top Middle East expert in the State Department. He was later followed by Alfred L. Atherton, Jr., Harold Saunders, Nicholas Veliotes, and Richard Murphy. Each had his own style and his own ways of solving problems, although their positions while in office, I now realize, were usually very similar regarding the gut issues involved in the Arab–Israeli conflict.

At the Israeli embassy, I closely observed ambassadors Simcha Dinitz, Ephraim Evron, Moshe Arens, and Meir Rosenne. Each of these men also had his own style. But, like their diplomatic brethren elsewhere, they had to learn that there are limits within which an embassy must operate no matter who is in charge.

This book, then, is the result of more than a dozen years of personal experience in covering the ups and downs of American–Israeli relations. I have had an opportunity to explore virtually every facet of this complex and unique relationship. In the process, I discovered that there was no shortage of books dealing with various aspects of Israel and its society or with U.S. policy in the Middle East. But there has really been no comprehensive volume exclusively focusing on the limits of the relationship between the two nations.

Because I write for Israeli newspapers, many people have understandably come to think that I am an Israeli. I am not. I am an American. When I lived in Israel, it was either to study Hebrew and other subjects at the Hebrew University in Jerusalem or to work for *Reuters*. I never became an Israeli citizen. But I did become fluent in Hebrew, and this has become one of my strengths as a correspondent. Although there are many Israelis who know English, in order to really come to grips with their hopes and fears, it is extremely important to speak to them in their own language. In Israel, as in most foreign countries, those people who speak fluent English are usually the elite of the society. There are still many Israelis who know no English. Just as important, Israelis whose vocabulary in English is limited will be more likely to speak to visiting American reporters in slogans and clichés than in precise terms. I have always lamented the fact that major U.S. news organizations continue to assign reporters to Israel who do not speak Hebrew. They do the same in other foreign capitals, and that is truly unfortunate for the ultimate consumer of news obtained through the filter of interpreters—the American public. No serious foreign news organization would ever dispatch a reporter to Washington who did not speak English. Can you imagine trying to cover a hearing in Congress or a national political convention by walking around with English translators?

Because the material for this book has been collected in the course of my work as a reporter covering many stories in Washington, Jerusalem, and elsewhere, I have come across a good deal of fascinating information not available to researchers who are restricted to archives and formal interviews. While I have reported on much of this in various publications over the years, my files have continued to bulge. For one reason or another, some of this material never got into print. A reporter always receives information "off the record," meaning that it can't be used. But, with time, it can be made public—which is something I have done in this book. I have gone over everything I have written on the subject—literally thousands of articles—as well as previously unreported information, mostly taken from my notes.

Thus, the bulk of the original source material comes from both personal observations and direct interviews. I have tried to make the sources of quotes, statistics, and other facts cited as clear as possible in the actual text, not in footnotes. Most of the statements quoted directly were made in one-on-one question-and-answer sessions with me. Excerpts from speeches, congressional hearings, press conferences, and other public forums were taken from my notebooks because I was present when the remarks were originally made.

Many people encouraged me to write this book, including many of my readers. It has been a wonderful experience working for my editors at *The Jerusalem Post*, Ari Rath and Erwin Frenkel. I learned much from them. I am also especially grateful to Helena Schwarz and Susan Rabiner of Oxford University Press in New York, who were instrumental in getting this project off the ground and seeing it through to the end. During the final stages of editing, Wendy Warren Keebler and Rachel Toor were most helpful. My beloved parents, Cesia and David Blitzer of Buffalo, New York, gave me the basic foundation and confidence I needed and for which I will always be indebted to them. And finally, my wife Lynn and daughter Ilana were the ever-present love and inspiration that pushed me in the right direction.

Contents

Introduction

The United States has always faced a dilemma in shaping its policy toward the Middle East: How can Washington manage to maintain strong ties with Israel—a reliable ally with many politically active friends in the United States—and at the same time develop strong relations with the strategically important and oil-rich Arab world?

Since Israel gained independence in 1948, successive Democratic and Republican administrations have managed to walk that delicate tightrope—some, of course, better than others. There can be no denying, however, that over this period American–Israeli relations have matured and improved. In areas of military, political, economic, and cultural cooperation, the two countries have consistently moved closer together.

Take, for example, the military relationship. In 1948, the Truman administration included Israel in a regional arms embargo, forcing Israel—then struggling in its war of independence against five neighboring Arab armies—to turn to all sorts of sources for badly needed weapons. There were gun-smuggling operations to Israel from the United States, leading to arrests and even jail terms for some Americans, Jews and non-Jews alike. It was the Soviet Union, of all countries, that gave the green light to Czechoslovakia to sell Israel some weapons during the war. The sale proved to be critical in enabling Israel to sign armistice agreements with its Arab neighbors in 1949.

In these days of close cooperation, it is easy to forget the fact that the initial Truman arms embargo against Israel basically remained in effect throughout the 1950s and that it was not until the early 1960s that the United States concluded its first-ever major arms sale to Israel, a sale involving an older version of the Hawk anti-aircraft missile. Since then, of course, the American–Israeli military relationship has expanded rapidly, especially after the 1967 and 1973 wars. For several years now, Israel has been the largest individual recipient of U.S. military credits.

Diplomatically, the same change has occurred. During Israel's first two decades, Prime Minister David Ben-Gurion did not receive frequent invitations to Washington. Years often passed before an Israeli leader was officially asked to come to the White House. But since 1967, such official Israeli visits have become commonplace. Former Prime Minister Menachem Begin, who assumed office in 1977, came to Washington nearly a dozen times, more often than any other foreign head of government during that same period.

Thus, it is clear that the American–Israeli alliance in the 1980s is on a totally different scale from that of earlier years. What is more impressive is the fact that U.S. relations with the Arab world have also improved during these same three decades. Washington, more than Moscow, is today a more attractive address for many Arab leaders eager to promote their countries' national interests. In part, this must surely be related to an Arab understanding that only the Americans have the political clout to change Israeli policies. Though the Soviets have provided the Arabs with military support, the military option against Israel has not proved effective in forcing changes in Israeli positions.

Of course, there continue to be sharp differences between Washington and Jerusalem in a host of areas. But both countries have come to recognize that they must keep those differences within limits, because—regardless of which political party is in power in the United States or in Israel—strong, close ties serve the national interests of both countries. That certainty is not intended to imply that the two will always agree on every important issue. No American ally, no matter how close, always agrees with Washington. There are regular strains between the United States and the Western Europeans, the Canadians, the Mexicans, the Japanese, and other close allies. But, as in Israel's case, these differences, even when serious, are not permitted to shake the foundations of the overall alliance.

For many observers, there has been a temptation to focus on the negative aspects of the American–Israeli relationship. Observers in both countries almost always seem ready to point out the many differences between Washington and Jerusalem in the search for Arab–Israeli peace. There are pundits in both capitals eager to point out that the two countries are on an "inevitable collision course" or that an all-out "crunch" or "confrontation" is just over the horizon.

Harvey Sicherman, writing in the Summer 1980 issue of *Orbis*, demonstrated an acute sense of these constraints:

The real condition of American–Israeli relations at any moment is difficult to discern. This may be attributed to the astonishing differences in their size, in their history, and even in their democratic political systems. Moreover, their association has been so close that the international equivalent of a domestic quarrel—no matter how petty—instantly captures the headlines of the media in both countries. Indeed, U.S.–Israeli relations may be subject to what one observer called the "gevalt" syndrome: on any give day, one has the impression that (a) the sky is falling down on both states; (b) it will fall down tomorrow; (c) it fell down yesterday but both governments are too stupid to understand it.

Especially since the 1973 war, these dark predictions have been made routinely, regardless of whether there is a Democratic or Republican administration in Washington, or a Labor or Likud government in Jerusalem. But no matter how tense or difficult the relationship has become— and at times it has been quite difficult—a complete rupture has not occurred. And based on this historical experience, such a rupture is highly unlikely to occur in the foreseeable future. The American–Israeli relationship even managed to survive the enormous strains of the Lebanese war in 1982.

Nonetheless, relations between Washington and Jerusalem have operated within a set of built-in constraints on both capitals, and understanding them is essential to understanding what makes American–Israeli relations tick today.

Clearly, it would not serve Israel's national interests to find itself in a real confrontation, for any prolonged period, with the United States. Because Israel, increasingly isolated throughout the world, has come to rely on the United States more and more—in economic, military, and political areas—every government in Jerusalem must always take the American point of view into consideration. Another factor weighing heavily on the minds of Israeli policymakers is the fact that the United States is the home of nearly six million Jews, making it the largest Jewish community in the world. These American Jews provide Israel with additional economic assistance through contributions to the United Jewish Appeal, purchases of Israel Bonds, and direct cash gifts to other Israeli causes. Every Israeli government will always start off its decision-making process with a built-in incentive to avoid putting itself in conflict with the American government or people. This does not mean that Israel will always do whatever the United States wants, but it does mean that the likely U.S. reaction will be factored into Israel's decisions.

It is equally important to recognize that the relationship is not a one-way street—certainly not in the 1980s. There are important reasons, other than those of compassion and identification, that have led U.S. administrations, whether Democratic or Republican, to support Israel. The long-standing moral factors involving the birth of Israel out of the ashes of the Holocaust are still persuasive, as are shared democratic values. But the strategic reasons are becoming even more important today, according to many American and Israeli officials. Israel does, after all, have the strongest military force in the Middle East. In hypothesizing a conventional confrontation with the Soviet Union or any other adversary, U.S. defense planners simply take Israel's support for granted. That support could be critical in the eastern Mediterranean.

In 1984, the United States maintained some 360,000 soldiers in Western Europe and close to 135,000 in the Far East; in the Middle East, there were only about 1200 serving as peacekeepers in Sinai. Two reasons help account for this difference. The Arab states, even the moderate ones, have rejected any permanent U.S. bases. Saudi Arabia and other Arab states friendly to the United States have preferred an over-the-horizon American presence. Secondly, U.S. defense strategists have concluded that a massive Western European or Far Eastern presence may not be necessary, in part because of the recognition that Israel, after mobilizing its reserves in seventy-two hours, could assemble a highly efficient, battle-tested, and reliable army of more than 400,000 troops, equipped with and capable of using some of the finest conventional weaponry in the world—most of it American-supplied.

Israel, of course, is not about to send those soldiers off to fight America's wars, unless the government in Jerusalem, with the support of the Israeli people, concludes that it is also in Israel's best interest to do so. But American strategic planners, at a minimum, can assume that in a cold-war confrontation in the Middle East it will not be the United States alone faced with the decision of either committing its own forces or seeing its surrogate defeated.

Thus, compared to what the United States has to spend every year to defend its other allies in Western Europe and the Far East, U.S. economic and military assistance to Israel would appear to be a real bargain. "It is a *metziyeh*," said Republican Senator Rudy Boschwitz of Minnesota, chairman of the Senate Foreign Relations Subcommittee on Near Eastern and South Asian Affairs, using the Yiddish word for "bargain." The senator recognized that most influential people in Washington do not necessarily see it the same way, largely because U.S. assistance to other allies is basically buried in the massive budget of the Pentagon, while American economic and military assistance to Israel is labeled as such in the worldwide foreign aid bill. But, to put the money slated for Israel in its proper perspective, Boschwitz said, it should be compared to what the United States has to spend annually to protect Western Europe and Japan. What he and some other members of Congress would very much like to do is move the annual U.S. military assistance package to Israel from the foreign aid legislation to the defense budget, "where it belongs"—a move that is unlikely to happen, since the State Department relies on the large-scale aid to Israel to carry the foreign aid bill through Congress every year. Foreign aid is not a winning issue for many lawmakers—but aid to Israel is.

In 1983, Boschwitz had his staff prepare a detailed memorandum outlining exactly how much the United States has to spend on its other allies. The figures, simply put, were staggering. Then Under Secretary of State for Political Affairs Lawrence Eagleburger, during questioning by Boschwitz before the Foreign Relations Committee on November 30, 1982, had estimated that the annual U.S. cost for protecting Europe in actual cash outlays came to between $50 and $80 billion. Johns Hopkins University Political Science Professor David Calleo, writing in the Spring 1981 issue of *Foreign Affairs,* estimated that $80 billion was spent by the United States on NATO defense in 1981. Calleo wrote:

> A precise cost for U.S. NATO forces cannot be provided since most force elements have more than one purpose and in any major confrontation with the Warsaw Pact all U.S. forces would be made available. Nevertheless, a recent U.S. response to the NATO Defense Planning Questionnaire estimates the cost of forces formally committed to NATO to be approximately $81 billion or around 51 percent of the total defense budget for FY (fiscal year) 1981.

Boschwitz also pointed out that, unlike America's other allies, who have consistently refused to devote as much of their financial resources to defense spending as has the United States, Israel in recent years has devoted about 25 percent of its gross national product (GNP) to defense—a basic reason why its economy is in such trouble today. (During the first term of the Reagan administration, the United States increased its defense spending to roughly 7 percent of its GNP.)

Boschwitz also noted that much of the assistance has been in the form of loans, which Israel has always repaid with interest. In 1984, Israel repaid the United States over $1 billion in earlier loans that came due and over the years has never failed to meet a payment to the United States. Between 1973 and 1984, Israel repaid the United States over $7 billion.

"From 1973 to 1982," the Boschwitz memorandum said, "Israel has received a total of $20.6 billion in economic and military aid; about one-half will be paid back. The same cannot be said for NATO expenditures. In 10 years, the Israelis received about one-fourth of what the U.S. spent on NATO in 1981 alone, and a little over one-sixth of what the U.S. will spend in FY 1983 on NATO." Boschwitz acknowledged that Israel, at times, can be a "prickly" ally. But, he insisted, so are America's other allies, usually more irritating than the Israelis. Japan, for example, has an $18 to $20 billion positive trade balance with the United States. "The Japanese, when it comes to trade, are an extremely difficult ally to deal with," Boschwitz said. That U.S. trade deficit with Japan alone, Boschwitz pointed out, directly affects America's unemployment problems. If Japan were to open its markets more fully to American products, America's unemployment rate would go down immediately and impressively. If Japan were to increase its defense spending from the tiny level of less than 1 percent of its GNP, moreover, it would not likely be able to sustain its competitive advantage over the United States. The same can be said about Western Europe and its aggressive efforts to take over some traditional U.S. markets, especially, Boschwitz said, in agricultural products. "Israel is not creating vast trade deficits for the United States."

Israel has demonstrated that it can play an important role in advancing U.S. interests in regional politics. The most dramatic example of this was in September 1970, when, at America's request, Israel massed troops along its border with Syria to deter a Syrian invasion of Jordan which was then involved in its civil war against the Palestine Liberation Organization (PLO). Israel did this despite the fact that it was still in an official state of war with Jordan.

Over the years, Israel also has made available to the United States captured Soviet-supplied military equipment. Cooperation between the U.S. and Israeli intelligence communities has been extensive and mutually beneficial.

Exactly how friendly Israel is to the United States was underlined in a remarkable but little noticed document submitted by United Nations Ambassador Jeane Kirkpatrick to the Senate Appropriations Subcommittee on Foreign Operations in March 1983. Her study showed that during the thirty-seventh session of the UN General Assembly in 1982, the country that voted with the United States more than any other was Israel. Washington and Jerusalem agreed in 86.2 percent of the votes, as compared to an 80.1 percent rating for Britain, 76.6 percent for West Germany, 70.7 percent for Canada, 67.9 percent for Italy, and 67.2 percent for Japan. On the opposite end of the scale, the Soviet Union and the United States agreed only 20.6 percent of the time, and Albania received an 8.8 percent rating. The moderate Arab states—such as Saudi Arabia, Egypt, and Jordan—received below 25 percent ratings. The radical Arab states—such as Libya, Iraq, and Syria—were below 20 percent. The Kirkpatrick study dramatically underlined what is not very often apparent: Washington and Jerusalem are natural allies with many synonymous international interests.

Domestic political realities, especially the existence of a strong, cohesive and politically active American Jewish community, have also influenced the behavior of every American administration. It is still good politics to support Israel and dangerous politically to oppose Israel.

Still, chronologically, these strategic and political considerations have trailed the moral factor. Israel was established only after the Holocaust of World War II. The United States, under Harry S Truman, became the first country to extend formal diplomatic recognition to Israel. Since then, this moral commitment has been supported by every U.S. president. An aspect of the relationship that cannot be ignored is that the United States supported Israel before any strategic advantage in doing so could be discerned.

This was very important during the 1983 Holocaust Survivors' gathering in Washington. Organizers of the gathering, which brought thousands of survivors and their children to Washington, were always careful in their public statements to characterize it as a nonpolitical event. But, from the start, those involved in the operation fully recognized the automatic political spillover benefit that the event would have for Israel in the U.S. capital and, indeed, around the world. Many of Israel's citizens are themselves survivors. In the United States, it always has been widely accepted that not all six million Jews would have perished if Israel had existed in the 1930s and 1940s. Even America had shut its doors to Jewish refugees in those days. Israeli officials and American Jewish political activists have agreed that raising public awareness of the Holocaust—the fact that one-third of world Jewry was destroyed during those few years—was bound to generate heightened sympathy and support for Israel. Only the most fanatically pro-Arab and anti-Israeli advocates could fail to appreciate the relationship. At the same time, however, there has been a deliberate effort not to go too far in making the connection, and many survivors have resented raising the specter of the Holocaust to justify every Israeli policy. Doing so, it has been said, merely cheapens the Holocaust and the memory of those who died in it.

The organizers of the gathering in Washington did not have to use a sledgehammer to press their point for strong U.S. backing for Israel. That was always understood. They could simply let their actions and their mere presence speak for themselves. President Ronald Reagan, who addressed 15,000 people at the Washington Capital Centre's opening event, appeared visibly moved by what he saw and heard. His wife Nancy seemed to have tears in her eyes as she witnessed the reunion of survivors and their U.S. army liberators. Other high-ranking U.S. policymakers were also sensitized to the Holocaust. Vice-President George Bush spoke at a congressional ceremony. The House and Senate leadership was invited to address the gathering. Many congressmen and senators met privately with their constituents among the survivors. Invariably, the subject of Israel arose. Without much advertisement or fanfare, Israel's cause automatically received a major boost. Israeli diplomats were well aware of this fact, as was Deputy Cabinet Minister Dov Shilansky, who was Begin's personal representative to the gathering.

In his speech before the gathering, Reagan promised the survivors that "the security of your safe havens, here and in Israel, will never be compromised." That statement drew a lengthy outburst of applause.

Some speakers at the events forcefully made the Israel–Holocaust connection. New York City's outspoken mayor, Edward Koch, was enthusiastically applauded at a closing ceremony at the Washington Monument when he called for stronger U.S. support for Israel and "Jerusalem, its undivided capital." He condemned the PLO as terrorists attempting to finish what Hitler had started.

The executive committee of the gathering, meeting on April 14, 1983, unanimously adopted a resolution that declared: "We are mindful that our time is precious, our responsibility is great and that we have a unique role to play." The document also said: "Our allegiance to the people of Israel is unshakable, and we must evidence that support."

Jimmy Carter had also been deeply sensitized to the Holocaust and its lasting impact on Israel. As president, he sent Elie Wiesel—Holocaust survivor, author, and philosopher—a series of reconnaissance photographs taken of the Auschwitz concentration camp from April 4, 1944, to January 14, 1945. The pictures were taken by American and British planes. They clearly showed the camp's gas chambers and crematoria, as well as prisoners undergoing disinfection and standing in line to be tattooed. The photographs, released by the National Archives and the CIA, revived the disturbing question of why the Allies did not bomb the rail lines that took victims to the camp. With the publication of the photographs, it was proven that the United States and Great Britain knew of the camp's existence at least a year before the end of the war. It was pointed out that the Auschwitz pictures were taken almost by accident. The planes were actually taking pictures of an I. G. Farben plant producing synthetic fuels less than five miles away. The plant was bombed during the last year of the war. Destruction of the rail lines to Auschwitz at that time would have hampered the transport of nearly a half-million Hungarian Jews who were being moved to Auschwitz.

Countering these pro-Israel pressures have been influential factors seeking to limit the degree of close American–Israeli cooperation and friendship. The need to maintain close ties with the Arab world is, of course, the most significant reason cited, especially since 1973, when a possible cutoff of Arab oil was threatened and petrodollar influence increased. Efforts to cool the American–Israeli relationship have intensified. America's big-business community, the major oil companies, the giant construction firms with heavy investments in the Arab world, and other Americans generally supportive of the Arab cause have become more actively involved in trying to influence the decision-making process. Their lobbying during the 1981 Saudi AWACS aircraft debate in the Senate was seen by many observers as decisive. The battle for public opinion—between pro-Israel and pro-Arab lobbies—heated up dramatically in the 1970s.

Since 1973, there have been several near-confrontations between Washington and Jerusalem. They involved the Nixon, Ford, Carter, and Reagan administrations and the governments in Israel headed by Golda Meir, Yitzhak Rabin, Menachem Begin and Yitzhak Shamir. There was, for example, the initial U.S. pressure during the final days of the 1973 war to free the encircled Egyptian Third Army near the Suez Canal; the highly publicized "reassessment" of U.S. policy toward Israel that followed Secretary of State Henry Kissinger's stalled shuttle effort to achieve a Sinai II interim agreement in March 1975; the repeated Israeli protests of proposed U.S. arms sales to Arab states (the Hawk anti-aircraft missile sale to Jordan in 1975, the Saudi F-15 "package" sale in 1978, and the AWACS sale in 1981); the severe tensions that developed during the sixteen months between the time of Egyptian President Anwar Sadat's historic trip to Jerusalem in November 1977 and the signing of the Israeli–Egyptian peace treaty in Washington in March 1979; the strains in the relationship following Israel's 1981 bombing of the Iraqi nuclear reactor; and generally negative American reaction to the Israeli aerial strike against PLO headquarters in Beirut, the Knesset's legislation to extend Israeli law to the Golan Heights, and, of course, the war in Lebanon. Yet, overall, the American–Israeli relationship remains vibrant. It has even managed to thrive in the face of all these strains.

When National Security Adviser Robert McFarlane spoke before the Hadassah National Convention in San Francisco on August 28, 1984, he elaborated on the nature of the American–Israeli relationship. "The United States," he declared, "maintains an enduring, unshakable interest in the security of the state of Israel and a strong bilateral relationship."

McFarlane, a former military officer who quickly moved up in the Reagan administration's foreign policy team, was in effect defining the unique relationship between Washington and Jerusalem as something other than puppeteer and puppet. Without saying so in as many words, he was clearly reminding his audience that the United States cannot simply snap its fingers and see Israel respond.

Arabs and their American supporters over the years have always yearned for a get-tough U.S. attitude toward Israel. They have consistently promoted the notion of direct U.S. pressure on Israel to make concessions in the peace process. Since the United States provides Israel with so much badly needed economic and military assistance, their thinking goes, why not hold back until Israel accepts some American demands? In recent years, a freeze on West Bank settlements has regularly been proposed as one such demand.

But U.S. policymakers, Republican as well as Democratic, have usually been reluctant to link Israeli financial assistance to political concessions. Many of them, of course, might have loved to try such a course of action. But for the most part their hands were tied by a combination of built-in political and military circumstances which have helped to shape the contours of the American–Israeli relationship.

Israel's critics have almost nostalgically recalled the days in 1956 and 1957 when President Dwight Eisenhower and Secretary of State John Foster Dulles used extensive economic and political pressure on the young government of Prime Minister Ben-Gurion to force a unilateral withdrawal from Sinai and Gaza, which Israel had captured during the just-concluded war. There were direct threats of the United States even joining with the Soviet Union at the UN Security Council to impose economic sanctions against Israel unless it withdrew from those territories. If such a resolution had passed, Israel might not have been able to trade with any other country. Security Council resolutions, as opposed to General Assembly resolutions, are legally binding on UN member states.

The Eisenhower and Dulles administration went one step further. It warned the Israelis through private diplomatic channels that if Israel did not withdraw immediately, the U.S. Justice Department might open an investigation into the tax-exempt status of the United Jewish Appeal and other charities providing vitally needed funds for Israel.

No military pressure could have been exerted against Israel in those days, for Israel was still not authorized to receive any major American weapons. With the establishment of Israel in May 1948, U.S. arms to Israel had been embargoed.

Still, this example of the Eisenhower–Dulles arm twisting is often recalled by the Arabs and their friends in defining a proper strategy for America's getting its way with Israel. If anything, they note, Israel has become even more dependent on the United States in the 1980s for continued and large-scale economic and military assistance. Why not attach a political price tag? former Under Secretary of State George Ball and other critics have often asked.

"It's not that simple," one veteran State Department Middle East hand replied when asked about this school of thinking. Off the top of his head, he cited several reasons why any U.S. president is going to think very hard and long before imposing a policy of directly withholding assistance to Israel in order to obtain political concessions. "We have to think of the chain of events which would occur if this blunt policy were adopted," the official said.

What would happen, hypothetically, if the Ball proposal were adopted to attempt to induce Israel to leave the West Bank and Gaza? Much, of course, would depend on the exact nature of the circumstances surrounding the decision—the political events leading up to the pressure—but here are some likely developments, as suggested by the State Department specialist quoted above.

For one thing, he said, a serious crisis would immediately erupt between the United States and Israel. This, in turn, would quickly result in a full-scale Israeli mobilization against the administration in office. The arena would be American public opinion, as reflected in Congress, the news media, the labor unions, the think tanks, churches, universities, and elsewhere. If the Republicans were in the White House, the Democrats in Congress and across the country would have an automatic partisan reason to come to Israel's defense. The opposite would be the case if there were a Democratic administration.

Naturally, the Jewish community would spearhead the anti-administration drive. All of the major Jewish organizations would unleash a sharp challenge to the administration's pressure tactics against a "friendly and democratic ally." Behind the scenes, they would promote stiff statements from members of Congress, including letters of protest. The threat of direct congressional legislation to mandate a halt to such an arms and financial aid suspension would materialize. There would also be many newspaper editorials and commentaries attacking the administration.

In short, this would be an acrimonious and very ugly period in domestic American politics—something no president is really eager to promote, especially because it could subject the administration to charges of anti-Semitism. In addition, many true anti-Semites would be emboldened. Responsible U.S. officials have always recognized that many anti-Semites come out of the closet when relations with Israel are strained.

But, the State Department official continued, that would not be the end of it. There would be a spinoff in the international arena as well, and mostly a negative one. How would it look, for instance, to other friends and allies of the United States—also dependent on American goodwill and support—to see Israel crunched? American credibility as a reliable and constant friend would come under question around the world. This, in turn, would enhance the stature of the Soviet Union and other U.S. adversaries.

Seeing the Americans lean on Israel would also suggest to the Arabs that they did not have to make any painful concessions in order to achieve peace. The late President Sadat, it is often recalled, did not come to Jerusalem in November 1977 because the United States was then holding back on assistance to Israel. He came, in part, because he concluded that the United States was *not* going to take that road and that if he wanted peace with Israel he would have to deal directly with Israel.

U.S. officials also agree that a dramatic suspension of arms and economic assistance to Israel would tend to unify the Israeli public and rally support for the government in power in Jerusalem. Even those Israelis inclined to oppose, let's say, a hard-line position toward the West Bank might see the U.S. pressure as a direct challenge of the country as a whole. Their patriotism alone might tend to stifle the debate within Israel, exactly the opposite of what the American administration in conflict with an Israeli government would want to see.

U.S. officials are aware of one other potential development such pressure tactics on Israel could trigger, namely an Israeli military response. Israel, they know, is still the most powerful military force in the Middle East. But an Israel uncertain of continued U.S. support might conclude that its qualitative advantage on the battlefield would soon erode in the absence of additional American arms shipments. Thus, there would be strong pressure within Israel—especially in the military—to embark on a preemptive strike against the Arabs before self-defense became impossible. Many Israelis would conclude that Israel should strike while still strong, rather than wait until its position was weakened.

The last thing an administration in Washington would want to see develop as a result of its pressure would be a war started by Israel, one that, because of perceived American ambivalance, might provoke Soviet intervention. Thus, a lot of talk about brutal pressure on Israel may be popular in certain quarters but turns out to be bankrupt in the face of real-world consequences.

Finally, if the U.S. administration did pressure Israel and was subsequently forced to back down in the face of reactions from Congress, the Jewish community, and others in the United States as well as in Israel and around the world, there would be another price to pay. The limits of U.S. policy would be advertised for all to see. No president wants to show off American impotence.

The above-mentioned scenario, which could unfold in the wake of American pressure against Israel, is by no means all that hypothetical. There is a historical precedent.

In 1975, President Gerald Ford and Secretary of State Henry Kissinger wanted Israel to withdraw from the Mitla and Giddi passes in Sinai, as well as from the Abu Rodeis oilfields. Kissinger's March shuttle had ended in failure. He returned to Washington deeply depressed. The president, within a few days, announced his "reassessment" of policy, during which no new arms contracts with Israel were signed and the new foreign aid bill for the Middle East was put on hold. There was, in sum, a deep chill in American–Israeli relations.

But things did not end there. This was no longer 1956, when the Jewish community and its friends were not nearly as well positioned to respond to what they had perceived as a threat to Israel, and the pro-Israeli lobby in Washington organized itself efficiently and quickly. Seventy-six senators, more than three-quarters of the Senate, sent a letter to Ford urging the immediate resumption of arms sales to Israel coupled with strengthened economic and diplomatic support. Ford and Kissinger had the rug pulled out from under them. They had to back down, setting the stage for the successful conclusion of the Sinai II accord on September 1, 1975. Israel made many of the concessions that the United States and Egypt had sought earlier, but it received a lot more in return, including increased U.S. political, economic, and military assistance as demanded in the Senate letter.

Nearly a decade later, the Reagan administration, in seeking to help Israel's beleaguered economy, attached some conditions for increased aid, but those were strictly economic conditions. The Americans wanted Israel to cut its budget in order to ease the enormous inflation and balance-of-payments problems of Israel. Israeli officials were among the first to agree that these steps were necessary, and they did not necessarily resent Washington's linking the measures to increased economic aid. But throwing political demands into the bargain would be deeply resented by Israeli officials and their U.S. supporters.

A demand for a West Bank settlement freeze, for example, was not made. Neither did the administration ask Israel to accept Reagan's September 1, 1982, Arab–Israeli peace initiative as a precondition for increased assistance.

Thus, despite occasional differences between the two countries, the United States continues to avoid any direct linkage between aid and political concessions. Under Reagan, as McFarlane pointed out in San Francisco, U.S. aid to Israel was increased and, even more important, restructured so that it now includes only outright grants and no more loans. During the four years of the first Reagan term, the United States provided Israel with almost $9.5 billion, more than during any other four-year period. The $2.6 billion in the 1984 fiscal-year budget represented 27 percent of the worldwide U.S. foreign aid program.

While there clearly are limits built into the American–Israeli relationship, the particular attitudes, positions, and personalities of key American and Israeli policymakers can play an important role in shaping the eventual state of the relationship. In Israel in the mid-1970s, there was the unusual situation that saw Prime Minister Rabin, a former Israeli ambassador to the United States and the leader of the Labor coalition, actually become stronger in domestic Israeli politics during periods of strain with Washington, while the opposite was the case with Begin. This stemmed from the fact that Rabin was often accused of being too pro-American. Begin, on the other hand, was often accused by his Labor critics of being overly dogmatic in his policies and ideologies, thereby threatening Israel's critical relationship with the United States. During the 1977 campaign, for example, Labor charged that a Begin victory could poison American–Israeli ties. Shimon Peres and other Labor leaders insisted that only they could "handle" Washington. Begin wanted to prove his Labor opponents wrong. He tried to project an image of close American–Israeli relations, and this, in turn, tended to strengthen his domestic political base.

In the United States, the shape of policy also can be changed by the personality and nature of a particular president, secretary of state, or other high official. Kissinger's style was obviously different from that of Cyrus Vance or Alexander Haig.

Remarkably, despite these personality differences, U.S. policy toward Israel (and vice versa) has remained rather consistent. It can be shown that U.S. policy toward the Arab–Israeli conflict has not changed very much since 1967. The United States still supports an Israeli withdrawal virtually to the pre-1967 lines. Eisenhower was the last American president to impose a U.S. solution on Israel. Since 1967's Six-Day War, successive Israeli governments have made it clear that they oppose any such withdrawal, and they have prevailed.

There has been, in short, a consistent pattern of shared purposes in the relationship going back to 1948. Whenever the relationship has threatened to develop into a real confrontation, a seemingly built-in—and often not very well understood—set of safeguards, powered by public opinion in both countries, has emerged to save the day. This is the hidden aspect of the relationship. Even in the aftermath of the Lebanese war and the enormous strains on the American–Israeli alliance that it produced, things managed to sort themselves out. Indeed, a strong case can be made that the relationship today, when seen over a span of three and a half decades, is stronger and more vital than ever before despite some highly publicized differences between Washington and Jerusalem. What follows in this book is an explanation for this phenomenon.

1

The Washington Bureaucracy

During a White House meeting two days before Israel was proclaimed independent in 1948, Secretary of State George Marshall told President Harry Truman that he would vote against Truman in the election later that year if the president recognized Israel. This statement was contained in a top-secret memorandum of conversation during that dramatic May 12, 1948, White House meeting, released for publication by the State Department on November 21, 1976, nearly twenty-nine years later. The memorandum was part of a 1197-page compilation of previously classified major documents concerning U.S. policy toward Israel and the Middle East in 1948.

The Marshall threat demonstrated the lengths to which he and other State Department officials were prepared to go to persuade the president not to recognize Israel. They were unsuccessful: Truman followed the recommendation of his White House advisers, particularly his special political assistant, Clark Clifford, who pressed for immediate U.S. recognition of the Jewish state. "I remarked to the president that, speaking objectively, I could not help but think that the suggestions made by Mr. Clifford were wrong," Marshall wrote in the memorandum. "I thought that to adopt these suggestions would have precisely the opposite effect from that intended by Mr. Clifford. The transparent dodge to win a few votes would not in fact achieve this purpose. The great dignity of the office of the president would be seriously diminished. The counsel offered by Mr. Clifford was based on domestic political considerations, while the problem which confronted us was international. I said bluntly that if the president

17

were to follow Mr. Clifford's advice and if in the elections I were to vote, I would vote against the president."

Under Secretary of State Robert Lovett, who also strongly opposed recognition of Israel, told Truman that it "would be injurious" because it was "a transparent attempt to win the Jewish vote." After making that point, Lovett said the U.S. should not recognize Israel because Washington did not know what "kind" of Jewish state would be established. "At this stage, Lovett read excerpts from a file of intelligence telegrams and reports regarding Soviet activity in sending Jews and Communist agents from Black Sea areas to Palestine," the memorandum said.

This was a period of intense U.S. fear of Communist expansion. Other documents released included numerous examples of this fear. William Burdett, then the U.S. vice-consul in Jerusalem, cabled Marshall on June 24, 1948, a month after the State of Israel was proclaimed, that "various sources indicate that guidance, money and arms were being provided to the Stern Gang by Russia through satellites, particularly Poland." He said the Polish consulates in Jerusalem and Tel Aviv "are believed to be in close touch with the Stern Gang. It is also believed Russia will make every effort [to] widen this support as effective means of gaining subversive foot-hold in Israel."

The documents also included an unpublished letter written on June 12, 1974, to the State Department's historical office by former Secretary of State Dean Rusk, who played a key role in the 1948 events leading up to the U.S. decision to recognize Israel. The letter provided a dramatic recounting of the shock and disappointment that took place at the U.S. Mission to the United Nations when Truman recognized Israel against the strong advice of the State Department. At that time, Rusk served as director of the Office of Special Political Affairs in the State Department.

Rusk wrote that when Clark Clifford asked him to inform the U.S. delegation at the UN that the United States was to recognize Israel fifteen minutes later, he replied, "But this cuts across what our delegation has been trying to accomplish in the General Assembly under instructions and we already have a large majority for that approach."

Clifford said, "Nevertheless, this is what the president wishes you to do."

Rusk later wrote in his letter: "I thereupon telephoned Ambassador Warren Austin [at the UN], who had to leave the floor of the Assembly to take my call. He made a personal decision not to return to the Assembly or to inform other members of our delegation—he simply went home. My guess is that he thought that it was better for the General Assembly to know very clearly that this was the act of the president in Washington and that the U.S. delegation had not been playing a double game with other delegations."

Rusk said "pandemonium" broke out when the U.S. announcement of recognition was read out from the press ticker. "I was later told that one of our U.S. Mission staff men literally sat on the lap of the Cuban delegate to keep him from going to the podium to withdraw Cuba from the United Nations." At about 6:15 P.M., fifteen minutes after the announcement, Rusk got a call from Secretary Marshall, who told him to "get up to New York and prevent the U.S. delegation from resigning en masse."

"Whether it was necessary or not," Rusk wrote in his 1974 letter, "I scurried to New York and found that tempers had cooled sufficiently so that my mission was unnecessary."

Thus, from the start, there has been a constant tugging of decisions within Washington's foreign policy bureaucracy. The battles between the White House and the State Department, for example, have become an almost constant feature in the making of U.S. policy toward Israel.

Ever since Israel was established in 1948, there have always been two major strains running through the formulation of U.S. policy toward the Middle East: that of the career State Department diplomat who sees things from the "global" perspective, and that of the astute politician who is more interested in the domestic implications of foreign policy decisions. There have been several wars, major realignments throughout the world as well as in the Middle East, and critical developments within the United States. They have had their impact on U.S. policy in the Middle East, but the political-versus-diplomatic struggle within the U.S. government has still continued, although less stridently.

Vice-President Walter Mondale and Ambassador-at-Large Alfred L. Atherton, Jr., were quintessential representatives of these two schools during the Carter administration. They both came from very different professional backgrounds, and, consequently, they tended to approach the problems in the Middle East quite differently. Each was sensitive to different points and nuances. Each stressed different issues. Still, the division separating the two men on the gut issues involved in the conflict—while in office—was not all that great, certainly much less than would have been the case thirty years earlier.

For a variety of reasons, the gap between the two camps has narrowed significantly over the years. Israeli officials are the first to acknowledge that the Middle East experts running the State Department today are by no means as virulently anti-Israel as were their predecessors back in the late 1940s and 1950s. For one thing, there are many Jews in today's State Department. The current batch of officials doing the staff work on the

Middle East—Jews as well as non-Jews—are clearly much more sensitive to Israel's concerns and security needs, even though they regularly disagree with certain policies.

Take Atherton, for example. He was deeply involved in the Middle East from 1965, when he returned to Washington from India. He served seven secretaries of state: Dean Rusk, William Rogers, Henry Kissinger, Cyrus Vance, Edmund Muskie, Alexander Haig, and George Shultz.

Atherton, who retired in 1985, was able to cast aside the sinister shadow of the earlier "Arabist" image. Like his former boss, Joseph Sisco, he was able to establish good working relationships, during exceedingly difficult periods, with both Israelis and Arabs—as well as with American Jewish leaders, who occasionally can be quite difficult.

"We always had great confidence in Roy's integrity," said I. L. Kenen, the retired chairman of the American Israel Public Affairs Committee (AIPAC). "Of all the people I have known in the Department of State over the years," he continued, "he has been the most available, the most helpful, the most communicative. Since the Six-Day War, he has always been completely frank, forthcoming, eager to interpret and to explain the situation as he saw it. He never once was inaccessible or unwilling to listen."

Who really shapes U.S. policy toward Israel? Whenever a president focuses his attention on the Middle East, assembling all the principals, as Carter did during the Camp David negotiations in 1978, there is no doubt that he is in the driver's seat. However, during other times, the decision-making process is diffused over a number of governmental departments and agencies. State and Defense Department career officials, special ambassadors, their advisers, and even anonymous aides in the departments of Energy and the Treasury and the Office of Management and the Budget, all have their input. The result is a process that from the outside often appears chaotic and sometimes contradictory.

When Henry Kissinger served as secretary of state, there was no doubt about who was making American policy toward Israel. He ran the State Department with an iron grip. Bureaucratic infighting was limited; Kissinger kept most of the cards very close to his vest. Information, the source of much power in Washington, was restricted to Kissinger and a handful of his cronies. Individual initiatives by lesser officials were virtually unheard of. This approach made life less complex for foreign diplomats in Washington; they knew the right address—Kissinger's—if they wanted anything important done.

This consolidation of power within one man's hands came to an end with the arrival of Jimmy Carter and his new team of foreign affairs advisers. During the Carter administration, the action once again was spread around, to the point where almost everyone, including State Department desk officers, often played significant roles in formulating policy decisions. Washington bureaucrats and political appointees, unlike those who followed along during the Kissinger years, were important actors who had a lot to say—and they often did speak up. At times, the large number of officials involved in the policymaking process created a sense of chaos about Middle East decisions; the waffling and indecisiveness that often characterized the administration's approach seemed remarkably different from the tight control of Kissinger. Israeli diplomats in Washington were the first to acknowledge this fundamental fact of political life in the new administration.

Especially on issues relating to the Middle East, these career officers at the State Department believe that only they, and not the political appointees in the White House, can fully appreciate the nuances of U.S. foreign policy interests. Historically there has long been a conflict of views between these two factions. At the beginning of any new administration, the career officers always seek to carve out an influential role under the new leadership, exploiting to the utmost the fact that they are the ones who have detailed knowledge and experience on very complex issues.

From Israel's point of view, the career officers are usually—but not necessarily always—less friendly than the political appointees. They have often spent a lot of time in the Arab world, where Israel is not on top of the popularity list, whereas the political appointees have spent a lot of time in America, where Israel is popular. But the political appointees usually do not have the necessary information at their fingertips, as do the career Arabists. A very pro-Israeli special assistant to the president, serving in the White House, may feel uneasy arguing over a diplomatic issue in which he has a weak background. Consequently, he may not initially get involved in the bureaucratic infighting that precedes the final debate and decision. But as the administration matures, those closest to the president tend to gain strength.

The bureaucracy is not a monolith. As Harvard political scientist Graham Allison has pointed out:

> Treating national governments as if they were centrally coordinated, purposive individuals provides a useful shorthand for understanding problems of policy. But this simplification—like all simplifications—obscures as well as reveals. In particular, it obscures the persistently neglected face of bureaucracy: The "maker" of government policy is not one calculating decision-maker, but is rather a conglomerate of large organizations and political actors.

Allison has demonstrated effectively that "what happens is characterized as a 'resultant' of various bargaining games among players in the national government." This was especially the case with a secretary of state like

Vance or Rogers, rather than with one like Kissinger or even John Foster Dulles, who ran Foggy Bottom with an iron hand, delegating very little authority to others.

Two early Israel-related decisions taken by Carter and Vance demonstrated the influence of the bureaucracy. One was the denial of concussion bombs to Israel. When President Ford and Kissinger had approved the sale of these bombs to Israel on October 8, 1976, they knew they were bucking the wishes of the many Defense and State Department officials who had opposed the sale for many months. But these officials were ultimately overruled. When Ford was defeated, these officials embarked on an intensive lobbying campaign within the new administration to block the sale. They helped themselves in this by selected leaks to *The Washington Post*. The opponents of the sale—whether they were dealing with the Bureau of Politico-Military Affairs at the State Department or International Security Affairs at the Pentagon—drafted memoranda detailing their reasons why Israel should not receive the bombs, among them the fact that Carter was committed to a reduction in arms traffic. Under Kissinger, most of these documents would probably have never been read at the top of the U.S. government. But Vance studied them carefully—after portions had been leaked to the press, published on page one, and subsequently condemned by editorial writers. At the same time, Arab ambassadors in Washington, themselves encouraged by publicity in the media, kept up a steady stream of official protests over the sale. By the time Vance had made his negative recommendation to Carter, the president was personally against the sale, having been strongly influenced by the press reports. In order to mollify Israel and its supporters somewhat, he had his spokesman announce that a worldwide ban was being imposed on the sale of concussion bombs and that the Pentagon was itself investigating the need for the bomb in the American arsenal.

The second Israel-related decision taken by the new president and secretary of state was the veto of Israel-made Kfir fighter exports to Ecuador. Because Kfirs are powered by U.S.-made engines, Israel needs permission from Washington for export sales. During the final days of the outgoing Ford administration, Kissinger indicated to Israeli Ambassador Simcha Dinitz that he had no objections to the sale, and, though Kissinger could not approve such a deal so late in the life of the administration, he did make a written recommendation on the matter to Vance. When Defense Minister Shimon Peres met with Defense Secretary Donald Rumsfeld and Kissinger in December 1976, there was no indication that approval of the sale was in question. Kissinger, had he stayed in office, might have dismissed the opposition of the Latin American bureau and other bureaucrats in the government, as he often did. But Vance and Carter sought everyone's advice and acted on their recommendations. The sale was vetoed.

Both of these decisions, which were made in the end by Carter himself, followed an extensive review by the government bureaucracy. The top decision-makers in the new administration—Carter, Vance, and National Security Adviser Zbigniew Brzezinski—were to a large extent dependent on the expertise of their advisers when it came to the Middle East because they initially had very little background in that area themselves. All three were relative newcomers to the Arab–Israeli problem. And the bureaucrats recognized this.

Who were the actors in the bureaucracy who exercised the greatest influence on the shape of U.S. policy in the Middle East at the start of the Carter administration? Interestingly, most of them were the same people who worked for Kissinger: Under Secretary for Political Affairs Philip Habib, Assistant Secretary for Near Eastern and South Asian Affairs Alfred Atherton, Deputy Assistant Secretary Arthur "Pete" Day. At the Bureau of Intelligence and Research, there was Harold Saunders. At the National Security Council was William Quandt, who worked for Kissinger until 1974 and returned to the NSC under Brzezinski. Both Brzezinski and Quandt served on the 1975 Brookings Institution panel on the Middle East, where they became friendly. At the Pentagon and the CIA, the only new actors were the ones at the very top; the rest were the same old hands. When it came to the Middle East, these bureaucrats fulfilled critical roles, as far as Israel was concerned, in the staff work that resulted in official policy. This was the group that drafted the statements, made the recommendations, formulated intelligence estimates, outlined the policy options, and, to a very large extent, influenced policy. Under Kissinger, their influence was limited; he could and would casually overrule them. Under Vance, their status was upgraded.

Israeli officials were aware of this challenge and tried to meet it. More importance was placed on contacts with the foreign policy bureaucrats. Determining the center of power and influence within the government bureaucracy became a priority demand.

In several administrations, Harold Saunders played a critical role in shaping U.S. policy toward Israel and the Middle East. He was, in many respects, the perfect bureaucrat, whose career exemplified the behind-the-scenes influence of a top-notch State Department Middle East specialist.

A highly publicized diplomatic spat between Israeli Defense Minister Ezer Weizman and Saunders, then assistant secretary for Near Eastern and South Asian Affairs, at a December 1979 diplomatic reception in Washington, focused the spotlight on the State Department's top Middle East expert. Who exactly was Harold Saunders, and what was his role in the formulation of America's policy toward the Middle East?

Saunders, a softspoken but decisive man, had reached a point in his professional career where he felt very comfortable with his analytical grasp of the Arab–Israeli problem and, therefore, was no longer threatened by personal attacks on him, especially those that periodically emanated from Israeli or pro-Israeli circles. At the State Department, that sense of easy confidence can come only after a career foreign policy bureaucrat has served for a long period in a rough area and under the intense pressure of hard-driving superiors. Saunders had.

His confidence was underscored when he took on the visiting Israeli minister at Ambassador Ephraim Evron's residence. As stunned guests and reporters watched and listened, Saunders and Weizman argued sharply about Israel's policy toward Lebanon. Four days later, after publication of the dispute, the two men appeared before television and newspaper reporters and tried to patch up their quarrel.

Quietly but persistently, Saunders had emerged as a key figure in the shaping of U.S. policy, both before and after the appointment of Sol Linowitz as President Carter's chief representative for the Middle East, replacing Robert Strauss.

Intellectual consistency—that's what Saunders brought most to U.S. policy. He had been around the White House, the State Department, and other branches of the government for a long time. In the get-tough world of Washington politicians and bureaucrats, he survived remarkably well in both Republican and Democratic administrations. Because most of his career involved the Middle East, Saunders gained a reputation as a typical State Department Arabist, an expert who has spent much time in the Arab world, is fluent in Arabic, and is basically unsympathetic to the Israeli cause. Did he fit this profile?

Academically, Saunders never studied the Arab world. After graduating from Princeton in 1952, he moved on to Yale, where he earned a doctorate in American studies in 1956. He enlisted in the Air Force and was detailed to the CIA, where he stayed as a civilian analyst after release from active duty until 1961.

It was only then that he began his Middle East involvement. President John F. Kennedy had just taken office, and Saunders, then thirty-one years old, moved to the National Security Council as a staffer on the Middle East, South Asia, and North Africa. Generally, NSC personnel are replaced with every new presidential administration, but Saunders remained. After becoming senior staff member for the Middle East in 1967, he was kept on the job until 1974.

In that year, Henry Kissinger, who as Nixon's national security adviser had worked closely with Saunders since 1969, moved him from the White House to the State Department as deputy assistant secretary for Near

Eastern Affairs. By then, Kissinger had already become secretary of state. It was immediately following the Yom Kippur War, and Kissinger felt he had to concentrate his best people at State. Diplomatic activity over troop disengagement agreements was hectic. Saunders was needed to fill out Kissinger's first-string team, which also included Joseph Sisco and Alfred Atherton. Saunders accompanied Kissinger on all of his Middle East shuttles and participated in all of the Arab–Israeli negotiations. Even after Kissinger had left his office, Sisco had become president of the American University in Washington, and Atherton had been named ambassador in Cairo, Saunders survived. He left the State Department with the start of the Reagan administration. The new secretary, Alexander Haig, did not ask him to remain. By then, Saunders had become too controversial.

November 12, 1975, marked a turning point in Saunders's career. Until then, he had been a virtually unknown U.S. official. But on that day, he testified before the House Foreign Affairs Subcommittee on the Middle East. The subject on the agenda was the Palestinians. Democratic Subcommittee Chairman Lee Hamilton of Indiana had asked the State Department to provide an in-depth analysis of the Palestinian question. Everyone at State realized that the subject was potentially explosive.

It was only two months after Israel and Egypt had signed the Sinai II accord. Before then, the United States had never really articulated a detailed analysis of the Palestinian question, certainly not in public. Hamilton's request, therefore, caused a flurry at State.

There were four possible candidates to deliver the testimony: Kissinger, Sisco, Atherton, and Saunders. A decision was made to send Saunders, who was the lowest-ranking of the four. Saunders prepared most of the eleven-page presentation, but he enlisted the aid of several other officials, including Atherton, who was then assistant secretary. Kissinger would later inform Ambassador Dinitz and others that he had only looked briefly at the document, but, in fact, he himself had edited two initial drafts prepared by Saunders and had personally cleared the final version. Thus began the "Saunders document" affair.

"In many ways," Saunders had told the subcommittee, "the Palestinian dimension of the Arab–Israeli conflict is the heart of that conflict." That was probably the most controversial sentence in the testimony, but Prime Minister Rabin, Foreign Minister Yigal Allon, Defense Minister Peres, and the rest of the Israeli government reacted very negatively to the entire testimony, possibly responding more to the scare headlines in the Israeli press than to the substance of the remarks. The Saunders appearance had been on a Wednesday. By the following Sunday, the Israeli cabinet had issued a formal communiqué sharply rejecting the document, resulting in a serious strain in American–Israeli relations.

Rereading the Saunders document a few years later confirms how much further the U.S.—and even the Israeli—government has gone on the Palestinian question since 1975. There was no proposal for recognition of Palestinian "legitimate rights and just requirements," as there later was at Camp David. There was no mention of the need to resolve the Palestinian question "in all its aspects." There was no call for the "participation of the Palestinian people in the determination of their own future." Obviously, there was no mention of Palestinian "autonomy" or the creation of a self-governing authority on the West Bank and Gaza Strip.

What the document did assert was that a final settlement would have to include "a just and permanent status for the Arab people who consider themselves 'Palestinians.' " (At that time, the State Department even felt that the word *Palestinians* had to be set within quotation marks.) Saunders had to accept a lot of personal criticism from Israel and its supporters during that episode; it would later prove beneficial in helping him cope with an even bigger brouhaha.

This second incident occurred during Saunders's trip to the Middle East in October 1978, immediately following the signing of the Camp David accords. President Carter and the U.S. government had taken it upon themselves to try to win broader Arab support for the agreements, and Washington began to prepare for the assignment.

Jordan's King Hussein, who initially reacted in a noncommittal manner to the accords, sent Carter a list of questions on the proposed autonomy scheme. Over several weeks, the United States carefully prepared the answers, which were included in some eighteen pages of double-spaced copy. Carter personally edited the final version and signed his name at the bottom of the last page.

It was already mid-October, and Begin was taking heat from his political opponents back home for supposedly selling out Israel's interests at Camp David. Carter asked Saunders to carry the answers to Hussein and, at the same time, to make a pitch for moderate Arab support, especially from West Bank and Gaza Palestinians.

Vance was concerned that the Arabs were not jumping on the bandwagon. The first Baghdad conference of Arab rejectionists had already been scheduled for November. Saunders's mission, therefore, was to try to enlist Arab support for Camp David. By highlighting Israeli concessions, especially the difference between Begin's initial "self-rule" proposals of December 1977 and the final agreements, the United States hoped Saunders would find new friends for Camp David among the Arabs. But the attempt was a failure, and, in the process, Israel reacted very negatively to the pitch.

There were Israeli press reports that Saunders, during his private conversations with the West Bankers and Gazans, was promising them everything, including a state and East Jerusalem. But those reports were inaccurate; Saunders merely reiterated existing U.S. policy toward those sensitive issues, and U.S. policy clearly differed from that of Israel. Instead of taking out its frustration on Carter and Vance, who had given Saunders his final instructions for the mission, Israel turned its anger directly on Saunders.

Saunders reacted to the Israeli uproar quietly and professionally. He and his superiors knew that he had not gone beyond the limits of U.S. policy. A few weeks later, when Begin came to New York for talks with Vance, the secretary of state made a point of asking Saunders along to the session. At the start of the meeting, Vance told Begin and the entire Israeli delegation that their personal attacks against Saunders would have to cease. "If you have complaints about U.S. policy, let's talk about them," one participant at that discussion quoted Vance as having said forcefully but politely. "I want all these personal attacks stopped." Later, Begin and several other Israeli diplomats told Saunders not to take the attacks personally. But given the background, it was hard not to.

Saunders was very sensitive to accusations that he was personally biased against Israel. One of the reasons why he and Dinitz never got along very well was because the ambassador had reportedly told Kissinger that Saunders was anti-Israel, and Kissinger had passed this on to Saunders.

The Israeli who probably knew Saunders best was Ambassador Evron. When Evron was the number two man at the embassy in the 1960s, he and Saunders—then at the White House—developed a good working and personal relationship. Evron probably explained more to Saunders about Israel's sensitivities and needs than anyone else. But, at the same time, Saunders became very sensitized to the plight of the Palestinians. He desperately wanted to find the best means of meeting their needs—without sacrificing Israel's real security interests. Trying to find the answer often pitted him against the Israelis.

Interestingly, Saunders probably had more knowledge about things Jewish than any other non-Jew in the State Department. In many respects, this became a deep and passionate interest for him, going back to the mid-1960s when he had participated in Passover seders at Evron's home in Washington.

But Saunders's attention in later years focused on trying to resolve the Palestinian question. And, like so many other officials in the Carter administration, he concluded that very little progress was likely without first bringing the PLO into the process. Israeli officials believed that Saunders had been overly zealous in trying to find moderation in the PLO's vague signals to the West. Because Saunders had the intellectual ability to convince other senior officials that his views were correct, Israelis accused him of being a bad influence on Vance, Strauss, Linowitz, and others.

Saunders, while advancing the Palestinian cause within the inner circles of the administration, simultaneously managed to convince other top policymakers that his views could also be fair to Israel. This double-barreled approach proved to be persuasive and effective—to Israel's chagrin. Perhaps this explained why Saunders was so greatly trusted by each of the political appointees for whom he worked over a period spanning two decades. He recognized his own limitations in pursuing the negotiations.

A Vance or a Carter could make a political deal with Israel and the Arabs; a Saunders could do the vital behind-the-scenes staff work in helping to make the advance arrangements. It was that blend of professional and political diplomacy that made Camp David a success. Saunders was most responsible for drafting the U.S. position on the initial framework accords; Carter later managed to push them through, more or less.

This was also the process that clearly emerged during Robert Strauss's brief tenure as Middle East envoy and continued as Linowitz assumed his responsibilities. In contrast to Saunders, Strauss recognized—even flaunted— the fact that he did not have much experience in dealing with the delicate nuances of Arab–Israeli diplomacy. Yet he was still asked by Carter to become America's chief Middle East negotiator. Even before the presidency of Lyndon B. Johnson, Strauss recalled in an interview with me, he started developing a "great reservoir of political strength and a good constituency" in the United States. "I've been very fortunate," he said.

Strauss was selected because he had political clout at home and because he understood politics, probably better than anyone else close to Carter. And the more Strauss focused on the key issues of the Arab–Israeli conflict, the more he came to believe—as Carter had before him—that having no more than a vague knowledge of the background of the conflict need not be a disadvantage during peace negotiations.

"If I can be evenhanded, creative, gain the respect of people involved, and if I wisely use the political power which has flowed to me over the years in this country, and if I commit it all to this project, which I am prepared to do, then I am beginning to think that instead of choosing someone else, maybe the president did choose the right man for this job," Strauss told me. "There are many people who bring far more knowledge to this job, who understand the nuances and the history much better than I do and probably ever will. There are many people who bring more intellectual accomplishment and ability to master every detail. But the deeper I get into this thing, the further I get into analyzing the problems of this equation, the more I realize that the plusses and the strengths of Bob Strauss are more important and by far overcome the weaknesses."

But the Arab–Israeli conflict quickly proved too much for Strauss. He walked away from it after only a few months.

The politics of the bureaucracy were very much evident during the ill-fated March 1, 1980, U.S. vote condemning Israel's West Bank settlements at the UN, a vote that Carter later declared a mistake. He cited the supposedly unauthorized inclusion of Jerusalem in the language of the resolution. Understanding the series of events and diplomatic history that led up to the vote is useful in appreciating the power of the bureaucracy in making American policy toward Israel.

Going into the vote, there had been a slow but steady erosion of Washington's willingness to defend Israel in the UN Security Council. Increasingly, the United States had refused to use its veto to block anti-Israel resolutions. The deterioration reached a dramatic low with the vote.

On the eve of the peace treaty signing in 1979, Jordan had asked the Security Council to consider the question of Israeli settlements in the territories captured during the Six-Day War. With UN Ambassador Andrew Young abstaining (as instructed by Washington), the Council passed a resolution establishing a special commission "to examine the situation relating to settlements in the Arab territories occupied since 1967, including Jerusalem." Few people were aware of this resolution and its wording, which prejudged the Camp David agreement on the ultimate sovereignty of the West Bank. The U.S. abstention was motivated by the administration's longstanding opposition to Israeli settlements, which the United States had rejected as "contrary to international law and obstacles to peace."

On the morning after the dramatic announcement of the Camp David breakthrough between Israel and Egypt, Begin and Carter found themselves publicly disputing the exact nature of the Israeli commitment to freeze new settlement construction. Begin said it was for only three months; Carter insisted that it was for the duration of the negotiations leading up to the establishment of a Palestinian self-governing body, which would then consider the issue together with Israel.

That dispute, which seriously damaged the Begin–Carter personal relationship, was exacerbated a month later when the Israeli cabinet announced plans to "thicken" some existing settlements. The announcement came just as the United States was in the midst of a major diplomatic initiative designed to enlist Palestinian, Jordanian, Saudi, and other Arab support for the Camp David framework. At that time, according to American officials, those "moderate" Arabs were still sitting on the fence, waiting to learn more about the details of the peace agreement. To this day, Carter believes that the settlements spat with Israel, and especially the "thickening" announcement, were decisive in pushing the moderate Arabs against

Camp David and toward the rejectionist camp. He makes this case in his memoirs.

Administration officials said their appeals to Israel to freeze new settlement construction were being ignored. They therefore felt comfortable ignoring Israel's appeal to block the Jordanian initiative. The special commission was formed, and Israel denounced it and refused to cooperate with it in any manner, even barring it from visiting Israel to gather information. Thus, the commission spent most of its time in Beirut, Damascus, and elsewhere in the Arab world listening to Palestinian and other Arab testimony. As expected, its final conclusions were less than sympathetic toward Israel. Israeli Ambassador Evron warned the administration at the time that its decision not to veto the formation of the commission would be regretted one day. Security Council commissions do not easily disappear, he said.

Though the United States, by its abstention, allowed the commission to be formed, Vance and other senior American policymakers promised Israel that the United States would "work against" any effort to make the Security Council an important forum for consideration of the settlements issue or any other in the Arab–Israeli conflict. The focus, American officials assured Israel, was going to be the Palestinian autonomy negotiations mandated by Camp David—and nothing else.

After the vote of March 1980, UN Ambassador Donald McHenry was asked about this previous American assurance to Israel. In a conversation with me, he confirmed Washington's understanding but insisted that Israel's February 10 announcement affirming the right of Jews to resettle in Hebron "guaranteed" that the settlements issue would come up in the Security Council. In his view, without the Hebron announcement, which was immediately condemned by the State Department, the Council would not have convened when it did. McHenry and other American officials believed that Israel had itself to blame for the Council resolution.

There was no doubt that the Hebron decision had infuriated everyone in the Carter administration, especially the president. The Carter people regarded it as needlessly provocative. It came just as Middle East Ambassador Linowitz appeared to be making some progress in the autonomy negotiations. There was deep resentment toward Israel—even outright anger. Several key American officials were ready to jump on the anti-Israel bandwagon. When Israel announced its Hebron decision, which merely stated the "right" of Jews to settle in Hebron but took no specific action, State Department officials recognized an opening to punish Israel on the settlements issue, probably Israel's most vulnerable point in terms of American public opinion.

"Israel should be pressed to stop settling the West Bank," urged *The*

New York Times in an editorial following the Hebron decision. "Further criticism of Israel on this issue is pointless," added *The Washington Post.* "So is wrist-slapping. More direct tactics are called for. Why not put a measurable value on the settlements and let Israel decide whether it wants to forfeit that much from its American aid?"

Ambassador Evron recognized that after the Hebron decision the Security Council might convene to examine the report of its special settlements commission. During a meeting with Secretary Vance, the ambassador asked for and received renewed assurances that Washington would "work against" any such Council session. Instructions were supposedly sent to McHenry to that effect. But in the middle of February, McHenry left on a familiarization tour of the Middle East, including a stopover in Israel. The United States did not work very strongly against the convening of the Council. Indeed, *The Washington Star* reported on March 5, 1980, that the initial American decision to vote in favor of an anti-settlements resolution at the UN was made "in principle" as far back as February 22.

With hindsight, Israeli suspicions should have been aroused on February 22, when Senate Majority Leader Robert Byrd, Democrat from West Virginia, inserted a statement into the *Congressional Record* warning that the American people "will be reluctant" to continue to provide Israel with "high-level amounts of aid" so long as Israel persists in building settlements. "I hope the government of Israel reconsiders," Byrd said. Seasoned diplomatic observers presumed that Byrd's remarks were an administration-inspired signal, since the Senate leader was no authority on foreign affairs, and the administration occasionally used Byrd to send indirect messages overseas.

The drafting of the UN resolution lasted for one week. McHenry was not looking forward to abstaining on an issue about which Washington itself had repeatedly disagreed with Israel. According to State Department sources, McHenry recommended that the United States inform other Council members that the United States could support a resolution that merely reiterated American policy on the settlements. Officials at the State Department were receptive. Ambassador Linowitz, who was in the Hague for autonomy negotiations during those critical days, recommended against an affirmative vote. He feared possible damage to the autonomy talks. Israeli officials believed that McHenry's signal to other Council members was a violation of the commitment to "work against" using the Security Council as a forum for considering the settlements issue. When McHenry was asked about this, he strongly objected. "We never made a commitment about how we would vote," he snapped.

The crucial decision to vote in favor of the resolution was taken during Carter's informal breakfast meeting with his foreign policy advisers on

Friday, February 29. Attending the meeting were Carter, Vance, Brzezinski, Secretary of Defense Harold Brown, White House Chief of Staff Hamilton Jordan, and presidential adviser Hedley Donovan. No formal notes were taken. Indeed, according to White House sources, the actual draft text of the resolution was not even on the table during the discussion. (These sources held that Carter actually never read the resolution until after the vote.)

To understand why the administration reversed itself on that UN Security Council resolution, the exact U.S. positions on Jerusalem and the West Bank settlements must be explained. Understanding Washington's official position toward the two explosive issues of the resolution helps put into some sort of proper perspective the incredible events surrounding that UN fiasco. In addition, it helps to determine whether Carter, Vance, McHenry, and other senior U.S. officials knew what they were doing when they agreed to vote in favor of the resolution, or whether it was merely an honest mistake, as they would have liked Israel to believe.

First, regarding Jerusalem: "We strongly believe that Jerusalem should be undivided with free access to the Holy Places for all faiths, and that its status should be determined in the negotiations for a comprehensive peace settlement," Carter said in his carefully phrased March 4 statement admitting the U.S. error in voting for the resolution. He insisted that the U.S. vote did not represent a change in America's position toward Jerusalem. When State Department spokesman Hodding Carter was asked to restate the U.S. position in Jerusalem, he referred reporters to the Camp David accords, which contained a letter from the president spelling out the U.S. position. That letter, however, was rather short. "The position of the United States on Jerusalem," Carter wrote, "remains as stated by Ambassador Arthur Goldberg in the UN General Assembly on July 14, 1967, and subsequently by Ambassador Charles Yost in the UN Security Council on July 1, 1969." The State Department spokesman refused to go beyond that Camp David formulation.

There was a reason for this strange U.S. behavior. According to Carter, Begin, Sadat, and others who participated in the Camp David summit, the entire "framework" package almost fell apart at the last moment because of Jerusalem. There was an eleventh-hour effort made to reach the sort of statement on Jerusalem acceptable to both Begin and Sadat. They made some progress, agreeing on the need for an "undivided" city with "free access" to the "Holy Places." But, in the end, they could not get beyond these generalities.

As a compromise, the three leaders agreed to drop any mention of Jerusalem from the actual agreement. Instead, they attached separate letters explaining their positions. But Begin could not bear even to hear the

U.S. position. He asked Carter not to actually spell it out. U.S. officials then proposed that they refer to earlier U.S. statements, sensitive to the depth of Israel's feeling.

There was a reason why the Americans at Camp David referred to both the Goldberg and the Yost statements. The Yost remarks went beyond those articulated by Goldberg, the latter noting only that the United States did not recognize Israel's "unilateral" action of June 28, 1967, formally annexing the eastern section captured during the Six-Day War. "I wish to make it clear that the United States does not accept or recognize these measures as altering the status of Jerusalem," Goldberg said. "We regret that they were taken."

At the same time, however, Goldberg never stated that East Jerusalem was "occupied territory." Later that year, in November, there was no mention of Jerusalem whatsoever in the UN Security Council Resolution 242. Writing in the *Columbia University Journal of Transnational Law* in 1973, Goldberg explained why:

> A most significant omission in the resolution is any specific reference to the status of Jerusalem and the resolution's failure to reaffirm past UN resolutions for the internationalization of the city. The logical inference from this omission is that 242 realistically recognizes the desuetude (disuse) of the prior UN internationalization resolutions.

Goldberg, in an interview with me, said he had deliberately avoided any reference to Jerusalem as "occupied" territory in order to clearly differentiate its special status from the other territories captured during the war. Israel's annexation was not accepted by Goldberg when he represented the United States at the UN. But he also never lumped Jerusalem in with the other "occupied" territories.

That subtle but diplomatically significant stance was abandoned by the time of the Nixon administration. Ambassador Yost was blunt when he addressed the Security Council on July 1, 1969. "The U.S.," he said, "considers that the part of Jerusalem that came under the control of Israel in the June War, like other areas occupied by Israel, is occupied territory and hence subject to the provisions of international law governing the rights and obligations of an occupying power. Among the provisions of international law which bind Israel, as they would bind an occupier, are the provisions that the occupier has no right to make changes in law or in administration other than those which are temporarily necessitated by his security interest, and that an occupier may not confiscate or destroy private property." Yost went on to "regret and deplore" Israel's actions "in the occupied section of Jerusalem."

Actually, there was no real need for Carter at Camp David to refer to both the Goldberg and Yost statements, since the latter fully spelled out the U.S. view. Politically, however, it made good sense for Carter to refer to Goldberg, who was recognized as a strong friend of Israel. Clearly, Carter and his aides wanted to use Goldberg to help justify their position. By only citing Yost, they would have been more likely to arouse opposition.

If the Yost statement still held, as Carter and the State Department insisted, then the United States still considered East Jerusalem "occupied" territory in which Israel had no right to establish civilian settlements. But, at the same time, Carter stated that Jerusalem should be "undivided," a word accepted (by Sadat) at Camp David. Thus, there was some ambiguity about the U.S. view. These two concepts have never been squared. U.S. officials prefer to leave it that way.

Despite the Yost statement, Ambassador McHenry was still wrong when he said on March 3 that the references to Jerusalem in the March 1 UN resolution did not represent a change in U.S. policy. They did. Even Yost only referred to the "occupied" section of Jerusalem. Neither he nor any other U.S. official ever previously recognized the phrase "the Palestinian and Arab occupied territories, including Jerusalem" as mentioned in the new resolution. In the world of diplomacy, this marked a major deterioration as far as Israel was concerned. Indeed, it represented a significant departure from the careful language of Resolution 242, which spoke only of "territories occupied" during the war, not stipulating "Arab and Palestinian."

What is fascinating about this particular change in policy, however, is that it was not the officially stated reason that Carter asked that all references to Jerusalem be deleted. According to McHenry, Carter merely wanted to continue to honor his Camp David deal with Begin not to actually restate the U.S. position.

In explaining the "failure in communications," McHenry said that he had been told that by removing only paragraph 7, Carter's concerns on Jerusalem would be removed. But paragraph 7, which was deleted, was a relatively innocuous call on Israel to refrain from interference in the "religious freedoms and practices in Jerusalem and other Holy Places in the occupied territories." Presumably, the person who instructed McHenry to get rid of paragraph 7 explained why it was unacceptable to Carter—the Camp David commitment to Begin. But paragraph 5, which remained in the resolution, was a much more blatant violation of that commitment. It said that "all measures taken by Israel to change the physical character, demographic composition, institutional structure or status of the Palestinian and other Arab territories occupied since 1967, including Jerusalem, or any part thereof, have no legal validity and that Israel's policy and practices of settling parts of its population and new immigrants in those territories constitutes a flagrant violation of the Fourth Geneva Convention relative to the protection of civilian persons in time of war."

Here, in paragraph 5, the United States was reissuing in spades a fresh and detailed iteration of the Yost position on Jerusalem—exactly what Carter had promised Begin would not be done. Yet it remained in the resolution. Surely even the most elementary understanding of Carter's rationale for removing paragraph 7 could have been expected to trigger questions among experienced U.S. diplomats about leaving paragraph 5 unquestioned. That was just one reason why the official explanation for the foul-up was so hard to believe. "The U.S. vote in the UN was approved with the understanding that all references to Jerusalem would be deleted," Carter said. "The failure to communicate this clearly resulted in a vote in favor of the resolution rather than abstention."

Incredible as it may sound, the most clear-cut departure from previous U.S. policy contained in the resolution—the call for the dismantling of existing settlements—was not by itself enough to warrant a U.S. abstention. "While our opposition to the establishment of the Israeli settlements is longstanding and well-known," Carter said, "we made strenuous efforts to eliminate the language with reference to the dismantling of settlements in the resolution. This call for dismantling was neither proper nor practical. We believe that the future disposition of existing settlements must be determined during the current autonomy negotiations."

But U.S. officials publicly confirmed that U.S. opposition to the dismantling of settlements was not enough to stand in the way of an affirmative vote. "The thrust of the resolution is consistent with U.S. policy," a spokesman explained. "Few resolutions turn out worded exactly as we would write them. Having expressed our opposition about the idea of dismantling settlements, we decided we should vote for the resolution."

Seen from this perspective, however, U.S. "opposition" to the dismantling language must have been very mild indeed, considering the fact that it was not enough to justify an abstention. Carter personally has confirmed that he had given the approval for the U.S. vote, despite the call for dismantling. "I instructed that we would abstain from the UN resolution that had any reference in it to Jerusalem, and that we would make it clear that we did not favor the dismantling of existing settlements," Carter said.

Supposedly making U.S. opposition "clear" was McHenry, who expressed "reservations" about the call for dismantling of settlements. "There are a number of factors of a practical character that make impractical the call in operative paragraph 6 of the resolution for the dismantling of settlements," he said. "Some projects are not easily dismantled. Moreover, whatever the future status of the occupied territories, there will be a need for housing and related infrastructure for the inhabitants."

Understandably, the entire episode had a strong impact on American–Israeli relations for some time. Despite Carter's public reversal, the impact was quite negative. There was no doubt that Israel's statement in February affirming the right of Jews to resettle in Hebron infuriated Carter, Vance, and all of their aides. When Security Council members predictably raised the issue, there was an instant readiness in Washington to go along with the guaranteed condemnation of Israel. Largely out of personal pique, the president, the secretary of state, the UN ambassador, and their aides wanted to castigate Israel publicly.

Until February 29, the day before the vote, there was no serious effort made to consult with Israeli diplomats in New York or Washington during the week-long drafting of the resolution. There was reason to believe that the administration wanted to keep its position secret from Israel in order to prevent an Israeli outcry which might have forced a U.S. about-face. When Israel asked about the U.S. position, the impression left was that the United States would abstain, as it had done in the past. It may be that in their headlong drive to punish Israel, Carter and his advisers got carried away. For several of them, this was easy; among many U.S. officials there was deep resentment toward Israel. But later the United States paid the price for its rashness—in Israel, in the Arab states, and around the world.

Individually, both Carter and Vance suffered severely as a result of the vote. It hurt Carter on the eve of the Democratic presidential primary in New York. Massachusetts Senator Edward Kennedy won the state, badly bruising Carter in the process. Vance certainly blundered in allowing McHenry to cast the U.S. vote. At the time, Carter was spending the weekend at Camp David. Vance later accepted responsibility for the "failure in communications," but it was the beginning of the end of Vance's tenure at the State Department. Syndicated columnist Joseph Kraft wrote in *The Washington Post* on March 6 that Vance was "a beaten man, discredited by the course of events in Afghanistan, demoralized by what has happened in Iran and no longer able to think with clarity." Within a few weeks, he would resign in protest of the failed U.S. military mission to rescue the American hostages in Iran. But the seeds of that resignation were planted earlier at the UN Security Council.

2

The Israeli Presence in Washington

In January 1981, Israel formally opened its new $5-million chancery building in Washington. District of Columbia Mayor Marion Barry, outgoing Secretary of Commerce Philip Klutznick, Under Secretary of State for Political Affairs David Newsom, AFL–CIO President Lane Kirkland, and Reagan foreign policy adviser Richard Allen were among the hundreds of guests who joined Ambassador Ephraim Evron at the ceremonial opening. The structure, located along Washington's new diplomatic row at the corner of Van Ness Street and Reno Road, was first planned in 1971, after the National Capital Planning Commission rezoned the exclusive area to allow foreign embassies. Eleven other countries, including Jordan, were authorized embassy construction here. Israel, the first to apply for space at the new international center, was also the first to have its building completed; actual construction took less than two years. Architecturally, the five-story building, complete with a sophisticated security system including remote-controlled outside television cameras, could have been lifted from the Jewish Quarter of the Old City in Jerusalem. The structure was designed by the Maryland firm of Cohen, Haft, Holtz, Kerxton, and Associates. Israeli architect Yeshayahu Mandell served as a consultant. Among the chancery's features are an atrium inside the lobby, a menorah design in the iron fence surrounding the corner compound, large arches both inside and outside the building, and a paved courtyard. The structure is well designed for diplomatic entertainment. Its large hall has replaced the ambassador's residence for many formal receptions. In fair weather, guests spill over from the ballroom to the adjacent courtyard. Many contemporary Israeli works of art adorn the walls inside.

Evron recalled that during Prime Minister Begin's first visit to Washington, Evron's predecessor, Simcha Dinitz, had signed an agreement with U.S. Chief of Protocol Evan Dobelle in 1977, officially leasing the land to Israel. Robert Kogod, a local developer and prominent Jewish community leader who personally supervised the entire construction program, received much credit for meeting the initial cost estimates and completing the building on schedule.

The new chancery is the third to be occupied by Israel since 1948. As American–Israeli relations rapidly expanded, the two older buildings became too small, and Israel was forced to lease additional rooms from the Congressional Quarterly building, two blocks from the old chancery just off fashionable Massachusetts Avenue. The new chancery can accommodate all of the nearly one hundred "official" embassy personnel in Washington, including diplomatic, consular, economic, and military officials. Unlike the old location, the new building and the adjacent streets have sufficient "legal" parking facilities for the staff, a fact that has helped ameliorate Israel's notorious record for amassing parking violation tickets. Among the many foreign diplomatic corps in Washington, Israeli diplomats traditionally had ranked second only to those of the Soviet Union in committing such parking violations, which go unpaid to the city government's treasury because of the embassy's diplomatic immunity. At the opening ceremony, a smiling Evron looked pointedly at Mayor Barry as he noted that the new building had adequate parking facilities. The guests laughed.

After May 1948, Ambassador Eliahu Elath and the first Israeli diplomats moved into the old Jewish Agency offices at a handsome rowhouse on Massachusetts Avenue. The second chancery, while considerably more spacious than the first, also came to be too limited as Israel's economic, military, and diplomatic interests in Washington expanded and developed. Indeed, the cubbyhole offices of several senior Israeli officials, including political and press counselors, were so small that it was very difficult to accept visitors. All that has changed in the new building, which has plenty of built-in room for growth.

This, then, is the physical Israeli presence in Washington. But Israel's ability to reach out to many other parts of the U.S. capital is not defined by the design of this one building.

How does one measure clout in Washington? If it means the ability to influence the most powerful political brokers in the capital, the Israeli embassy certainly has it—in the administration, Congress, the news media, the organized labor movement, the academic community, and elsewhere. The approximately twenty Arab embassies also have it, especially at the State Department, at the Pentagon, and among the big-business community. American Jewish political activists in Washington also have clout, certainly more than their Arab–American counterparts and most other organized ethnic groups that lobby the government. But the clout of American Jews in the formulation of U.S. foreign policy toward the Middle East, while significant, is not as instrumental as that of the Israeli embassy, in part because so many administration and congressional leaders simply believe that the Israelis have the decisive say in determining American Jewish policy preferences.

Edgar M. Bronfman, president of the World Jewish Congress, underlined this point in a controversial February 1, 1983, address before that organization's board of governors' meeting in Washington. The thrust of his speech defended the right of Jews in the Diaspora to dissent from the views of the Israeli government, even on issues involving Israel's national security. "Many argue that open dissent in the Diaspora should not be tolerated," he said. "It would weaken us, they say, and make us less effective with our own governments in trying to advance the cause of the State of Israel. Others hold that we lose our credibility when we march in predictable lock-step with whatever [the] Israeli government [does] on each and every issue. Indeed, it has been said by many American secretaries of state that they don't need to hear from so-called leaders of American Jewry—they hear exactly the same song from the Israeli ambassador."

An Israeli recognized this problem when he offered some advice to a concerned American Jew, a leading public relations executive, on improving Israel's *hazbara* (or public information) campaign in the United States. Responding to a proposal for an Israel information service staffed and funded by American Jews, the Israeli wrote:

Since my position—and a bit of direct experience—has at times put me close to Israel's information tangles, and since the subject has long concerned me, permit me the liberty of a comment. The stuff of political image-making is political "news." Ultimately, this news is about power—the institutions in which power reposes and the people who control them. It is the real or perceived link with power that makes a "source" interesting for the press. If an American–Israeli information service would have no such link with the power centers in Israel it would not get very far with the press. And I am prepared to guarantee that it won't develop such a link, for the same Israeli reasons that have prevented all Israeli governments from creating an effective and coherent information machinery.

What American Jewry can do, however, is translate its own political power into an information effort, and that could then be deployed subtly and wisely on Israel's behalf. It would be an indirect but more promising approach. This would require some fresh thinking by American Jewry. I am not certain the disparate nature of the community and its organizations would make that possible. But I am convinced it is the only direction.

It is, in a word, engagement in politics, not public relations, with the media a political target. The aim: to hold the media accountable to the Jewish interest. A precondition: to keep that aim lashed firmly to a larger American interest, as for example the need for more intelligent, credible and sophisticated reporting on international affairs as prerequisite for a more effective and sophisticated American foreign policy. There could be many avenues of approach under the general heading of bringing American Jewry's political power to bear on affecting American opinion regarding Israel. For that, American Jews must put their heads together. They should not expect (or seek) much help from Israel.

American Jewish organizations have spent much time in recent years, especially since the 1973 Yom Kippur War, in trying to come up with a more effective *hazbara* campaign. The need for better public relations was, of course, underlined during the war in Lebanon by the criticism Israel suffered in the U.S. news media. The ambassador in Washington, Moshe Arens, who later became Israel's defense minister, was particularly sensitive to the public-image problems of his country in the United States. Indeed, he argued strongly and repeatedly that the real battle for the direction of U.S. policy toward Israel and the Middle East would be waged in the news media and other public forums.

In an interview with me, Arens noted that the U.S. government, like Israel, was stepping up its public relations campaign. But in the U.S. case, he said, the focus of attention was on the American Jewish community and other traditional pro-Israel supporters in the United States as well as the Israeli public. The U.S. embassy in Tel Aviv in recent years has become increasingly effective in presenting the official U.S. point of view to influential Israelis. Arens saw some silver lining in the fact that the president of the United States and the prime minister of Israel were each seeking to influence the public opinion of the other's constituency; this confirmed the democratic nature of both countries. Yet Arens, who was very talented in making Israel's case on American television, agreed that a large chunk of Reagan's original September 1, 1982, Middle East peace initiative was geared toward influencing the American Jewish community. At first, Reagan had succeeded in weaning away some American Jewish leaders from the official Israeli position. Even AIPAC's Tom Dine and Jack Spitzer, then president of B'nai B'rith, issued statements that contrasted sharply in both substance and tone with the official Israeli cabinet reaction.

"I think that in the final analysis," Arens said, "if you ask where all this is going to lead, public opinion will determine and decide—and the side that is more successful in swaying public opinion about the justice of their views will be the side, on this particular issue, which will probably come out on top." Arens noted, however, that one thing that greatly undermined the Israeli government's efforts to influence American public opinion was the fact that some opposition Labor leaders in Israel had spoken out in favor of U.S. positions and against those of the Israeli government. He would have liked to see more of these Labor personalities follow Begin's example when he had led the opposition. In a debate between Washington and Jerusalem, they should limit their criticism of the government to their appearances at home and not use the platforms offered them in America (especially on television) for that purpose.

Though Arens conceded that the Reagan administration had made some inroads during the war in Lebanon in influencing a few recognized American Jewish leaders to back away from their traditional support for Israel, he did not believe that the Jewish leadership would move away from the Israeli position to any significant degree. "This is an intelligent administration of people who have a considerable degree of sophistication," he said. "They are great friends of Israel, and in many ways, President Reagan may be the greatest friend that Israel has had in the White House in many, many years. But I think I am telling you nothing new if I say that this is an administration that plays hardball. When they want to achieve a certain objective, they go at it very seriously. And so trying to appeal to people in the Jewish community, trying to appeal to people in Israel—that's an obvious part of the tactic and they are doing their best to be successful at it."

In countering the U.S. effort, Arens said, Israel itself has to wage "a very active campaign to explain our positions—and we are in the process of doing that."

For Israel, the ambassador in Washington is in the forefront of that information campaign. Arens, during his one-year tenure, demonstrated that a solid, responsible, and articulate envoy can make a difference and that the selection of an ambassador in Washington is crucial to Israel's relations with—and image in—the United States. What qualities are needed? How does one succeed in Washington?

First, the ambassador must be one who has clout with the Israeli government in Jerusalem. One of Arens's strong points was the widely held perception in Washington that he was an Israeli government insider. His immediate predecessors, Dinitz and Evron, had many excellent attributes, but among their recognized weaknesses was that Begin and other members of the cabinet did not really rely on their views. This stemmed from the fact that both Dinitz and Evron had earlier served Labor governments. Dinitz was a close aide to former Prime Minister Golda Meir, and Evron to David Ben-Gurion. Arens is a former chairman of the Knesset Foreign Affairs and Defense Committee and a heavyweight in the Herut faction of the Likud inner circle.

Second, the ambassador must be a skilled diplomat. As Israel's representative in Washington, the ambassador must promote Israel's interests, first and foremost among the senior echelon of the executive branch of the U.S. government. He must also know when to turn to other sources of support for Israel in the continuing struggle over the making of U.S. policy—Congress, the media, the Jewish community, organized labor, academics, and others—always remembering that support for Israel has traditionally been bipartisan, that Israel has both friends and enemies in the Democratic and Republican parties, and that the same holds true across the left-to-right political–ideological spectrum. Because there are both conservatives and liberals who support and oppose Israel, the ambassador must know when to keep his or her mouth shut on contentious domestic American issues. The ambassador must always be on guard.

Third, the ambassador must be an investigative and diplomatic reporter, acting as Israel's eyes and ears in the United States, giving reports to Jerusalem that explain cogently and precisely the current thinking in Washington and around the country on issues of special concern to Israel and identifying negative trends in U.S. policy early, before they are set in concrete. It is in this area of intelligence gathering, by the way, that Arens's one glaring failure occurred during his year in Washington. Like so many others in the nation's capital, he was surprised by the timing of the Reagan peace initiative in the Middle East. To the embarrassment of Arens, the president and his aides had successfully managed to keep the secret. As a result, Begin, Shamir, and other members of the Israeli cabinet had no advance warning.

Fourth, the ambassador must be a crackerjack speaker who is not afraid to appear on television. In fact, the ambassador's ego should be large enough so that he or she actually loves to go before the cameras at every possible opportunity. It is here that the battle for the hearts and minds of 220 million Americans is fought virtually every day. Because the ambassador is always in demand on the lecture circuit, this person must love to orate and must speak gramatically correct English, not with a heavy accent. The ambassador, moreover, must have full command of all the nuances of the language, as well as being familiar with the history of the Arab–Israeli conflict, and must always be eager to debate with critics. It is in this area that Arens excelled, as did Dinitz and Abba Eban. They were both eager and effective in arguing Israel's case.

Fifth, the ambassador must be likable. There is a well-supported theory that personalities, not just issues, shape policies. Particularly, an ambassador to Washington must know how to deal with Americans, how to laugh and be "one of the gang," especially in establishing personal relationships with key administration figures, senators, congressmen, columnists, and other influential Americans. This involves knowing how to operate in small, private meetings and how to make private backroom deals.

Finally, the ambassador must be a good administrator. The Israeli embassy in Washington is a large operation, employing scores of people, and the ambassador is also responsible for nine other consulates around the country. The bureaucracy is large and can be unruly if not controlled. The ambassador has to know how to delegate responsibility and how to get things done quickly and efficiently.

In short, the ambassador needs the oratory skills and diplomatic experience of Abba Eban, the backroom political acumen of Ephraim Evron, the ability to get along with Americans of Simcha Dinitz, and the credibility back home of Moshe Arens or Yitzhak Rabin.

Exactly how have Israeli ambassadors operated in Washington? What follows are three case studies using some of the experiences of ambassadors Evron, Dinitz, and Arens.

When Ephraim "Eppy" Evron drove through the northwest gate of the White House on Thursday, December 28, 1979, for an introductory courtesy call with National Security Adviser Zbigniew Brzezinski, the veteran Israeli diplomat recalled an earlier Thursday encounter he'd had at the White House a dozen years before.

It was May 25, 1967, a few days before the Six-Day War. Egypt's President Gamal Abdel Nasser had just closed the Straits of Tiran to Israeli shipping, had ordered the UN peacekeeping forces removed from Sinai, and had massed troops along Israel's frontiers. Foreign Minister Abba Eban arrived in Washington following frantic visits to Paris and London in an eleventh-hour diplomatic effort to try to head off a new war. Was President Lyndon B. Johnson prepared to honor the Eisenhower–Dulles commitments of 1957, when the United States had promised to guarantee freedom of passage through the Straits of Tiran in exchange for a total Israeli pullback from the Sinai?

A meeting between Eban and Johnson was scheduled for Friday noon. The foreign minister spent all day Thursday and Friday morning meeting with other senior U.S. officials, including Secretary of State Dean Rusk, Under Secretary Eugene Rostow, and Defense Secretary Robert McNamara. Evron, at that time, was the minister at the Israeli embassy in Washington, the number two man behind Ambassador Abraham Harman. Since taking up the post in 1965, Evron had established an impressive network of contacts with some of the most powerful people in the nation's capital, especially at the White House.

On Friday morning, while Eban and Harman were across the Potomac at the Pentagon for a session with McNamara and the senior U.S. military brass, Evron received a disturbing telephone call from Walt Rostow, the national security adviser at the White House. "The president wants to postpone the meeting with Eban," Rostow said. "He's still studying the material," apparently referring to the Eisenhower–Dulles documents. An American official had been sent to the Eisenhower Library at Gettysburg, Pennsylvania, to find the exact wording of the commitments. But it was already clear to Evron that the United States was stalling. Johnson and Rusk apparently wanted to receive a report from UN Secretary-General U Thant, who had still not returned to the United States from a visit to Cairo, before articulating an official U.S. policy.

When Eban returned to the embassy from the Pentagon, he was upset to learn that the meeting had been postponed. The foreign minister was under intense pressure from his government to leave Washington that same evening in order to catch a flight back to Jerusalem for Sunday's scheduled cabinet meeting. It was to be one of the most fateful in Israel's history.

Eban, Harman, and Evron sat in the ambassador's office waiting for the telephone to ring. But the afternoon ended without the call from the White House. It was already 5:00 P.M.

Eban asked Evron to telephone Rostow and inform the U.S. official that the foreign minister could wait no longer; he would be leaving Washington that evening for Jerusalem, with or without the session with the president. Rostow asked Evron to come over to the White House, but alone.

"The president is unhappy with all the theatrics," Rostow told the Israeli diplomat as they sat down in Rostow's basement office in the West Wing of the White House. Johnson, it seems, had been deeply disturbed by Canadian Prime Minister Lester Pearson's decision a few days earlier to disclose publicly in Parliament certain delicate matters that he had discussed with the U.S. president. Evron was told that the president wanted to make certain that Eban would not follow Pearson's example and that he would not speak to the press after the session. The fact that the meeting took place could be announced, but no details could be given. In addition, Rostow wanted Eban to agree that the session would be described officially as a "courtesy call" and that the foreign minister would enter the White House through the back "diplomatic" entrance rather than through the northwest gate, where the press would see him.

Evron quickly assured Rostow that Eban was not seeking publicity. Israel faced a life-or-death situation, he said. The foreign minister would not speak to the press, Evron said, but it would be ridiculous to characterize the meeting as a mere courtesy call, given the gravity of the unfolding events.

At that point, Evron told me in an interview, Rostow spoke by telephone with the president. The foreign policy adviser sat upright in his chair as he repeated, "Yes, Mr. President. Yes, Mr. President." He informed Johnson of Evron's assurances. The president agreed to meet with Eban at 7:00 that evening.

After hanging up the phone, Rostow stunned Evron by saying that the president wanted to meet with both of them first—immediately—even before Eban drove over to the White House. "Let's go upstairs," Rostow said, putting on his suitcoat. "He wants to talk to you."

During the interview, Evron told me that he had nervously agreed but asked if he could first telephone the Mayflower Hotel, where Eban and Harman were anxiously awaiting word on the meeting, to inform them of the 7:00 P.M. appointment. He made the call.

Evron and Rostow then spent the next half-hour in the Oval Office with Johnson, who did most of the talking. He spoke about congressional limitations on the power of the presidency. "Without congressional approval," he said, "I'm nothing but a six-foot-four-inch Texan friend of Israel." He said he needed more time. He urged restraint on Israel's part. "I appreciate that Israel is not a satellite of the United States," he continued, "but the United States is not a satellite of Israel's either."

It was only at that point that Evron recognized the limited nature of a U.S. presidential commitment.

"Israel is not Czechoslovakia," Evron replied, politely but emphatically referring to 1938. "We will fight for our existence."

Johnson sought to reassure the Israeli diplomat. "Don't worry," he said. "Everything will turn out okay."

By the time the extraordinary meeting had ended, Eban and Harman were already on their way to the White House. Evron drove back to the Mayflower but just missed them. Here he was, the number two man at the embassy, having just spoken with the president of the United States on the most sensitive matters affecting Israel's security, and his superiors did not even know about it. He had to brief them before their own "official" meeting with the president.

He rushed back to the White House, where he just managed to get hold of Eban and Harman as they were about to go upstairs to Johnson's private living quarters. Understandably, Evron's conversation with Johnson was factored into Israel's subsequent decision to preempt. Johnson later refused to go along with Soviet leader Alexei Kosygin's effort at the Glassboro summit to condemn Israel at the UN. The president no doubt recalled his private chat with Evron at the White House.

This episode in diplomatic history underscored the truly unique relationship that developed between Johnson and Evron during their joint tenures in Washington. It was not, however, going to be the last time the president would work directly with the relatively low-level Israeli official, bypassing normal diplomatic channels. Abba Eban would later write in his autobiography that Evron was "one of the most astute and experienced diplomats in Israel's service."

Seven months later in 1967, during the last week of December just a few days before Prime Minister Levi Eshkol's scheduled visit to the United States, Evron's direct pipeline into the White House was again activated.

Shortly after the Six-Day War and Israel's brilliant victory, Johnson imposed an arms "suspension" against Israel in an effort to encourage the Soviet Union to do likewise with the Arabs. But Moscow scorned the U.S. overture and began a massive resupply operation to Egypt and Syria. Meanwhile, France's President Charles DeGaulle ordered an embargo on the delivery of already ordered and paid-for Mirage fighter planes and other military hardware to Israel.

Thus, in the autumn of 1967, Ezer Weizman, then chief of military operations, came to Washington and made Israel's first official request for the supply of F-4 Phantoms. The Johnson administration agreed to study the request. But no decision was forthcoming in the weeks ahead. Eshkol hoped that the final approval for the sale would be extended during his visit to the United States in early January. But, by late December, there was still no indication that the approval would be granted. Evron was asked to see what he could do. He telephoned one of Johnson's advisers at the ranch. Could Evron and the adviser meet in San Antonio?

It was raining in San Antonio a few hours later when Evron arrived there. He was expecting to have a discussion with the adviser at the airport, but, once again, he was in for a surprise.

"The president wants to see you," Evron was told. "I naturally informed the president that I was going to meet with you today and he told me to bring you to the ranch."

Evron later told me he was nervous as they drove to the Texas White House.

"What's on your mind?" Johnson asked the Israeli diplomat as they sat down in the living room for the first round of drinks. They discussed Phantoms and the overall situation in the Middle East. They also talked about the Eshkol visit to the United States. But Johnson's mind drifted elsewhere as they spoke.

"In retrospect," Evron said in an interview a few days after arriving in Washington as the new ambassador, "he must have already been considering the possibility of not running for reelection."

"Eppy," he recalled Johnson as having said, "if anything happens to me, you shouldn't worry because Hubert [Humphrey] will be president and Israel has no more committed friend than Hubert." At that time, Evron conceded, he had no idea why Johnson had made the comment. He let the president's remarks slip by.

Near the end of the discussion, Johnson did ask Evron for one favor. Nearly $500 million in Israel Bond purchases and United Jewish Appeal contributions had gone from the United States to Israel during the weeks and months since the Six-Day War. The outflow in dollars was going to be reflected in the relatively negative year-end balance-of-payments deficit. Would it be possible for the Bank of Israel to transfer some of the funds to an American bank for a few days, so that the economic situation would not appear as bad on paper as it really was?

Specifically, Johnson asked that the Bank of Israel transfer about $250 million to an American bank. Later, after Evron's cable reached Jerusalem, Prime Minister Eshkol and Foreign Minister Eban, after some doing, finally managed to convince David Horowitz, the president of the Bank of Israel, to make the transfer. Horowitz, the typical banker, complained that Israel would lose about $100,000 in interest during the few days of the transaction. But he reluctantly agreed. Johnson and the administration were grateful.

During the Eshkol visit, Johnson informed the prime minister that the United States would provide Israel with Phantoms if (1) the Soviets continued to pour arms into Egypt and Syria (they did), (2) the French continued to embargo the shipment of Mirages to Israel (they did), and (3) the Arabs stood by their August 1967 Khartoum Resolution refusing to negotiate peace with Israel (they did).

The United States, in a politically significant communiqué released at the end of the Eshkol visit, pledged for the first time to follow closely the military balance of power in the Middle East. Later that year, McDonnell-Douglas began to manufacture Phantoms for Israel.

"Just think about it," Evron repeated several times during our interviews. "Me, Eppy Evron, from Kiryat Chaim, meeting with the president of the United States."

On Monday night, October 8, 1973—just two days after Egypt and Syria attacked Israel—Ambassador Dinitz attended a small, informal party at the home of David Brody in Chevy Chase, Maryland. What was the ambassador doing at the party at a time when Israel's very survival was endangered? Was it important for him to be there? The answers to these questions are keys to understanding how Israeli ambassadors operate. This also sheds light on Dinitz's controversial role during the first week of the Yom Kippur War, his general attitude toward Congress and the administration, and his own personality.

Brody is the director of the Washington office of the Anti-Defamation League of the B'nai B'rith. The party had been planned weeks before the war. Invited guests included senators, representatives, and administration officials. Dinitz had been asked to come as guest of honor, and he had accepted. But Dinitz's father died on the Friday before the war, and he flew home to Israel for the funeral, intending to stay for the *shiv'a*, the seven-day period of mourning.

On Saturday morning, Golda Meir summoned Dinitz, her long-time assistant, to her Jerusalem office. She told him that Syria and Egypt were about to attack and that he would have to return to Washington immediately. By 5:00 on Sunday afternoon, Dinitz was at the State Department for his first meeting with Secretary of State Kissinger.

Meir had instructed the ambassador to ask the United States to accelerate the delivery of those arms already on order. She said that, despite Israeli intelligence's optimistic predictions, there would be heavy losses, and it would be important to have equipment to replace what would be lost. But the contingency of a military airlift was not even discussed at that time.

At the State Department, Kissinger told Dinitz that U.S. intelligence reports agreed with the Israeli assessment that it would be a short war, perhaps even shorter than 1967's Six-Day War. Dinitz left very confident.

Next morning, Dinitz was at his office early. He asked his secretary to tell Brody that if his party was still going to take place, he would be there. The secretary was told that senators Frank Church, Walter Mondale, Gale McGee, and Philip Hart, as well as Arthur Burns of the Federal Reserve, had all accepted invitations and that it would be a good opportunity to push Israel's case among influential Americans.

At the party, the ambassador was asked to brief the guests on the course of the war. Dinitz gave a very optimistic analysis, which he said was based on the latest Israeli military intelligence reports. Israel had suffered early losses in aircraft—the Soviet-supplied SAM 6 missile was effective—but Dinitz insisted that the war would be a short one. He still had no idea of the real situation.

Afterward, Dinitz began to mingle with the guests. When he so wanted, he could be the diplomat's diplomat. He talked to Senator Church, who later took over as chairman of the Foreign Relations Committee. Dinitz was clearly courting Church. For Israel, it was crucial that all members of the Foreign Relations Committee be friendly.

It was no secret in Washington that when Dinitz arrived in April 1973 relations between the embassy and the Democratic Party were in need of repair. Ambassador Rabin had virtually endorsed Richard M. Nixon in 1972. Dinitz had his work cut out for him. He recognized the challenge and began to rebuild the traditionally close ties to the Democratic Party. In the process, Dinitz did not alienate the Republicans, whose friendship he also continued to seek. He treaded the delicate line between partisan rivalries, certain that American support for Israel needed commitment from both parties. Brody, who spent much of his time on the Hill, said Dinitz was "highly regarded . . . very effective . . . persuasive . . . and very well-liked." Others generally concurred.

At Brody's party, Dinitz spoke privately in a corner with Church for about fifteen minutes. The next day, Church made the following statement in the Senate: "In view of the rapid replenishment of weaponry being furnished Egypt and Syria by their Arab neighbors, we must see to it that Israel is promptly supplied with such replacement of equipment as she may need to defend herself." Those insiders who were at Brody's party would have been naive to assume that Church's strong statement—which had reverberations in the State Department, the Pentagon, and the White House—was unrelated to his private chat with Dinitz. Even though Dinitz was still optimistic in his hopes for a short war, he was taking no chances. He was beginning to lobby quietly within Israel's best source of supporters—the Congress—in case the administration was not forthcoming and pressure was needed.

The war raged on. On Tuesday, October 9, Dinitz received the first information from Israel that things were not going well. He would have to go to the administration with much more substantial requests. Israel needed many tanks, planes, armored personnel carriers—even ammunition—and the need was so urgent that the only solution would be for the United States to begin a massive resupply operation, an airlift. Dinitz officially asked Kissinger for an airlift for the first time on that Tuesday night.

The versions of the events that followed until the airlift actually began on Saturday night, October 13, differ significantly. Television correspondents Marvin and Bernard Kalb argue in their biography of Kissinger that the secretary tried desperately to get the airlift moving but was challenged by bureaucratic resistance in the Pentagon, which was fearful of an Arab oil embargo as well as a depletion of its stockpiles of conventional arms. Other writers, among them Tad Szulc in *New York* magazine and Edward N. Luttwak and Walter Laqueur in *Commentary*, accused Kissinger of tricking Dinitz into believing that the delay was caused by the Pentagon, when in fact Kissinger himself was to blame. Luttwak and Laqueur charged that Kissinger's objective was to try to persuade Dinitz to refrain from "going public." They wrote: "If Dinitz could be persuaded that matters were best handled by 'high-level' diplomacy, he would refrain from soliciting the support of Israel's friends on Capitol Hill. In other words, Dinitz could help to contain public pressures for aid to Israel that the administration could resist in no other way."

Did Dinitz in fact fail to mobilize Israel's friends? During those four days (after the Tuesday request) Dinitz did try to arouse his supporters publicly, but he did it privately and behind the scenes so as not to antagonize the administration, whose goodwill would, in the end, be necessary. The subject of the relationship between officials of the Israeli government in the United States and American Jews is a sensitive one. American Jews do not like to be accused of dual loyalty. During that first week of the war, however, pro-Israel senators, representatives, journalists, and others began telephoning the Israeli embassy, looking for guidance. What could they do to help? Resolutions? Rallies? Statements? Until Tuesday morning, October 9, Dinitz maintained that things were going well. But by that afternoon his tone began to change. He began recommending action, though on a quiet level.

There can be no doubt, however, that Dinitz believed the Kalb version, that Kissinger was sincerely trying. Senators were asked to call the Pentagon, which they did. Israel's friends were told that "bureaucrats" at Defense were to blame. Many of those involved in the struggle to get the supplies moving have conceded that from Wednesday to Saturday night, when the airlift secretly began, was a very confusing time. No one was certain about what was happening and what they should do to help.

Diplomats at the embassy gave out conflicting reports. This was probably because Dinitz ran a very tight embassy. He was, in fact, accused of running the embassy in the same manner in which Kissinger administered the State Department; only their most trusted senior aides, the small group who formulated and executed policy, were actually made aware of events. However, there can be no doubt that Jewish lobbyists, their friends on the Hill, and the embassy itself were pressuring for action. According to sources close to the late Senator Henry Jackson's office, for example, the senator and Dinitz spoke often during those days. And Jackson was busy speaking to Defense Secretary James Schlesinger, demanding an airlift. Several House and Senate members of the Armed Services Committees were contacting their friends at Defense on Israel's behalf.

Was their action directed to the wrong place? Should those calls have been made to State, where Luttwak and Laqueur claimed the delay really began? Today, it seems a sterile argument, since the airlift, which eventually became more extensive than the 1948 Berlin airlift, did begin and helped to turn the tide of the war. And within a fortnight, the administration had asked Congress to allocate $2.2 billion to pay for those arms. Certainly Dinitz cannot be credited with singlehandedly getting the airlift and the money. He was joined by a conglomeration of powerful forces determined to help Israel, including a basically sympathetic U.S. president. But the Israeli ambassador did his share.

Moshe Arens did not have an easy time establishing close personal relations with senior officials in the Reagan administration. Even before coming to

Washington to succeed Evron in February 1982, the Likud member of Knesset had managed to rub Secretary of State Alexander Haig and other top Reagan policymakers the wrong way by publicly criticizing U.S. policy in the Middle East. The Americans recognized that Arens was an outspoken hawk, not a career diplomat well versed in the nuances of international diplomacy. But they still were genuinely puzzled and miffed by his decision to join Prime Minister Menachem Begin, Defense Minister Ariel Sharon, and Foreign Minister Yitzhak Shamir in openly lambasting the Reagan administration. It was one thing for political leaders back in Jerusalem to speak that way and another for an incoming ambassador to Washington to follow suit. Indeed, U.S. officials suggested privately that the administration might initially try to undercut Arens's effectiveness by simply ignoring him. Important American–Israeli diplomatic business would be conducted through the U.S. embassy in Tel Aviv. Requests by Arens to meet with Haig and other senior officials would be denied, forcing him to see only lower-level functionaires. The administration, if it so wanted, could make Arens's life in Washington rather miserable. What exactly did Arens say that so upset Haig and other heavyweights?

First, he charged that the American–Israeli strategic cooperation agreement, which the administration had suspended in December 1981 following the passage of the Golan Heights Law, was really meaningless and that "both countries will be better off without it." Haig himself had worked very hard behind the scenes to pressure Secretary of Defense Caspar Weinberger and the Pentagon into accepting the strategic accord in the first place. They had been reluctant to elevate Israel officially to the status of America's strategic ally because of the expected political cost in the Arab world. But Haig won the day. While the agreement did not contain as much substance as Israel would have liked, it still represented a step forward—and in a direction Israel had been trying to move for many years.

Second, Arens said that the administration "in effect had decided to adopt the Saudi Arabian positions on Middle East issues. When they do that, I think they don't realize the Saudi Arabians don't have any positions of their own. The Saudi positions are those of the PLO." That sweeping accusation, which ran as a front-page story in major U.S. newspapers, angered not only Haig and the State Department but also President Reagan and other White House officials. Arens's comments during two separate interviews with Israel Radio at the end of December 1981 received extensive publicity in the U.S. news media; all the senior officials were well aware of what he had said. As a result, they said Arens was not exactly starting his assignment on a positive note.

Every ambassador assigned to Washington (there are currently more than a hundred) has as a first priority the establishment of a smooth working relationship with the top echelon of the administration in office. That is where the most crucial, immediate decisions affecting another country can be made. Congress, the news media, the business community, and other influential sectors of American society, while important in long-range planning, are clearly secondary in day-to-day relationships. It is extremely unusual for an ambassador to get to know personally, or even to meet with, the president. Indeed, many ambassadors never see even the secretary of state. Depending on the importance of their business, they will see an under secretary, the assistant secretary for their region, or the desk officer dealing specifically with their country's affairs.

Israeli ambassadors in Washington, especially since 1967, have traditionally had direct access to the secretary of state himself. In fact, Dinitz was often accused in the Israeli press of being too close to Kissinger. With the possible exception of Soviet Ambassador Anatoly Dobrynin, Dinitz saw Kissinger more than any other foreign envoy. Kissinger has even joked about this. With Dinitz sitting at his side, he told a farewell luncheon sponsored by the Conference of Presidents of Major American Jewish Organizations in New York in January 1977: "I have had the privilege of dealing with the ambassador of the only country in the world where its representative in Washington can be criticized for having too close a relationship with the Secretary of State." Kissinger, of course, was right. Other countries would have been delighted with ambassadors who had established such direct access to the secretary of state.

Arens had his work cut out for him. He had special problems related to his image as a hardliner. As chairman of the Knesset Foreign Affairs and Defense Committee, the Herut politician had voted against the Camp David accords in 1978. The American news media, reflecting a high level of U.S. concern, picked up on that theme, and in early March *The New York Times* diplomatic correspondent Bernard Gwertzman wrote that Arens was "living up to his reputation as a plain-spoken hawk whose views on most Middle Eastern issues sometimes make Prime Minister Menachem Begin seem like a moderate." A few days later, ABC television's popular *Nightline* host Ted Koppel said that Arens had brought to his new post "a reputation for toughness. Mr. Arens voted against the Camp David agreement and he remains skeptical as to its worth."

Yet, only six months after arriving in Washington, key Reagan administration officials were openly praising Arens. Those same officials who earlier had predicted a chilly reception for him were now going out of their way to compliment him on his work. This change in attitude was most vividly demonstrated as word filtered back to the United States about Arens's apparently critical role in influencing Israel during the crisis in West Beirut in early August 1982. The Israeli envoy was described by U.S.

officials as a "secret weapon" in convincing Jerusalem that Israel's long-range interests could best be promoted by helping the United States obtain a badly needed foreign policy victory. This meant further Israeli flexibility in special U.S. envoy Philip Habib's negotiations to secure a peaceful PLO evacuation from West Beirut. On Sunday, August 8, Arens suddenly left Washington for Jerusalem. His mission, according to Israeli officials, was to bring to the cabinet a first-hand assessment of the thinking in the United States. As one Israeli diplomat explained, "There is a limit to what can be conveyed in cables."

During the previous six months, Arens had become immersed in getting to know the United States once again. Although he had grown up in New York City, served in the U.S. Army, and studied at the Massachusetts Institute of Technology, he had returned to the United States after two decades in Israel. He had to establish new contacts and to get his finger on the pulse of the country. He did so in numerous speaking engagements and other public and private meetings. He quickly became a familiar face on American television. At the same time, he managed to establish close ties with Haig and other senior U.S. officials, including Under Secretary for Political Affairs Lawrence Eagleburger. Administration officials later pointed out that it was no mere coincidence that the new secretary of state, George Shultz, decided to meet Arens before any other ambassador. Later, Arens continued to meet with Shultz; they also spoke regularly by telephone.

The Americans came to recognize that Arens was no "right-wing kook" as one U.S. official had described him only a few months earlier. But the ambassador became effective in Washington for another reason as well: policymakers concluded that he had clout in Jerusalem.

Arens exploited the fact that he was a politician rather than a professional diplomat. As such, he had greater leeway in making statements and taking decisions. He could go to Jerusalem on the spur of the moment; meet with the prime minister, the defense minister, the foreign minister, and the chief of staff; and sit in on cabinet meetings as a virtual equal. Precisely because of his well-known reputation as a hardliner, a recommendation by Arens that Israel be more sensitive to U.S. concerns could be persuasive in formulating Israel policies.

Rightly or wrongly, the Americans believed that Arens's visit to Israel during the summer of 1982 was a turning point for Habib. They gave the Israeli ambassador much of the credit for the breakthrough. Arens, they said, simply explained how deeply U.S. public support for Israel had eroded since the fighting erupted, and the cabinet responded by compromising on the remaining obstacles in the negotiations. Such an analysis may be somewhat oversimplified, given the nature of Arens's personal views on the use of military force. Still, the Americans believed that Arens bluntly laid out before the Israeli leadership the very likely negative U.S. response to an Israeli assault against the remaining PLO strongholds in West Beirut. He also pointed out how Israel would benefit from an agreement. Again, rightly or wrongly, Washington suspected that Arens's report was essential in avoiding further bloodshed.

For Arens personally, the immediate impact of a Habib success was very positive. Practically all of Washington's important doors were quickly opened to him. At a nationally televised news conference, Reagan referred to Arens by name in making a particular point. Arens was realistic enough to recognize that he had not turned America's thinking around. He had scored some points, especially on television, but he knew that the situation remained tenuous as the administration began to press for broader agreements in Lebanon and on the Palestinian question. But there was a widespread consensus that Arens had gotten off on the right foot.

Arens was clearly on the front line dealing with the Reagan administration and its Middle East peace initiative. After Reagan unveiled his blueprint during a nationally televised address on September 1, 1982, Arens was extremely busy trying to assess the short- and long-term impact on the overall American–Israeli relationship. In an interview with me, he said: "I think the bottom line of the relationship has not been fundamentally affected by what is a very strong divergence of views that almost borders on the confrontational in its intensity—the fact that the president has taken a position which he himself has described in his position paper as 'unalterable' and the Israeli government has rejected those positions. At its root, I think the relationship continues to be one of very solid friendship, essentially an alliance. I think that by the very nature of that relationship, it cannot be disturbed by differences of opinion—even if they are heated, even if they are strident—about how our common goals are going to be attained."

Arens had his own explanation for the timing of the Reagan plan. "Clearly," he said, "they thought they saw what they call here a 'window of opportunity.' And if they saw a window of opportunity, it should have been associated in their minds with the one major event of the past few months, namely, the Peace for Galilee operation in Lebanon. I think also that as a result of Israel's operation in Lebanon, they perceived themselves to be under strong Arab pressure and, therefore, felt called upon to demonstrate, at the earliest possible moment, that they were not always yes-sayers to everything that Israel said, everything that Israel did, and that they were ready to take positions that were not consistent with Israel's positions."

Arens said he had discussed the whole subject of a new U.S. peace initiative on several occasions with Secretary Shultz and that it had become clear that the Americans felt a sense of urgency on the matter. "My position—and the position of Israel—was at least to put first things first, let things fall into place in Lebanon, exert a concerted and common effort in the pursuance of our common goals there; and that coupling events in Lebanon with some new initiatives directed at the autonomy negotiations could exacerbate the problems and maybe prejudice our ability to gain our objectives in Lebanon." After a few such conversations, Shultz agreed with Arens that they should first work to remove the PLO from Beirut.

Referring to the Palestinian question, the ambassador said he and Shultz had been discussing this matter "during the entire period that the Israeli army stood at the gates of Beirut." The various issues connected with the eventual evacuation of the PLO were discussed and sometimes argued about. The discussion invariably came back to "what is called here the Palestinian problem" and the need to address this problem urgently in the light of the lessons learned from the operation in Lebanon. At one stage it had become clear that there was a possibility that a U.S. initiative might surface even before the withdrawal of the PLO from Beirut. Despite all those conversations, the timing of the Reagan peace plan and its actual form came as quite a shock to Arens, who was then in Israel for U.S. Defense Secretary Caspar Weinberger's visit. "The form I didn't know," he said. "The form nobody knew until it was actually presented to us."

Arens complained that the United States had not sufficiently informed Israel of the Reagan plan despite the discussions with Shultz. He distinguished between "discussions" and "consultations"; the latter were indispensable in what was essentially an alliance between Israel and the United States. "We have constant discussions with the secretary—if not on a daily basis, certainly on a weekly basis. But these are not the kind of consultations we are talking about. What we would expect as friends and allies of the U.S.—and what I think we have every right to expect—is that before launching an initiative, the U.S. would specifically consult us about that initiative and there would be a meeting either with me here or with the prime minister in Israel where the U.S. representative would put the position paper that was eventually delivered to us on the table and say: 'We are suggesting presenting this list of American positions. What is your opinion about the content and what is your opinion about the timing and what is your opinion about the very presentation?'

"I don't for a minute suggest that we should expect to have a veto on that kind of an initiative although, by the way, there are some contractual commitments which President Ford took upon himself in 1975 where, in essence, there was an American commitment that there would be no American proposals without prior consultations with Israel in order to avoid proposals which are not consistent with Israel's approach."

"I think," continued Arens, "we should have expected and could have expected that there would be prior consultations on this specific move and that we would have a chance to comment on it, and maybe then there would be a change either in content or in procedure. There was nothing of the sort. I hadn't the faintest notion—and I must admit that I was shocked while I was in Israel accompanying Secretary Weinberger. I was informed that Ambassador Lewis had gone to see Prime Minister Begin at Nahariya and had presented him with this position paper. In that sense, there was no consultation whatsoever. And by the way, the position paper was presented to King Hussein before it was ever presented to us."

He also disclosed that Weinberger himself appeared to have been surprised. "I'm sure that Secretary Weinberger must have been aware that there was a discussion process going on and maybe he was even a party to some of the discussions. But it is my impression that he did not know that on the eve of his arrival in Israel, this position paper was going to be presented to the prime minister."

What was clearly upsetting to Arens was that the administration had deliberately avoided informing Israel of the new strategy. "In our discussions with administration officials here, you could almost sense a certain glee about the secretive way in which this thing was handled and about the very few people in the administration who knew of it, and about their great success in aborting any leaks of this initiative. So clearly it was a deliberate decision to do this in a very secretive manner and not to have any prior consultation with Israel on the subject."

It was Arens's opinion that the administration had simply concluded that it would be "more effective" to launch the new initiative that way, even without a hard advance commitment from King Hussein to join the talks.

The differences between Washington and Jerusalem over the Reagan plan did not affect other American–Israeli issues such as military supplies, economic assistance, and political support. On this Arens was firm. Even then, he was also convinced that Israel would share fully with the United States the military lessons it learned during the fighting in Lebanon, "for the very simple reason that Israel is a member of the democratic community of nations and the United States is the leader of that community of nations. . . . It may take a little time. It is not easy to summarize, to categorize, to classify, to digest all the information that has come out of this complex operation in Lebanon. But I have no doubt that once this is done, the information will be supplied to the United States." It was, shortly after Arens succeeded Ariel Sharon as defense minister in early 1983.

Arens disagreed emphatically with a then popular notion in the American media that American–Israeli relations had slipped to an all-time low. Admittedly, there had been ups and downs over the years, but looked at from a historical perspective, the curve seemed to Arens to be going up continuously. "If you try to compare U.S.–Israeli relations today, in 1982, with U.S.–Israeli relations in 1952, or in 1962, or even in 1972, I think probably you would state that they were better in '62 than in '52 and better in '72 than in '62 and better in '82 than in '72.

"Certainly, there is a much bigger appreciation now of Israel's strategic value in the partnership than there was in the past. We started with a relationship that was based almost solely on common values and common traditions and today, clearly, it is common values, common traditions and common interests—a recognition of Israel's ability to contribute to the protection of these interests. That's really a very solid foundation. And I think you will probably not find many countries in the world regarding which you could say there is a more solid foundation existing for their relationship with the United States."

Arens's life became quite hectic in the months that followed. December 6, 1982, for example, was typical. On that Monday, Arens was, as usual, trying to win friends for Israel—not always an easy job. He flew to New York from Denver, where he had addressed the Union of American Hebrew Congregations. That speech must have been somewhat uncomfortable since earlier in the convention, the UAHC's president, Rabbi Alexander Schindler, had further distanced himself from Prime Minister Begin by declaring that the incorporation of the West Bank into Israel "represents a threat to the Jewish essence of the State and the unity of the Jewish people." Schindler told the Reform Jewish leaders: "While I understand and appreciate Israel's historical claims to Judea and Samaria, I believe it necessary for the sake of peace and justice that these claims be moderated." In New York that same morning, Arens met privately with former President Richard Nixon. They discussed the situation in the Middle East as well as other global problems facing America and Israel. Nixon had requested the unusual meeting. (In earlier months, he had become increasingly critical of the Israeli government and especially of Begin.) From New York, Arens flew to Washington for an important meeting with Deputy Secretary of State Kenneth Dam, the number-two man in the department. The issue: the administration's sharp opposition to congressional initiatives to increase financial assistance to Israel.

If that schedule were not enough, Arens also faced the extraordinary complication of having to work that same day at an Israeli embassy that was on strike. The approximately 1000 foreign service officers of the foreign ministry in Jerusalem had called a one-day, around-the-world strike to protest their compensation (less than their colleagues in the defense and finance ministries) and related working conditions. Arens, a political appointee, was blunt in letting everyone know that he opposed the strike.

He had absolutely no intention of cooperating with it. "He comes from a different background than us," one of the strikers said. "I grew up in the socialist movement: Labor Zionism. We were taught not to break strikes. He grew up with a different mentality."

That, of course, was quite true. In many respects, Moshe Arens was not a typical Israeli. For one thing, he did not look like one. He did not, for example, dress like most Israelis. As Lars-Erik Nelson, the Washington bureau chief of the New York *Daily News* wrote just prior to the ambassador's arrival in Washington, Arens preferred "an Ivy League tweed jacket." He also liked button-down, light blue shirts, preppy style. He wore his MIT graduation ring. The envoy, Nelson said, walked into a room "talking mile-a-minute American. . . . It is hard to remember that he is not in fact an American. He is an Israeli hawk."

Nelson's analysis was certainly true when it was written. But later there were some important changes in Arens's political style, changes that called into question his earlier, well-earned reputation as one of Israel's leading hawks. He had voted against the Camp David framework agreements because he opposed the withdrawal from Sinai. He had thought the price Israel was forced to pay was too high. He had also turned down Begin's offer to become defense minister after Ezer Weizman's resignation. Arens did not want to be in charge of implementing that painful pullback. Ariel Sharon, who voted for Camp David and who was later reluctantly tapped by Begin to become defense minister (after a nearly one-year gap in which Begin himself filled the office), could partially thank Arens, who was then chairman of the Knesset's Foreign Affairs and Defense Committee, for his job. Only several months later did Begin manage to persuade Arens to succeed Evron as Israel's ambassador in Washington.

So how does one adequately describe the flap that developed in November 1982 when Israel Radio reported that Arens, the alleged hawk, had sent a cable to Jerusalem recommending that Israel impose a three-month freeze on new settlement construction on the West Bank? It was, simply stated, a bombshell. Arens later refused to comment on the news reports. He simply said his views on settlements were well known and had not changed since he had arrived in Washington. Still, he would not react directly to the reports. "I cannot refer to our communications," he said. Several other Israeli officials confirmed that Arens had indeed sent such a communication, which Begin quickly rejected. The *Middle East Policy Survey* reported that Arens premised his proposal on the assumption that Jordan's King Hussein would first enter into direct talks with Israel. Asher Wallfish, who covers the Israeli cabinet for *The Jerusalem Post*, reported that Arens had in fact made a number of proposals in September for thawing relations between Israel and the United States, including one for a three-month settlement freeze. Israeli officials were quoted by Wallfish as saying that Arens's recommendations were "purely tactical since the ambassador was known to be as inflexible on the Israeli claim to Judea and Samaria as any hawk in the cabinet—if not more so." One Israeli official surmised that the leak to Israel Radio was part of an effort by rivals in the Herut Party to smear Arens.

Whatever the specifics of the cable, the fact remained that Arens quickly came under sharp criticism at home from some of those very same politicians who were once his closest political and ideological friends. Interior Minister Yosef Burg said he was shocked. Science and Infrastructure Minister Yuval Ne'eman said that it was not an ambassador's job to suggest government policy. Deputy Prime Minister Simcha Erlich said an ambassador should be limited to reporting on the mood and the currents of the host country. The Council of Jewish Settlements in Judea, Samaria, and Gaza sent a telegram to Arens expressing its anger at the reported suggestion.

Shmuel Katz, who once served as Begin's adviser on overseas information but who split with the prime minister over Camp David, asked: "Does Arens not understand the implications of such a 'freeze'? That by agreeing to it, Israel would be embracing the principle that the settling of Jews in *Eretz Yisrael* [the land of Israel] is a bad thing; is in fact, an 'obstacle to peace'? That it will be interpreted as acquiescence in the monstrous Arab charge that the absence of peace is due to the presence of Jews in Judea, Samaria and Gaza, and not to successive Arab aggressions?" Katz continued: "The list of questions is endless. The truth is that Arens knows all the answers. Moreover, he has always been (and remains, as he reaffirmed a few days ago) a vigorous proponent of Jewish settlement in every part of *Eretz Yisrael*—as a vital element in Israel's security and in consummation of the right of the Jewish people to its homeland. The idea, so alien to his outlook, of making this 'gesture' is purely the consequence of intimidation, of the fear that 'intransigence' (the label attached by State Department propagandists during the last twenty years to any refusal by Israel to be dictated to) might be met by 'sanctions'—that is, a stoppage of economic aid."

While Katz and the others were clearly charging that Arens's basic positions had weakened in the face of Washington pressure, *The Jerusalem Post*, in an editorial, quickly came to the opposite conclusion. "One of the better decisions of the second Begin government, which came into office in the summer of 1981, was the appointment of Moshe Arens as ambassador to Washington," it wrote on November 1. Despite Arens's hawkish background, the newspaper said, he was "one of the most capable of the group of men who took over the reins of government with the Likud's advent to power five years ago. His appointment as ambassador put an end to the anomaly of Israel's envoy in Washington—a post more important than most of the ministries in the cabinet—not having the constant ear and confidence of the prime minister, which was the case in the four years of the first Begin government."

Referring to the reported call for a temporary settlement freeze, the editorial said that "Arens is no more 'soft' on the intention to keep the territories in perpetuity than is Mr. Begin. He would seem to be, however, an intelligent hawk, aware of the real forces operating in that great big world out there, which Israel must take into account at least tactically, even if strategically its government is intent on a policy of creeping annexation. . . . Arens's presence in Washington is a special asset to Israel in the context of the Begin government and its basic policies. But it is an asset in danger of being frittered away if his reasoned advice is consciously ignored. The degree of Israel's military, economic and political dependence on the U.S. has grown so great it is foolhardy indeed to send a leading political figure of the ruling party to keep a finger on America's political pulse and then deliberately ignore his readings of that beat."

That Arens had moderated the tone, if not the substance, of his policies after arriving in Washington could not be denied. But that should not have come as any great surprise. Like all previous Israeli envoys serving in the U.S. capital—Eliahu Elath, Abba Eban, Abraham Harman, Yitzhak Rabin, Simcha Dinitz, and Ephraim Evron—Arens was influenced by what he had seen and heard in Washington and throughout his travels around the country. There are limits within which any Israeli ambassador in Washington must operate if the ambassador is to be at all effective in this country.

What Arens and his predecessors heard from senior officials at the State Department, the White House, the Pentagon, and elsewhere in the U.S. government had, of course, been important in affecting their views. But these largely predictable official statements were by no means as critical in shaping and moderating earlier positions as those comments privately expressed by Israel's best friends in Washington. Arens was deeply impressed by the statements he heard from Israel's most sincere and loyal supporters in the U.S. Congress and the Jewish leadership. He saw them all the time. He knew that what they had to say came from the heart and the mind. He knew they represented the foundation of overall American support for Israel, with a proven track record. Without their support, Israel would be in very big trouble.

When they talked, therefore, Israeli ambassadors listened. Those with the most credibility included such senators as Democrat Henry Jackson of Washington State and Republican Rudy Boschwitz of Minnesota and they, too, for tactical reasons, urged Israel to adopt a temporary settlement freeze. They also proposed that Israel take a less hostile stance toward Reagan's peace initiative, as did many other well-regarded American Jewish organizations and leaders. To get a sense of the real mood of the United States, Arens often called in several other longtime pro-Israel Washington hands, such as lawyers Leonard Garment and Max Kampelman or columnists William Safire and George Will. He came to respect their views, and, clearly, they affected his thinking on tactics.

This is not to suggest that Arens, after arriving in Washington, became a veritable dove. He still shared Begin's long-range objective—namely, that Israel should forever control the West Bank and Gaza. Yet, at the same time, the two men developed different tactics to achieve that goal. Arens was clearly much more sensitive to American public opinion. Begin was more concerned about his right-wing critics and their hold on his government.

Arens clearly made a reputation for himself in the United States during his one year as Israel's ambassador. He may have been chairman of the Knesset Foreign Affairs and Defense Committee and a well-known figure in Israel before his arrival in the U.S. capital, but he was virtually unknown in America, even within the Jewish community. All that changed very quickly. Arens became a very well-known personality in the United States. Whether it was ABC's *Nightline*, NBC's *Meet the Press*, CBS's *Face the Nation* or Public Broadcasting's *MacNeil-Lehrer Newshour*, he was often seen on national television news shows defending Israel's case. He was also a regular on the lecture circuit, and as a result he returned to Jerusalem to succeed Sharon as defense minister in February 1983 with a sizable following of American admirers, among them, several senior Reagan administration officials who were impressed with his ability to keep cool under fire.

Arens was always on good terms with former Secretary of State Alexander Haig, who was recognized as a pro-Israel advocate in the administration. George Shultz may not have shared Haig's overall world view as far as Israel was concerned, but that did not prevent Arens from establishing a very good personal rapport with the new secretary as well. Thus, it was not altogether surprising that Mr. and Mrs. Shultz invited Mr. and Mrs. Arens to the Kennedy Center for the Performing Arts just before Arens returned to Israel, even though American–Israeli relations were very strained at that moment. "We had a very enjoyable evening," Arens recalled later. State Department officials pointed out that it was exceedingly rare for the secretary to invite a Washington ambassador to such a private social occasion.

National Security Adviser William Clark, not among the most ardent of Israel's supporters in the administration, was also deeply impressed with

Arens, despite disagreement on important issues. Clark was not supposed to meet with foreign envoys under Reagan administration ground rules. Nevertheless, he wanted to meet Arens, so Senator Paul Laxalt of Nevada, the chairman of the Republican National Committee and a close friend of Reagan's, set up a meeting for Arens and Clark in his own Capitol Hill office. Deputy Secretary of State Dam and Under Secretary for Political Affairs Eagleburger also came to work closely with Arens on a wide range of Israeli-related issues. Like so many other Americans, they appreciated Arens's intelligence and candor. They knew he had a credible voice in the inner circle of the Israeli cabinet, as, of course, was confirmed by Begin's subsequent decision to tap Arens for the defense post.

Arens learned much during his stay in Washington. He came to understand U.S. decision-making and the mood in America, which added an important new dimension to cabinet deliberations in Jerusalem. He also gained a fresh perspective on the American Jewish community. He came to appreciate Jewish political power, expecially in helping to use Congress as a counterweight to the administration. Although a lifelong Herutnik— he had been active in the Betar youth movement in the United States before immigrating to Israel—Arens came to appreciate the fact that other pro-Israel political movements could also generate support for Israel. This was underlined for him by the number of editorial pieces backing Israel that appeared in the pages of *The New Republic* magazine, whose editor, Martin Peretz, came from a Labor–Zionist background.

Over the years, the United States and Israel, like all nations, have conducted their relations through regular diplomatic channels. At the same time, however, there have often been some informal back channels developed in order to skirt around the official foreign policy bureaucracies, which can be stifling in both countries. In Washington, for example, some presidents and their politically appointed aides have been suspicious of the traditionally pro-Arab bias among some State Department Middle East specialists. In Jerusalem, some prime ministers have gone over the heads of the careerists at the Foreign Office to conduct Israel's foreign policy more directly.

There are many ways for American and Israeli policymakers to convey messages to each other. The most direct, of course, involves formal communication through diplomatic channels. The Israeli ambassador in Washington might be called into the State Department for a meeting with the secretary of state. But sometimes a less direct approach is desired. The United States can get its ideas across to officials in Jerusalem through selected leaks to the news media or by using congressmen, American Jewish leaders, and other parties to convey some thoughts. The same, of course, holds true for an Israeli government that might prefer a more subtle method of talking to Washington. The United States and Israel have similar relationships with other states as well, friends as well as adversaries.

Over the years, the American Jewish community has played a unique role as communicator between Washington and Jerusalem. "We do what we can to help Americans understand why and how Israel and the U.S. are good for one another," said Hyman Bookbinder, the Washington representative of the American Jewish Committee, at the Commonwealth Club in San Francisco on March 25, 1983. "We try to counteract false arguments and false charges. We make the moral case for Israel."

Less publicized but equally as important over the years has been the quiet, behind-the-scenes role played by prominent American Jewish leaders in explaining various aspects of U.S. policy to officials in Jerusalem, with the same overall goal of a more harmonious American–Israeli relationship. At times, that might take the form of a respected Jewish leader meeting with the Israeli ambassador in Washington or even going to Jerusalem to make an important point directly to the foreign minister or the prime minister. The advice and insights of these Jewish Americans are very often, but not always, well received in both the U.S. and Israeli capitals. As Americans and as Jews, they have a special interest and ability in promoting close ties between the two countries.

Former President Jimmy Carter has confirmed publicly that one American Jew played a particularly significant role in helping him communicate with the Israeli government during the sixteen months between Anwar Sadat's historic arrival in Jerusalem in November 1977 and the signing of the Israeli–Egyptian Peace Treaty in Washington in March 1979. That person was Leon H. Charney, a New York lawyer who happened to be a close friend of both White House Counsel Robert Lipshutz and Defense Minister Ezer Weizman. As such, Charney had unique access to the highest echelons of the U.S. and Israeli governments.

After the signing of the treaty, Carter wrote to Charney, thanking him for his efforts. "As a private citizen of the United States," the president said, "you personally have been very helpful to me and my administration in our efforts to reach this goal."

"From the very first time I met Leon late in 1977, I think it was, I found him to be a source, if a somewhat mysterious source, of advice," Carter later recalled. "Admittedly, at first, it was a source I regarded with some trepidation for I did not know him well. Since then, I got to know him better through Bob Lipshutz. I found him knowledgeable of the situation in Israel in matters that didn't come to me from the State Department and other official sources, offering me inside advice, Ezer's advice, and his own advice."

Lipshutz had once said that Charney was "one of the unsung heroes of the peace process." Asked about that comment, Carter replied, "I don't want to exaggerate what Bob Lipshutz had said, but there were very few people who played such a significant role and were so unsung. There were, on the other hand, so many sung heroes. I agree wholly with Bob."

For his part, Charney looked back very fondly on those heady days when he shuttled between Washington and Jerusalem, carrying private messages between the top American and Israeli leaders. Most of those messages, of course, never appeared in the formal diplomatic record, although both Charney and Lipshutz kept detailed notes. When Carter was in Jerusalem in early March 1979, trying to wrap up the final details of the peace treaty, Charney was seen speeding in an escorted limousine between the King David Hotel, where Carter stayed, and the Jerusalem Hilton, where Weizman was based.

In an interview with me, Charney recalled that he had at least twice cautioned Carter about taking certain steps that Charney suspected would have severely irritated Begin, thereby setting back the peace process. "I was able in many instances to support Israel's position in the White House," Charney said. "My conduit to the president was normally through Bob Lipshutz, who had immediate access to the president, but I had been asked to report to the president directly if necessary. Bob and I worked as a team to eliminate bureaucracy and to formulate ideas which at the time were vital because of the speed and nature of the process. The president wanted this channel to operate." So did Weizman and the Israeli government.

One of the most spectacular but unpublicized incidents in Israel's history of diplomatic back channels occurred in 1972. Prime Minister Golda Meir and Finance Minister Pinchas Sapir met secretly with American oil magnate Armand Hammer, who was known to have a direct pipeline to the top Kremlin leadership. Hammer was asked to intercede on behalf of Soviet Jews and their desire to emigrate. It was a time of financial crisis for the Soviet Union, and the Israeli proposal—conveyed by Hammer to Moscow—called for a cash transfer of $500 million in exchange for permission for 1 million Jews to leave for Israel. The emigration would be spread out over several years. The money would be raised among world Jewry. But Hammer could not persuade the Kremlin to go along with the scheme, reminiscent of earlier plans in the 1930s to purchase the freedom of German Jews. In late 1984, Foreign Minister Yitzhak Shamir flew to Los Angeles to honor Hammer at an Israel Bonds dinner.

Throughout his diplomatic career, the latest Israeli ambassador, Meir Rosenne, has always tried to put his assignment into some sort of historical perspective, as a Jew and as an Israeli. "You should always remember whom you represent," he told me. "You represent a small country, and you represent not only the Jews who live in Israel today, but you represent all the generations that did not have the privilege to see a Jewish state. It's as simple as that. You represent those who fought in the Warsaw Ghetto, who died in the concentration camps. You represent the soldier who is now in the Golan. . . . You represent the member of the kibbutz, the worker in the factory, the professor in the university, and your task is to make sure that when you leave your job, Israel is stronger than when you became ambassador."

In the United States, Rosenne has made a major effort to be in close contact with the Jewish community, "because, after all, the entire Jewish people are the shareholders of what we call Israel. One should not forget this. This is my belief, and I am very deeply convinced of what I am saying."

3

Strategic Cooperation

On Yom Kippur 1973, Israel was surprised by the coordinated Syrian–Egyptian strike across the Golan Heights and the Suez Canal. Israel's highly respected intelligence organizations had witnessed the extensive military activities across the frontiers in the days leading up to the war, but political analysts had concluded that the Egyptians and the Syrians were simply conducting joint training exercises. The likelihood of a war was believed to be remote.

The previous June, Israel had mobilized its reserves when similar maneuvers were observed along the Egyptian and Syrian borders. The mobilization had been quite expensive for the Israeli economy. Beyond the direct costs, there was the matter of lost productivity as factory workers, farmers, engineers, scientists, and others left their normal jobs to join their army units.

Israel did not mobilize in October, partly because of the earlier costly experience. It was, as the Agranot Commission of Inquiry later concluded, a bad blunder. The surprise attack found the very limited number of Israeli troops along the front lines in disarray. There were extremely heavy losses during the first few days. Indeed, until the Israeli army was able to regroup and fully mobilize, the overall situation looked bleak. During the three weeks of fighting, more than 2500 Israeli soldiers were killed. Several thousand more were injured, many of them very badly.

The first few days also saw some terrible setbacks for Israel in the air war, normally an area of Israeli advantage. Nearly 100 Israeli planes were downed by the Egyptians and the Syrians, most by the Soviet-supplied surface-to-air missile systems installed along the Suez Canal and on the Golan Heights. Many Israeli pilots were killed. Of those who managed to eject themselves from their aircraft, some were badly injured or taken prisoner.

The damage to the Israeli economy from that three-week experience, of course, is still very much felt in Israel.

Nearly a decade later, Israel was considerably stronger militarily, having learned its lessons about defending aircraft from missiles. This was dramatically demonstrated during the summer of 1982, when Israel used recently developed tactics to demolish the Syrian air defense system in Lebanon. The Syrian air force, facing the Israeli pilots without help from the Soviet missiles, was humiliated, losing nearly 100 planes.

But only three years after that war, yet another new situation existed. Both Israel and Syria were heavily influenced by their respective setbacks in 1973 and 1982. The conventional wisdom suggests that neither country wants to see another head-to-head conflict erupt. For its part, Israel suffered greatly during the fighting in Lebanon. The Syrians, for their part, are very much aware of Israel's continued air superiority, despite the fact that the Soviet Union has more than totally rearmed the Syrian forces with even more advanced weapons systems.

Israeli defense planners are still affected by the surprise of 1973. As a result, they continue to plan on the basis of the worst-case scenario. The conventional wisdom before the 1973 war also ruled out another full-scale conflict. The Arabs had been routed during the 1967 Six-Day War, and with brimming confidence Israel presumed they would not start another. That confidence turned into disaster on Yom Kipper 1973.

U.S., Israeli, Arab, and other independent analysts are in general agreement that Israel today would win any fresh round of open warfare with the Syrians, even if other Arab states were to join in. But as Israeli defense officials have noted, this is not a victory Israel seeks. Another full-scale Israeli–Syrian war would result in many more Israeli soldiers being killed and injured, considerable loss in military equipment, and heavy financial expenditures, making an Israeli economic recovery even more remote. Certainly, the damage to the Syrian army would be even more horrible, and the Soviet Union knows it. The Kremlin has made a heavy investment in Syria; it cannot afford to see its allies, using equipment that is designed to intimidate potential opponents, humiliated once more. Thus, the potential for a localized Israeli–Syrian war spreading to include the superpowers cannot be ignored.

Syrian President Hafez Assad was bolstered by the U.S. and Israeli political setbacks in Lebanon. His influence in that war-torn country is very high, as evidenced by the forced abrogation of the May 17, 1983,

Israeli–Lebanese security agreement. He was unusually blunt in advertising his objectives in an interview with ABC's Peter Jennings in late 1984. Assad said Syria would have to achieve "strategic balance" with Israel before embarking on any peace negotiations. "This is what we strive for," he said. "We are serious in our search for peace as much as we are serious in our efforts to achieve military parity."

Assad's alliance with the Soviet Union and his drive for pan-Arab leadership are recognized in Washington as a threat not only to Israel but also to the United States and its other friends in the Middle East. This was made obvious in a revealing speech delivered by a senior Pentagon official on April 29, 1984, to a Jewish audience in Washington. The carefully drafted address, cleared for publication by the Defense Department, was delivered by Assistant Under Secretary for Policy and Resources Dov S. Zakheim.

In the speech, Zakheim spoke of the dangers resulting from this Soviet–Syrian alliance. "Beginning in 1980 with the Soviet–Syrian Treaty of Friendship," he said, "the Soviet presence in Syria has grown from around 2000 to perhaps 7000 to 9000 now. For the first time, there are organized Soviet air defense units in Syria.

"Quite clearly, the Soviets are building a serious military presence in Syria. They have developed an integrated and layered air defense network that they largely control."

Zakheim, a former defense analyst for the Senate Budget Committee, noted that this was the same practice used by the Soviets in Egypt prior to their expulsion in the early 1970s. Syria's SA-5's, he said, now cover part of Israel's own airspace. They are "only a portion of this network that includes a whole array of other SAMs and 'state of the art' equipment and technology that the Soviets have not previously provided outside the Soviet bloc."

Along with this advanced air defense equipment and electronics, he continued, the Soviets are now also providing the Syrians with SS-21's, which are highly accurate surface-to-surface missiles, "undoubtedly useful in Syrian eyes for targeting northern Israeli air bases and weapons depots." All this means, the Pentagon official concluded, that the Soviets "see Syria as the key to their positions and interests in the Middle East. The Syrians, in turn, see Lebanon as a vehicle for extending their own influence throughout the region."

Zakheim said that Assad "may not be a puppet of the Soviets, but he knows very well that his own objectives converge with Soviet interests of undermining moderate Arab regimes and U.S. influence in the area. The Soviets increasingly see that growing Syrian leverage in the area serves these interests. Not surprisingly, the Soviets are doing all they can to provide Syria with an umbrella of protection. That is why we are in constant consultation with the Israelis on the Soviet–Syrian threat.''

It is also why Washington has moved impressively in recent years to strengthen its strategic coordination with Israel. The first steps involved joint medical evacuation exercises in Israel, using existing Israeli facilities, including the Hadassah Medical Center in Jerusalem. Beyond that, the talks are moving ahead speedily in the areas of combined planning, aerial and naval exercises, access points, and requirements for prepositioning U.S. military equipment in Israel. In 1984, Israeli ports received visits from the battleship *USS New Jersey*, the amphibious helicopter carrier *USS Guam*, and many other U.S. vessels. In addition, General P. X. Kelly, commandant of the U.S. Marine Corps, journeyed to Israel—the first time in Israel's history that a Marine commander has done so. General Donald Keith, commander of the U.S. Army's Military Readiness and Development Command, also came to Israel to discuss joint military training exchanges. Israel's chief of staff, General Moshe Levi, came to the United States for a two-week tour in September 1984.

All this highly visible enhanced military cooperation, of course, is in marked contrast to the deliberate U.S. distancing from the Israeli military two years earlier, reflected in the ugly incident in Lebanon when a U.S. marine captain jumped on top of an Israeli tank to prevent it from entering some disputed territory outside Beirut.

Why is Israel interested in closer strategic ties with Washington? What worries Israeli military planners is the prospect of a Soviet–Syrian strategy of trying to bleed Israel by waging an incessant limited war against it. Israeli officials recognize that they simply would not be able to sustain the vitality of the country for long against such strategy; the cost would be enormous.

The massive quantities of military equipment now facing Israel along its eastern front are also very much on the minds of Israeli officials. The number of tanks in Syria, Jordan, and Iraq is now greater than the total number of tanks in the Central Command of NATO in Western Europe. There is clearly a potential for a major Arab offensive should the time come when Israel seemed to be sufficiently worn down.

The Arabs, even without Egypt's forces figured in, can still field considerably more troops than Israel, according to authoritative estimates. Israel's army, when fully mobilized, can amount to nearly 500,000 troops. But Syria's regular army already has some 425,000 soldiers, and, according to its defense minister, Mustafa Tlas, it can rapidly grow to 750,000 when fully mobilized. Iraq currently has over 1 million men in arms.

Tom Dine, executive director of the American Israel Public Affairs Committee (AIPAC), testified before the Senate Appropriations Committee on March 21, 1984, in support of increased U.S. military assistance to Israel. "The resources of the Arab confrontation states make it possible for them to maintain a combined military budget that is double the size of Israel's entire gross national product," he said. "This allows the Arab confrontation states to spend more than $10,000 on war preparations per Israeli citizen, while Israel spends less than $140 per citizen of the hostile Arab states."

Dine pointed out that a wide circle of Arab states openly profess that they will, as in the past, send aircraft and expeditionary forces to join the battle if there is a future war against Israel. Many of these, such as Libya, are armed far beyond the requirements of home defense. Some, like Saudi Arabia, worsen Israel's problem by bringing to the battle the latest European and American weapons. This means that Israel must not only match the best that Soviet science and industry can offer, but also combat the state of the art technologies of Western nations." Dine concluded that though "Israel is a small nation of 4 million people . . . it must have the fighting strength to defeat combined armies comparable in their totality to the whole of NATO on the central front."

Israeli leaders are also very much aware of one additional factor: many more Arabs have been killed by fellow Arabs than by Israelis. Tens of thousands of Arabs have been killed in recent years by Arabs in Lebanon. The Syrian army slaughtered between 10,000 and 20,000 of its own citizens in Hamma in February 1982, following rioting and some guerrilla activities against the Assad regime. And arousing special anguish within Israel recently is the evidence that the Iraqis have used poison gas against civilian concentrations in Iran. Thus, Israelis worry about what the Arabs might do against Israel, if given the chance.

Those fears help to explain what motivates Israel's defense establishment today. As former Defense Minister Moshe Arens told me, "Israel exists in the Middle East, not in the Middle West of the United States," the implication being that wars are not necessarily fought according to the Geneva Conventions in the Middle East.

More than ever before, Americans are finally coming around to recognize the special character of the region. America's own experience in Lebanon was quite bitter and eye-opening. The United States has since packed up and left Lebanon. But Israel, even after withdrawing from Lebanon, has to exist in that difficult part of the world.

Readers of American and Israeli newspapers and viewers of American and Israeli television could not help but notice the very real difference in the treatment that the news media in the two countries gave to the mounting casualties in Lebanon in 1983. As of that time, more than 550 Israeli soldiers had been killed in the aftermath of the June 6, 1982, invasion. Over 250

American marines died. On the front pages of *Yediot Ahronot* and *Ma'ariv*, for example, there were bold, black-framed photographs and short biographical sketches of virtually all of the dead Israeli troops. On Israeli television's nightly news program, there was an almost saturated coverage of the funerals of the slain soldiers and their wailing friends and family.

The United States, of course, is a much bigger country. Thus, the numbers of U.S. service personnel killed in Lebanon, while no less tragic, did not have the personal impact on 220 million Americans as did the deaths of 650 soldiers among the 4 million Israelis. *The New York Times* and *The Washington Post* listed the names of the marines killed in Lebanon, as did most other major American newspapers. But those lists usually were in very small type, buried on inside pages.

Certainly, there was extensive grief and outrage throughout America as a result of these deaths. This was especially the case when a publication or a television network poignantly focused on one individual case. But the overall national trauma in Israel and the deleterious impact on that country's morale, most people will agree, were considerably more intense. There is little doubt, moreover, that it was a major factor leading to the premature retirement of Menachem Begin.

Begin, while prime minister, met often with the parents of slain soldiers. It was, understandably, a terrible ordeal, knowing as he did that his decisions were directly responsible for the initial march into Lebanon and the resulting casualties. Begin told some of his closest aides, as did Ronald Reagan in later weeks, that these direct confrontations with distraught parents were among the most difficult experiences of his life. The pain was very evident in Begin's face.

But for Begin there was another element of pain. Because of the time span from the end of World War II, a very large number of the Israeli men killed in Lebanon were sons of Holocaust survivors—those who had managed to survive Auschwitz and the other death camps, only to resettle in Israel after the war and to create new lives for themselves. They had raised sons on kibbutzim and moshavim as well as in the towns and villages around the country. It is difficult to imagine the personal grief that these parents suffered when their sons, mostly in their twenties and early thirties, were killed in Lebanon. For them, the Holocaust was once again rekindled. Most had already lost their parents during one war; now they had lost their sons, many of whom were named after their murdered grandfathers. Begin, who himself had gone through a rough period of his life in Europe before World War II, could personally relate to these people. Like him, many had come from Poland. He, too, had a son who was raised in Israel after the war. There can be no denying that Begin's personal encounters with these parents in 1982 and 1983 were among the factors leading to his deteriorating physical and emotional health. In the end, he too became a casualty of the war.

For years, Israelis and their most active Washington political supporters have pushed hard to convince successive U.S. administrations that Israel is America's major strategic asset in the Middle East and that closer military cooperation between the two countries should be promoted. Many Americans have long feared a negative spillover in the Arab world, where the United States also has important economic, military, and political interests, should such closer cooperation be undertaken openly. But such openness is desired by the Israelis, who receive extensive amounts of economic and military assistance from the United States every year and who are understandably eager to appear less beholden.

In recent years, an increasingly vocal chorus of Americans and Israelis has come to promote the concept of close strategic cooperation. Their arguments appeared to pay off at the end of 1983, when President Reagan and Prime Minister Shamir announced closer American–Israeli strategic ties in a host of areas vital to both countries.

A joint political–military group was established to coordinate strategic activities in Lebanon and elsewhere in the region. The group was to meet twice a year or at the request of either side. Shamir, during an interview with me, was very confident that the strategy sessions would lead to joint American–Israeli military exercises, prepositioning of U.S. medical and military equipment in Israel, and joint planning for various contingencies.

Former Vice-President Walter Mondale issued a statement around the same time, strongly endorsing greater strategic cooperation between Washington and Jerusalem. "In an effort to promote peace and deter the Soviets," he said, "Israel is an important ally. No Soviet strategist can consider an offensive operation in the eastern Mediterranean without weighing the strength of Israel's defense forces. No Soviet proxy can undertake aggression without risking a crushing rebuff." Other candidates for Presidential nomination also stepped forward to support closer strategic ties.

But this bipartisan appreciation of the potential value of a militarily strong Israel was not always so evident, and in fact, it is a relatively recent development in the maturing of the American–Israeli relationship.

Thus, it was not all that long ago when most Americans tended to cite primarily moral and emotional reasons for their support of Israel. There was the tragic reality of the birth of Israel out of the ashes of the Holocaust. There were the shared democratic traditions and values. Finally, there was a domestic American political consideration—namely, the existence of a strong, well-organized, and politically active pro-Israeli community in the United States, spearheaded by Jews but also including many non-Jews.

The strategic basis for the American–Israeli alliance was seldom cited.

But the case for stressing the strategic side of the story has intensified in recent years. Israeli officials themselves have encouraged this trend, fearing that the massive sums of U.S. economic and military assistance to Israel every year might cease to be acceptable to the American public and Congress unless explained in such a hardnosed way. If Israel were to be demonstrated to provide a useful military and strategic service to the United States on the other hand, the aid becomes justified on the basis of self-interest as well as national morality.

Early pioneers in raising the strategic arguments were largely young military specialists with extensive knowledge of Pentagon thinking. They had seen firsthand how a whole generation of senior U.S. defense planners had simply ignored the Israeli factor in considering U.S strategy around the world. Though the United States and Israel had dramatically strengthened their overall relationship, including ever larger sales of U.S. military equipment to Israel, at the Pentagon itself there was very little actual planning of how the United States might be able to take advantage of Israel's considerable assets. The fear, again, was that such open collaboration in the military area might upset the Arab world.

Among the most active in advancing the strategic argument since the 1973 Yom Kippur War have been Dr. Steven J. Rosen, a former defense analyst at the Rand Corporation in California who later became director of research at the American Israel Public Affairs Committee(AIPAC); Dr. Steven L. Spiegel, professor of political science at the University of California at Los Angeles; and Dr. Joseph Churba, a former Middle East intelligence analyst at the U.S. Air Force who today heads a private consulting and research institute in Washington.

More recently, they have been joined by many other academic specialists who have come to recognize the advantages to the U.S. military itself of closer cooperation with Israel. Naturally, major American Jewish organizations have publicized these advantages. The Jewish Institute for National Security Affairs (JINSA) in Washington was originally established in large measure to promote this line of thinking. (Its other mission was to encourage traditionally liberal American Jews to support a stronger U.S. defense policy, including additional funding for the Pentagon.)

On Capitol Hill, these efforts were bolstered by the late Democratic senator from Washington State, Henry Jackson, who often spoke out on defense issues. Many politicians in Washington have supported Israel over the years because it was good politics back home, but Jackson, with no large Jewish constituency, was among those who sincerely believed it was vital for America to have a solid alliance with a strong, battle-tested, militarily reliable, and democratic Israel. The late Hubert H. Humphrey of Minnesota, another outstanding friend, was more emotional in his dedication to Israel, although he too often underscored the military advantages to the United States of this special relationship.

More recently, Republican Senator Rudy Boschwitz of Minnesota, as chairman of the Foreign Relations Subcommittee on the Middle East, has taken the lead in advancing Israel's strategic importance to U.S. national security interests. Israel can, after all, assemble a 400,000-troop army within seventy-two hours. That partially explains why the United States does not have to maintain a huge ground presence in the Middle East, as it does in Western Europe (300,000 soldiers) and the Far East (150,000 troops).

In fact, Boschwitz, along with Republican Congressman Jack Kemp of New York, often said he would like to remove the military portion of assistance to Israel from the worldwide foreign aid legislation and put it in the Defense Department's budget, where all the indirect assistance to Western Europe and the Far East is buried. But these lawmakers recognize that any such change is extremely unlikely. The State Department, for one thing, knows that removing Israel from the foreign aid bill would practically ensure defeat of the legislation. Aid to Israel, by far the most popular of America's aid recipients, often has carried the entire foreign aid bill through the appropriations process in both houses every year.

Today, the American–Israeli relationship has matured to the point where close cooperation between the two countries is simply taken for granted. This was underlined in an important address delivered on June 12, 1983, by Under Secretary of State for Political Affairs Lawrence Eagleburger. After pointing to the traditional moral rationale for strong U.S. support for Israel, he said: "It also rests on a broad base of common, strategic interests. . . . [Israel's] military power is seen by the Soviets as standing in the way of their expansionist ambitions in the Middle East. The security of Israel is vital to American interests, and we will not stand idly by in the face of Soviet threats to that security." In March 1985, Defense Secretary Caspar Weinberger invited Israel, together with the NATO allies, Japan, and Australia, to participate in the Strategic Defense Initiative (SDI), the so-called "Star Wars" research program. Israel's emergence as an important strategic player in the Middle East and Eastern Mediterranean has not been easy for Israel. Through an enormous amount of hard work, financial sacrifice, creative thinking, and, most unfortunately, heavy loss of life and limb, Israel's military machine has become the most powerful in that part of the world. Israelis would have preferred things to work out differently. They have no great desire to see their sons and daughters serve in the army for three or four years when they turn eighteen, and then serve in the reserves for thirty days a year—lately, even sixty days a year—until they reach the age of fifty-five. They would much rather do more productive and less dangerous things with their lives. But the small population base and the struggle for survival have been such that they have had no real alternative. Had there been no strong military there would be no Israel today.

In the process, Israel also has had to devote more than 25 percent of its gross national product to defense spending, as opposed to some 7 percent in the United States, 5 percent in Britain, 3 percent in West Germany, and 1 percent in Japan. The Soviet Union spends about 13 percent of its GNP on defense. If Israel could limit its defense spending to only 5 percent, or even 10 percent, of its GNP, it would not be plagued by triple-digit inflation and balance-of-payments deficits. Its people would not be subjected to the highest per capita tax in the world. Its external debt would not be so onerous. It would be able to concentrate more of its limited resources on strengthening the nonmilitary domestic infrastructure of the country and improving the day-to-day lives of its people through better education, health, and welfare. It would not have to appeal to the U.S. government and to private American citizens for additional assistance. But that is simply not possible, given the tremendous security problems confronting Israel's leaders.

In addition to its huge defense budget, Israel also has been seriously set back by the crushing cost of importing oil—nearly $2 billion a year. This would not have been the case if Israel had retained the Sinai.

As Israelis witnessed the worsening state of their relationship with Egypt—and the spectacle of embattled PLO Chairman Yasser Arafat receiving a warm welcome by Egyptian President Hosni Mubarak in Cairo—they began to ask whether the sacrifice of returning Sinai (and its precious oilfields) was worth it. If Israel had kept those Sinai fields, the country today would have been 100 percent energy-independent. Oil from Sinai would have met all of Israel's daily needs. But instead, the country is almost 100 percent energy-dependent, having only two tiny oil deposits, one at Ashdod along the Mediterranean and the other down near the Dead Sea. They provide Israel with barely 2 percent of its needs.

This was a very painful Israeli concession, but one for which Israel received very little credit around the world. And when Israel made this sacrifice in 1978–79, there was no oil glut. There was a crunch. Even great countries like France and Italy were willing to provide nuclear technology to Iraq in exchange for long-term oil commitments.

Yet, despite Israel's economic, military, cultural, and political burdens, Americans in larger numbers, in and out of government, are beginning to appreciate that Israel can still serve as a useful ally for the United States. The impression conveyed in many of the American news media reports, of course, was that in the November 1983 Reagan–Shamir summit, the

United States did all the giving while Israel did all the taking. But careful analysts have concluded that the United States gained when it helped to strengthen Israel. As Professor Spiegel of UCLA wrote in *Commentary* in June 1983:

> The facts speak for themselves. Israel is a unique and impressive ally. It influences political developments in its own area, causes the Soviets embarrassment and military difficulties, facilitates the evaluation of American weapons, conveys lessons which can be learned only from combat experience, provides intelligence on the region and saves U.S. defense costs through innovations and modifications of U.S. weaponry. Despite claims that Israel is a strain on the U.S. treasury, the types of assistance it provides more than compensate for U.S. aid.

Until recently, people in the Pentagon simply took Israel for granted. They assumed that during a conventional confrontation against any hostile adversary in that part of the world, the United States could count on Israel's support. ABC News correspondent Ted Koppel, for example, reported in March 1979 that a U.S. Navy study had concluded that Israel's air force alone could destroy the entire Soviet fleet in the eastern Mediterranean.

Thanks to a greater willingness to work closely with Israel out in the open, Defense Department specialists are taking a much more detailed look at what Israel can do for the United States, even if this might not be so welcomed in the Arab world. The Pentagon has authorized all sorts of studies on improving strategic ties with Israel. The results already have become evident.

As AIPAC's Steven Rosen pointed out, the Arabs were never pleased by earlier manifestations of closer U.S. ties to Israel, going back to 1948 when President Truman recognized Israel's independence against the opposite recommendation of the State Department. But as American–Israeli relations have warmed up, the Arabs have come to accept this development as a fact of life.

Critics of closer ties warned President Johnson that the sale of tanks to Israel would poison America's relations with the Arabs. They warned President Nixon that the sale of F-4 Phantom jet fighters to Israel would weaken America in the Arab world. They later made the same argument against closer strategic ties between Washington and Jerusalem. But all of those earlier fears were largely unfounded. The moderate Arabs are going to stay with the United States—regardless of the American–Israeli relationship—because they have nowhere else to go. The problem, of course, is that many officials in Washington continue to take Arab rhetoric at face value.

Ironically, now that the two countries actually are involved in open strategic cooperation, some serious questions are being asked in Jerusalem about the actual wisdom, from Israel's point of view, of this entire course of action.

Shamir, when he was prime minister in 1983 and 1984, found himself on the defensive in explaining what strategic cooperation actually meant. Criticism surfaced not only from the opposition Labor alignment but also from within his own coalition government. He had to come before the Knesset to deny that there were any secret agreements with the United States that could result in Israel's being dragged into another head-to-head confrontation against the Syrians. "The accusations and suspicions against us to the effect that we have allegedly conceded our national independence and become a satellite are ridiculous," he declared. "The U.S. and Israel have simply reached the conclusion that they have a common interest in Lebanon and in standing up to an aggressive Syria. Therefore, it behooves them to work together, to consult with one another, and to try to arrive at a coordinated agreement."

Israelis were worried, moreover, that Israel might have to get involved in direct military clashes to promote largely American—as opposed to strictly Israeli—security concerns. Thus, they were asking whether Israeli soldiers should get killed keeping the Straits of Hormuz open to shipping or bolstering U.S. credibility in the region. There were cries in Israel warning against its becoming America's Cuba in the Middle East.

In earlier years, Israel had served broader U.S. strategic interests in the region, but those cases did not generate much controversy or publicity. One example was Israel's decision to help save King Hussein's regime in 1970, at the specific urgings of President Nixon and National Security Adviser Henry Kissinger. Kissinger, in the first volume of his memoirs, and Yitzhak Rabin, in his 1979 autobiography, included detailed chapters disclosing exactly what had occurred during that initial period of burgeoning American–Israeli strategic cooperation, disclosures that can shed some light on the potential benefits in the future of close cooperation—and the pitfalls.

Hussein, a close ally of Washington for many years, was on the verge of collapse at the time, the PLO having opened a deadly challenge to his regime. Intelligence reports reached Washington that time was quickly running out for the king. The Syrians already had started to move troops and tanks across their border into Jordan to come to the PLO's assistance. There was silence from Hussein's moderate Arab allies. The West Europeans were gun-shy. The American government was already under heavy criticism over its role in Vietnam and, therefore, unable to send in the marines, as they had done in 1958 in Lebanon. Nixon and Kissinger, at that point, turned to Israel.

Rabin, the ambassador in Washington, was summoned to the White House. He was asked to help. The Israeli cabinet in Jerusalem was convened, and a decision was made to mobilize the army, mass troops along the border with Syria and Jordan, and send a diplomatic message to Damascus through third-party channels warning that a continued Syrian thrust into Jordan would result in a fight not only against the Jordanian legion but also against the Israel Defense Forces. Memories of Israel's dramatic 1967 Six-Day War victory were still very fresh in the minds of officers in Damascus. The air force chief of staff at that time was young Hafez Assad, who would later organize a coup and assume power. Apparently, Assad did not then want to tangle with Israel, for the Syrian drive into Jordan was reversed. Hussein, as a result, was able to put down the challenge of the PLO, which was now demoralized by Syria's change of heart. Hundreds, if not thousands, of Palestinians were slaughtered by Hussein's fierce Bedouin troops. The rest were expelled from the country, and most eventually wound up in a basically weak Lebanon, where they succeeded, until Israel's 1982 invasion in achieving their mini-state within a state. Hussein remained in power, largely because Israel was prepared to risk its own soldiers' lives in what the PLO later called "Black September," referring to the large number of Palestinian fighters killed.

Certainly, the Soviet Union has had to take this Israeli military prowess into consideration. That has been translated into some automatic strategic cooperation between the United States and Israel, even if not highly publicized as such.

But now there is a new potential for a changed relationship, one that will bring cooperation out of the closet. "I am pleased to announce that we have agreed to establish a joint political–military group to examine ways in which we can enhance U.S.–Israeli cooperation," President Reagan said on November 29, 1983, at the White House, with Shamir standing at his side. "This group will give priority attention to the threat to our mutual interest posed by increased Soviet involvement in the Middle East. Among the specific areas to be considered are combined planning, joint exercises, and requirements for prepositioning of U.S. equipment in Israel." Shamir, already sensitive to some initial alarm bells sounded in Israel, put a slightly different spin on this strategic cooperation. "The aim of this cooperation," he said, "is to strengthen Israel and deter threats to the region."

When NBC News commentator John Chancellor and other critics complained that the United States gave Israel everything during the Reagan–Shamir summit and received nothing in return, they basically ignored the fact that the United States had received something very tangible from the Israelis: a stronger, more viable Israel, which can, in a crisis, be of critical support in defense of U.S. interests.

Tragically, the United States is still not always taking full advantage of this fact. When U.S. aircraft fighters went into action on December 4, 1983, against Syrian positions in eastern Lebanon, only second-rate A-6's and A-7's could be used. More advanced F-16's could not be used because they can't take off or land from aircraft carriers.

This would not have been the case if the Carter and Reagan administrations had accepted Israel's urgent appeals to take over Etzion and Eitam airbases in eastern Sinai following the Israeli withdrawal. Those bases were among the finest in the world, complete with many underground, reinforced concrete hangars. The United States never really made a major push to persuade the Egyptians to permit a U.S. military presence in eastern Sinai. Elements at the State Department feared it would weaken the Egyptians politically in the Arab world, since the United States would be seen as taking over some parts of Sinai, as opposed to encouraging the departure of the Israelis. Today, as the Saudis and other friendly Gulf states find themselves in trouble and turn to the United States for assistance, they too have probably come to regret the shortsighted decision to abandon Etzion and Eitam.

U.S. and Israeli officials in Washington agree that there has been considerable progress in strengthening the mutual military relationship in recent years.

What appears to be developing, slowly but surely, is a radically new American–Israeli defense alliance, a partnership that is most likely to result eventually in Israel's playing an increasingly more important strategic role for the United States. This represents a fundamental breakthrough, according to both American and Israeli specialists. "Israel is becoming integrated into the U.S. global defense system, much like Italy, Turkey, and South Korea," one American expert noted. "There will be important benefits for both sides."

Indeed, those developments on the bilateral strategic and military front that have been allowed to surface would certainly appear to confirm this trend. Every branch of the U.S. armed forces and the intelligence community is directly involved. The U.S. Air Force, which has traditionally been the closest of the U.S. services to Israel, has exchanged the most sensitive information on aerial warfare with its Israeli counterpart. Most recently, of course, there was a lengthy exchange on the lessons learned by Israel during the fighting in Lebanon in the summer of 1982. Other branches of the U.S. military are finally following the lead of the Air Force.

Despite the highly publicized strains with the American marines early during the participation of the marines in the multinational peacekeeping force in Lebanon, General P. X. Kelly, the marine commandant, visited

Israel in 1984 and was described by his associates at the Pentagon as having returned to Washington a true believer in the strategic importance of Israel to America.

Not coincidentally, the U.S. Marine Corps is moving ahead toward closer cooperation with Israel. The marines have purchased from Israel a powerful antitank weapon. According to U.S. reports, the marines want to upgrade the weapon to destroy heavily armed fortifications. Israel has also designed for the marines a new tactical assault bridge, which Israel will coproduce with an American firm.

The U.S. Army is also involved in the emerging alliance with Israel. At least one year before the October 1983 bombing of U.S. marine head-quarters in Beirut, the Army had entered into prearranged emergency medical procedures with Israel. There was some political foot dragging, resulting in the failure to use Israeli medical facilities in the immediate aftermath of the tragedy. But since then there has been speedy and im-pressive progress. In December 1983, for example, there was a formal agreement designed to make Israeli facilities available to U.S. service per-sonnel. As Secretary of Defense Caspar Weinberger later disclosed in Washington, Americans already are taking advantage of that arrangement.

So far, the most impressive improvement in American–Israeli military ties involves the U.S. Navy, which traditionally had been the least friendly of the U.S. military services toward Israel. Historically, this was the result of the Navy's search for port facilities in the vast geography of the Arab world. There was fear that any public cooperation with Israel might jeop-ardize that effort.

But the Arab states, including the most moderate, have not gone out of their way to assist the U.S. Navy. With the exception of Oman, none of the Arab countries is prepared to grant permanent basing rights to the Americans, not even Egypt or Saudi Arabia.

As a result, there has been serious disillusionment in Washington, and Israel's ports, especially Haifa, have now become more enticing. There has been a dramatically stepped-up use of Haifa by U.S. battleships, in-cluding the *USS New Jersey,* whose powerful sixteen-inch guns had pounded away at hostile targets in Lebanon. This highly visible profile of cooperation is very significant.

U.S. and Israeli officials agree that the change in the Navy's mind set toward Israel began in large measure with the arrival of Navy Secretary John Lehman during the early days of the Reagan administration. Lehman, a former National Security Council staffer under Henry Kissinger, is a strong supporter of Israel. He is also a fighter pilot in the naval reserves who has come to appreciate Israel's talents. He has set a new tone of friendliness toward Israel in the Navy.

The increased visits to Haifa are not the only by-product. Weinberger, during his address on May 23, 1984, before the American Jewish Press Association, also revealed that the United States and Israel were involved in a joint project to develop a new attack patrol boat for Israel's needs in the 1990s, using both American and Israeli weapons. Earlier, the administration had gone ahead with Israel's requests for technical and financial assistance for the new Lavi fighter.

Beyond that, Weinberger specifically cited the U.S. Navy's decision to purchase Israeli-made pilotless reconnaissance aircraft, known as remotely piloted vehicles or RPVs. This sale represented an important breakthrough in Israel's continuing search to win a slice of the Defense Department's procurement pie. The U.S. Navy has leased twelve Israeli-made Kfir fighters to simulate Soviet MiGs in training exercises.

The American–Israeli Joint Political–Military Group holds regular meetings, rotating between Washington and Jerusalem. There are full plenary sessions as well as separate "military to military" and "political to political" discussions. The two sides are reviewing some of the most sensitive subjects on both countries' agendas. "There are certain things which the Americans are exploring with us which they don't even raise with some of their NATO allies," one Israeli official commented. Some of the meetings have been publicized, but most have not. There was a general consensus among the U.S. and the Israeli delegations that as little as possible should be allowed to surface.

It would be a mistake to conclude that this enhanced relationship is going to totally revolutionize U.S. thinking toward Israel overnight. There is still very little likelihood that the Americans would seek any Israeli assistance in a crisis in the Persian Gulf. The only realistic way the Americans might bring Israel into the picture would be if a massive U.S. military involvement in the Gulf were required. That, in turn, would demand air cover, basing, and logistical support, which only Israel could provide. But since few in Washington believe that any such U.S. involvement in the Gulf is going to materialize, Israel is pretty much staying out of the current U.S. strategic thinking regarding the Iran–Iraq war and the possibility that it might spread.

There are certainly critical benefits for Israel in expanding this military alliance with the United States. For one thing, Israel is most anxious to check any direct Soviet involvement in a future round of fighting. Quite logically, the closer the Israeli and American militaries are linked, the less likely it is that the Soviet Union would strike directly at Israel.

Israel's defense strategists recognize their enormous disadvantage in trying to maintain some sort of quantitative arms balance with the Arab states. The Arabs are currently spending some fourteen dollars in weapons purchases for every one dollar spent by Israel, according to a recent study released by the U.S. government's Arms Control and Disarmament Agency. This compares to a three-to-one or four-to-one ratio in the 1960s.

Given the skyrocketing costs of weaponry, there is simply no way that Israel can ever hope to compete in such an arms race. Israel's long-range security interests, according to American Defense Department officials, involve the establishment of a broader strategic deterrent. That means bringing the United States into the equation. The Arabs and the Soviet Union must come to conclude that the Washington–Jerusalem alliance is so solid that any thought of a strike against Israeli armed forces would simultaneously be a strike at the U.S. military. While certain elements within the Arab world are prepared to risk provocation against the United States, the Soviet Union is more cautious about taking any action that would end any partisan divisions within the American foreign policy establishment and might escalate into a superpower conflagration.

The mutual benefits that have been obtained from limited military cooperation suggest that some sort of American–Israeli defense pact is very much a live possibility down the road. On a personal level, U.S. and Israeli military personnel are establishing close relations. There are always several senior Israeli officers at the Army and Navy War Colleges in the United States as well as at other military installations around the country, including Fort Knox and Fort Hood. There are also many American soldiers visiting and serving in Israel. There is a constant rotation of personnel in both directions, resulting in the development of a common language and, most importantly, mutual respect.

All of this may seem incredible to those who recall that the United States embargoed major weapons shipments to Israel until the early 1960s. Israel's president, Chaim Herzog, told me that in the early 1950s, when he served as the military attaché at the Israeli embassy in Washington, he had to work feverishly for months to get one Israeli soldier admitted to a special course for foreign troops in the United States to learn how to drive a jeep. In the end, Israel was allowed to send the soldier, provided there was no publicity.

In short, these indeed are exciting times in the expansion of the American–Israeli military relationship. It is most unlikely that the clock will be set back, regardless of the party in power in Washington or whether a Labor- or Likud-led coalition government rules in Jerusalem. There are new needs determining the new American–Israeli military relationship, beginning a new era of cooperation between Washington and Jerusalem.

4

The CIA and
the Mossad

How close is the current cooperation between the U.S. and Israeli intelligence communities? Are the Central Intelligence Agency and its Israeli equivalent, the Mossad, working closely together? What about the various U.S. Defense Department intelligence agencies and their relationship with Aman, the intelligence arm of the Israel Defense Forces?

These questions are tough to answer for several reasons. For one thing, people involved in intelligence do not tend to be talkative types. When they offer behind-the-scenes information, one never knows whether it is all that reliable, or simply part of some broader disinformation campaign. There are built-in political reasons why getting the true picture is not all that easy.

From the traditional U.S. point of view, any widely held perception of a very close American–Israeli relationship on intelligence or other strategic matters is expected to upset the Arabs. Therefore, U.S. officials rarely advertise their usually close ties with Israel. They fear that such exposure would undermine U.S. interests in the Arab world.

The opposite, of course, is the case in Israel, where officials are often trying to paint a picture of almost uniquely close American–Israeli cooperation in a wide range of areas, including intelligence. By doing so, they hope to convince the Arab states that their continued refusal to deal with Israel directly is futile, that those countries waiting for a real split between Washington and Jerusalem are indulging in wishful thinking. The more the Arabs come to recognize the deeply rooted alliance between the United States and Israel, the more readily they will abandon their challenge to Israel's very right to exist.

Clearly, the late Egyptian President Anwar Sadat was in part motivated to make his historic November 1977 breakthrough visit to Jerusalem because he came to sense that American–Israeli relations were very strong and not about to change radically in his lifetime. He recognized that a continued refusal to deal directly with Israel would result only in continued frustration for Egypt; the option of a decisive military victory over Israel was dead, given Israel's unshakable partnership with Washington.

Still, despite the difficulties involved in trying to assess the current state of American–Israeli intelligence cooperation, there are ways to probe the mystery. Interviews with well-informed and authoritative American and Israeli sources have confirmed that the present intelligence climate between the two countries is quite good. More important, however, there is considerable cooperation. Indeed, there is almost a division of labor in certain highly sensitive intelligence areas.

Take the spread of international terrorism, for example. Israel has an understandable interest in the subject. Its experts have been at the forefront in confronting terrorism for many years. The sharing of information, therefore, can be quite beneficial to the United States. The Federal Bureau of Investigation, for instance, has often looked to Israel's equivalent organization, the Shin Bet, for assistance in this field. It is not widely known, but the FBI usually has one or two resident agents assigned to the U.S. embassy in Tel Aviv, serving as liaison with the Israeli police authorities. The Israel police, at the same time, have a representative attached to the consulate in New York.

"We do coordinate very closely with Israel," said Stan Klein, the chief of FBI's counterterrorism division. "We exchange views with them on threat assessment. We have a very good dialogue with them." He praised Israel's effectiveness in fighting terror, conceding that the FBI itself has learned from some of Israel's techniques.

Israel has come to the United States for help in other matters, especially in those fields where Israel's capabilities are limited. This primarily involves such high-tech matters as electronic eavesdropping, satellite reconnaissance, and photography. Israel traditionally has been stronger in the "human" areas of intelligence gathering—namely, planting competent agents in foreign countries who develop access to useful information. Israel is uniquely equipped to establish these spy networks, since the Mossad can draw talent from new immigrants who have come from almost every country in the world.

One former Mossad station chief in Washington recalled how at one point in his career he had been sent to Syria, posing as a West German businessman. He spoke German fluently, of course, and he had a light complexion with reddish-blond hair. He had a harrowing experience while walking down a Damascus street. He heard someone shout out his real Hebrew name. The person who spotted the Mossad agent was a diplomat from the U.S. embassy who had known the Israeli in Washington. Keeping his cool, the Israeli never turned around and just kept walking. Fortunately, the American quickly realized what was going on and started to move in the opposite direction. The Mossad man was able to finish his work in Damascus successfully before leaving the country.

In 1982–83, the American–Israeli political relationship went through some very difficult ups and downs. The war in Lebanon severely strained the ties between the Reagan administration and the Begin government. But while the political relationship may have bounced around badly, the intelligence relationship was steady throughout. It was almost as if the two countries were on the same wavelength in intelligence matters. The Mossad representative at the Israeli embassy in Washington was in close touch with the CIA, as was the CIA station chief at the U.S. embassy in Tel Aviv with his Mossad counterparts in Israel. The Mossad and CIA agents working at their embassies have a "cover" title, although their real identities, of course, are well known to their respective host governments. That has to be the case since they deal with each other on sensitive intelligence-related material all the time.

This was underlined at a 1976 dinner party at the Israeli embassy in Washington, hosted by Ambassador Simcha Dinitz. The prime minister at that time, Yitzhak Rabin, was in Washington for talks at the White House. At the black-tie affair, I was talking with Secretary of State Henry Kissinger when the Mossad representative at the embassy was introduced to Kissinger. "What is your job at the embassy?" Kissinger asked. The Israeli responded matter-of-factly, "I'm the liaison to the CIA."

At first, that might seem somewhat surprising, given this apparent breaking of cover. But this Israeli official, after all, was dealing with the CIA leadership almost every day; they were exchanging information on all sorts of matters, picking each other's best brains for some tidbits that might prove useful in the national interest. Kissinger, then secretary of state, was obviously well aware of the close ties between the two intelligence communities. The Mossad representative was also aware that I knew his real identity.

Exchanging information is, of course, a two-way street. In the American–Israeli talks on the war in the Persian Gulf between Iran and Iraq, the basic focus was on sharing intelligence, but in this case the Americans did most of the talking, briefing their Israeli counterparts on what actually was happening on the ground. U.S. officials said Israel had some excellent sources of intelligence on much of the Arab world, but that was not so much the case in the Arabian peninsula.

"When it comes to Lebanon, Egypt, Syria, Jordan, and the PLO," an American government source said, "Israel really knows what's going on. But that's not true in Saudi Arabia and elsewhere in the Gulf." The source said that Israel relies on Washington for a great deal of what it knows about the internal scene in these countries. The Israeli embassy in Washington has a full-time diplomat assigned the specific task of collecting such information from U.S. experts at the State Department, the National Security Council, the Pentagon, and the CIA. He winds up spending almost all of his time obtaining U.S. assessments on the Arab world and then passing them along to Jerusalem.

Israeli officials in Washington concede that they get a tremendous amount of information from the Americans, but they still maintain that Israel does have other sources of information about Saudi Arabia and the Gulf. Over the years, there have even been some—but not many—clandestine contacts between high-ranking Israeli and Saudi officials in the United States, Western Europe, and other Third World countries.

The failure by Israeli intelligence to predict the Egyptian–Syrian attack in 1973 returned to haunt Israel, as well as the United States, during the escalating turmoil in Iran in 1978. This time, however, Israel's intelligence estimates were right on target, pointing out for the first time exactly one year earlier that the shah was in deep trouble. But the U.S. intelligence community deliberately ignored repeated warnings from Israel. By the time the United States came around to accepting the Israeli assessment of the instability of the shah's regime, it was too late.

The fact that the CIA discounted the Israeli predictions was partially the result of Israel's intelligence failure in 1973. Until the Yom Kippur War, the United States had come to rely heavily on Israeli intelligence sources for raw information and sophisticated analysis, especially on events in the Middle East. Indeed, President Nixon once said that he was not all that surprised to discover that the CIA had failed to predict the outbreak of hostilities, but he wondered how Israel's highly regarded intelligence officials could have misread the signals.

American intelligence officials were barred, under instructions from Washington, from penetrating organizations opposed to the shah. This followed the standard U.S. practice of not stationing in friendly countries covert agents unknown to the host government. As a result, the United States relied almost exclusively on Savak, Iran's secret police, for information on the strength of the opposition. Savak's assessments were imprecise, to say the least.

Israel, apparently, was under less restraint. Its people in Iran were more willing to try to find out the score, even at the risk of upsetting the shah. More important than the superior Israeli understanding of the Islamic religious forces at work in Iran was Israel's inside information on the behind-the-scenes role played by Libya and several of the Palestinian organizations that were providing extensive support to the shah's opponents. Israel could find out about the inner developments of the Iranian opposition through its outside sources, such as those close to the Palestinians and Libyans. By the time of the revolution, the Palestinian–Libyan connection with the shah's opponents had been well documented in the general press. It was widely known, for example, that radical Palestinian groups, most of which were supported politically and financially by the Soviet Union, were deeply involved in fomenting turmoil on Iran's streets.

That the next regime in Iran severed ties with Israel and ended the export of oil to the Jewish state should, therefore, have come as no surprise. The removal of the shah represented a major strategic victory in the Palestinian struggle against Israel. It obviously also represented a major defeat for the United States, which had come to rely on Iran as a linchpin of U.S. interests in that part of the world. No wonder President Carter was so upset by the U.S. intelligence failure.

When the first cable warning of serious troubles for the shah reached Jerusalem a year earlier, Israeli officials were naturally skeptical. Like their American counterparts, they had come to believe that the shah's giant military machine automatically guaranteed stability. But the Israeli envoy, Uri Lubrani, was persistent in his reporting, and by May, Israel was already warning the Americans of potential disaster. Yet the U.S. intelligence community's preconceived assessments, most of which were based on political wishful thinking rather than on realities, tended to dismiss the Israeli warnings.

There was little doubt that the United States would have been able to salvage something positive in Iran if it had acted decisively upon receiving the first Israeli estimates. An effort could have been made, for instance, to persuade the shah to step down, at least temporarily, and let his son take over. A new government would have been installed, and it would probably have remained pro-American. Oil supplies would have continued to flow to Israel. And the military would have remained solidly pro-American. But as late as September, the CIA was still drafting rosy intelligence estimates on Iran. Under the circumstances, it was not very comforting for Israeli officials to know that American respect for their intelligence operations was once again on the upswing.

In fact, U.S. intelligence estimates on the Middle East have been frequently wrong over the years. The United States, like Israel, did not predict the outbreak of the 1973 Yom Kippur War. Despite the massive Soviet arms shipments to Egypt and Syria, beginning in February 1973 and continuing until the October War, the intelligence community argued that all-out warfare would not erupt. Even after the war had actually started, the Defense Intelligence Agency—the Pentagon's intelligence organization, which is separate from the CIA—was still dismissing the likelihood of major hostilities. The DIA assessment continued for some six hours after Egypt and Syria launched their surprise attack.

Over the years, Israeli defense ministers have usually met with the director of the CIA during visits to Washington. These sessions are never included on their public schedules, but they take place regularly. On Friday, July 29, 1983, for example, Defense Minister Moshe Arens met with CIA Director William Casey at the end of his Washington visit. Foreign Minister Yitzhak Shamir had returned to Israel the night before, but Arens stayed on in Washington basically to exchange some views with Casey and other CIA specialists.

Bob Woodward of *The Washington Post* reported on May 19, 1984, that Casey, during his tenure at the CIA, had provided Israeli intelligence with access to sensitive satellite photographs and other reconnaissance information that had been denied the Israelis in the late 1970s. "The extent of U.S.–Israeli cooperation on intelligence matters is a matter of some concern in the CIA," Woodward said. "Some officials believe that Casey has gone too far. Others say, however, that the United States gets much critical information in return from the well-respected Israeli services." Woodward quoted retired Israeli chief of military intelligence, Major General Yehoshua Saguy, as saying that the CIA now gives Israel access to data from reconnaissance satellites—"not only the information but the photos themselves. Casey now says 'yes' all the time."

The head of the Mossad is a frequent visitor to Washington, although such trips are not made public. On a rare occasion, he might make himself visible. Yitzhak Hofi was head of the Mossad until 1982. He accompanied Prime Minister Begin to Washington for the signing of the Israeli–Egyptian Peace Treaty in March 1979. I saw him sitting quietly at one of the tables under the tent on the South Lawn of the White House during the gala dinner party celebrating the peace treaty. He obviously was not identified as head of the Mossad in the official guest list. His identity in Israel, unlike the identity of the head of the CIA in the United States, is supposed to be kept top secret, although most insiders usually know who he is. Certainly, he is known to the U.S. government, since he spends a considerable amount of time in contact with his American counterparts.

Israel's relationship with the CIA has been close for many years. It was most actively nurtured while the legendary James Jesus Angleton served as head of the CIA's counterintelligence division and as chief liaison to the Israelis. Tad Szulc, the respected American foreign affairs writer, has quoted sources close to Angleton as saying that he had indeed secretly aided Israel with technical nuclear information during the late 1950s. Seymour M. Hersh, the former *New York Times* reporter who wrote a scathing book on Kissinger, reported in *The New York Times Magazine* on June 25, 1978, that Szulc's report "fits in with something I had been told by a high-level CIA official—that Angleton, then in charge of CIA liaison with Israeli intelligence, gave the Israelis similar technical information in the mid-60s." Angleton, who was forced out of the CIA during the Ford administration, some say at the urgings of Kissinger, has refused to comment on the allegations over the years, although everyone agrees that he was a strong supporter of Israel during his years at the CIA.

In fact, CBS News reported back in 1975 that Angleton had lost his job in December 1974 because of policy disputes over Israel and not because of allegations of CIA domestic spying, as originally reported. The network reported that Angleton found Kissinger's policy of detente with the Soviet Union "too soft." Angleton was said to have argued with CIA Director William Colby over Middle East policy questions as well. It was reported that Colby, for example, had ordered Angleton not to visit East Jerusalem during one trip to Israel because it was "occupied Arab territory." CBS News said that one week before *The New York Times* published its story charging domestic spying by the CIA, Colby told Angleton that he would no longer handle Israeli affairs at the CIA. Angleton was offered two options: retire early, or write a manual on counterespionage. Angleton resigned at that point, according to CBS.

Angleton was by no means an exception in the U.S. intelligence community. Over the years, there have been many specialists who have come to appreciate Israel as America's major strategic asset in the region, the assessment often based on Israel's contributions to America's intelligence. At a May 1978 Washington symposium on the strategic balance in the Middle East, for example, former U.S. Air Force intelligence chief, Major General George F. Keegan (retired), said: "Today, the ability of the U.S. Air Force in particular, and the Army in general, to defend whatever position it has in NATO owes more to the Israeli intelligence input than it does to any other single source of intelligence, be it satellite reconnaissance, be it technology intercept, or what have you."

Keegan also disclosed that Israeli intelligence had thwarted a radical coup in Saudi Arabia and that Sadat had been saved from an assassination attempt by information provided to the United States by Israel.

"There were at least three attempts in the last fifteen years to overthrow Saudi Arabia through assassination of the king," Keegan said. "We know that in two of those attempts it was Israeli intelligence alone that made it possible to frustrate and thwart those attempts, as it was Israeli intelligence on one occasion, and possibly two, that prevented radical Arab KGB-backed efforts to assassinate Sadat."

The former U.S. intelligence chief declined to spell out the details, but he did say that Israel's intelligence capability "has kept the Soviets at bay in the Middle East, and thus far has prevented the more radical Arab regimes from capturing and seizing Saudi Arabia."

Keegan also provided the first confirmation of an Israeli air strike against Soviet transport planes bringing weapons to Syria in 1973. "When the Soviets in '73 began to introduce the heavy An-22 transports through Aleppo, the Israeli air force took off, flew 750 miles, and shot one down. The Soviets got the message."

The other three members of the 1978 Washington panel—Admiral Elmo Zumwalt, Jr., retired former chief of naval operations; Lieutenant General Arthur Collins retired, former deputy commander-in-chief of the U.S. Army in Europe; and Lieutenant General Benjamin Davis retired, former deputy commander-in-chief of the U.S. Strike Command—agreed with Keegan's evaluation of Israel's strategic importance. Keegan said that the United States has been supporting Israel over the years because this support is in America's best national security interests. It has little to do with domestic American politics, Holocaust guilt, morality, or anything else, according to Keegan.

Dr. William Kintner, a retired American ambassador who moderated the panel discussion, summed it up this way: "I think the most important thing that has come out of this discussion is the strategic value which a strong Israel provides, not only to itself but to the security of the western world and the U.S. in particular. I think that is a lesson that has to be disseminated throughout every possible avenue of information in the U.S."

Keegan, in an earlier interview with me, had high praise for Israel's "unparalleled intelligence." The United States has benefited greatly from it. "I could not have procured the intelligence on the Soviet air forces, their combat capabilities, their new weapons, their jamming and their electronics and their SAMs with five CIAs," he said.

Admiral Zumwalt described Soviet objectives as wanting to complete the encirclement of China and weaken the West. "The importance of a stable ally in the Middle East, to work with the U.S. to restabilize that area cannot be overstated," he said. Zumwalt pointed to the 1970 crisis in Jordan, when Syria had threatened to intervene against King Hussein's pro-Western regime. "It was insufficient that the U.S. went on an alert and reinforced its Sixth Fleet," he said. "It took, in addition, the willingness and the expressed intention of the Israeli government to send its forces in to support Jordan and to restore the situation to bring together that set of forces necessary to persuade the Soviets to lean on Syria to withdraw." It is for that reason that U.S. military supplies to Israel enhance the security of the United States, he added.

That does not mean that all U.S. intelligence officials have necessarily shared that positive view of Israel. Many have been much more concerned with the U.S. standing in the Arab world. Their assessment of the U.S. national interest has dovetailed more with the traditional Arabist view at the State Department than with the Angleton or Keegan school of thought.

In 1975, for example, there was increasing concern among Israel's intelligence officials over what appeared to be a growing pro-Arab tilt among several senior analysts in the CIA. The November 1975 closed-door testimony on the Middle East arms balance offered by outgoing CIA Director William Colby was one of the first indications of this attitude. Colby, who had just been dismissed by President Ford but was asked to remain in office until his designated successor, Ambassador George Bush, returned from China and won Senate confirmation, argued in his testimony that the balance of power in the Middle East was shifting in Israel's favor. His testimony, which disputed figures offered by Israeli officials, was widely seen as having damaged the administration's own pending request before the Congress for $1.5 billion in military aid for Israel during that fiscal year.

Israel's cause in the CIA bureaucracy, of course, had suffered a serious setback earlier that year when Colby fired Angleton. Angleton, a hardline anti-Communist, bitterly opposed Kissinger's policy of detente with the Soviet Union and had made his views known within high-level policy circles. His strong stance against the Soviets led him to believe that American national interests demanded a strong Israel in the Middle East to counter increasing Soviet gains. Angleton had dominated Israeli affairs in the CIA for many years, refusing to relinquish control of his duties to other intelligence officers, many of whom were less pro-Israel. Colby's controversial testimony against Israel was the further expression of the same attitudes that had drawn Angleton from the CIA.

Washington correspondent Daniel Schorr, working in 1975 for CBS, reported that there was a strong pro-Arab faction in the CIA and only a small pro-Israel faction, and he said that this pro-Arab group strongly influenced decisions. According to Schorr, even before the 1973 war, several analysts had argued that Sadat would not resume hostilities. "Those [CIA] reports were abysmally and catastrophically wrong," he said. Kissinger later used this faulty assessment before the war in attempting to weaken Colby's arguments on the Middle East arms balance. Kissinger bluntly told congressional committees that the CIA evaluation should not be regarded as errorless, and he pointed to the fact that the CIA had misread situations in the past.

The relationship between the intelligence agencies of the two allies continued to deteriorate until, on September 28, 1979, *The Washington Star* called upon the U.S. Justice Department to begin an immediate inquiry into allegedly illegal Israeli spying activities in the United States. Noting that Attorney General Benjamin Civiletti said he had not received a request from Congress or any of its committees to look into Israeli espionage activities, the newspaper said in an editorial: "Well, we hope such a request will materialize." The editorial went on to assert: "It strikes us that the reports of Israeli bugging have been sufficiently informed that Mr. Civiletti would show more concern, in his official capacity, over who's doing what to whom."

Over the previous weekend, Civiletti had issued a statement saying that he had received "no information or evidence" to suggest that outgoing UN Ambassador Andrew Young's meeting with PLO representative Zehdi Labib Terzi had been "bugged or surveilled."

One Israeli source complained that Israel's intelligence services had themselves been partly responsible for the wave of negative publicity because of their tendency in the past to "glorify" their intelligence successes. As a result, this source said, "today's headlines appear credible, when in fact they are just a bunch of vicious lies."

Still, Israeli officials were upset by what they charged was a new wave of "fiction" being written in the U.S. news media about the Mossad. They suspected that the controversial articles and editorials, like the one in *The Washington Star*, may have been prompted by some "anti-Israel" U.S. officials and by several former U.S. officials. They doubted that the Carter administration as a whole had made a concerted decision to encourage such stories.

The allegations involving supposedly illegal Israeli intelligence activities had, of course, come to the forefront in the wake of Ambassador Young's forced resignation for having a secret and unauthorized meeting with a PLO official.

The stories began appearing just as the Young affair unfolded, first with a report in *The Atlanta Constitution* which suggested that Israeli intelligence agents may have bugged Young's meeting with PLO representative Terzi at the home of Kuwait's UN ambassador, Abdullah Yacoub Bishara. Israel denied that report, and the State Department repeatedly stated that the United States had no evidence to confirm that Israeli intelligence agents had learned of the meeting. Civiletti requested a formal inquiry into the allegations and reported that the study had found nothing to confirm them.

Yet the stories continued to appear, and Israeli officials as well as other Israeli supporters believed that Israel's generally popular image was being seriously damaged as a result.

This particular Mossad story appeared in *Newsweek* magazine under the headline "Israel's Spies in the U.S." The magazine charged that "the Israelis routinely spy on their U.S. allies." It quoted one unnamed "U.S. intelligence expert" as saying that Israel has "penetrations all through the U.S. government. They do better than the KGB." The magazine said that "with the help of American Jews in and out of the government, Mossad looks for any softening in U.S. support and tries to get any technical intelligence the administration is unwilling to give Israel." A former CIA agent, also unnamed, was quoted by the magazine as saying, "Mossad can go to any distinguished American Jew and ask for his help." The article said, "The appeal is a simple one: when the call went out and no one heeded it, the Holocaust resulted." According to *Newsweek*, Israel "is not likely to use its information against the U.S., but CIA officials still think Mossad's U.S. operations threatened American security. One intelligence source says that what data the Soviets can't get in the U.S., 'they can steal back from the Israelis.' "

Israeli officials were especially incensed by that accusation, claiming that Israel's intelligence network was considerably more secure than that of the United States and other allies, such as Britain, France, Italy, West Germany, and Japan.

Most of the Mossad stories stressed one recurring theme: the James Bond-like abilities of Israel's intelligence services. "Mossad is perhaps the most cunning in the world," said *Newsweek*. According to the magazine, the United States "tolerates" Mossad's activities because of "a reluctance to anger the American Jewish community and partly because the U.S. has too much to lose. Israel has given the Pentagon complete access to Soviet military equipment captured from the Egyptians and Syrians. Mossad's Jewish contacts in the Soviet Union and Eastern Europe are among the CIA's most valuable sources of intelligence. A Mossad agent, for instance, obtained a copy of Khrushchev's famous speech denouncing Stalin." All this was done, *Newsweek* said, with only about 1000 Mossad agents worldwide, far fewer than the CIA or the KGB.

An article in the December 1983 issue of *Washingtonian* magazine raised the sensitive matter of American Jews serving in U.S. national security jobs involving Israel and the Middle East. Is there still a built-in suspicion of a dual loyalty that has kept Jews out of these positions, especially at the CIA? Yes, according to Dale Van Atta, the author of the article, which was entitled "God and Man at the CIA." Van Atta is an investigative reporter who works for nationally syndicated columnist Jack Anderson.

Over the years, Van Atta has specialized in national security issues. He noted that Jews "have come a long way" in making advances in recent years, but there are still problems.

"Because they were considered to be naturally pro-Israel and therefore suspect, Jews were not actively recruited," Van Atta said. A former senior CIA official was quoted as saying: "It was an unwritten rule that we didn't want any Jews working on the Middle East problem. So most of the analysts were Arabists—they had studied in Egypt, Syria, and the like, or were the children of businessmen and others who had lived there."

Van Atta pointed out that for two decades, the Israeli desk in the CIA was "tucked away in the counterintelligence staff because its chief, James Jesus Angleton, was chief liaison with Israeli intelligence. . . . The desk has since been moved out of counterintelligence, and a number of Jews have attained prominent positions within the agency."

But he added that "suspicion lingers." He cited the circumstances surrounding the resignation of Max Hugel as chief of clandestine services only a few weeks after CIA Director Casey named him to that slot in 1981. Thus, Van Atta wrote, "the old-boy network successfully aided the ouster" of Hugel by "playing on this mistrust of Jews."

Understandably, that suggestion in the article infuriated Hugel, a wealthy New Hampshire businessman who had worked closely with Casey during Ronald Reagan's 1980 presidential campaign. Shortly after Casey named Hugel to the sensitive position, *The Washington Post* published front-page allegations from two of Hugel's former business associates, charging that he had been involved in some improper deals many years earlier. Hugel strongly denied the charges but resigned in order to spare Casey and the president any further political embarrassment. Since then, he has worked aggressively to try to clear his name. He successfully filed suit against his two accusers, Tom and Sam McNell, but they have mysteriously disappeared.

Of course, there had been resentment to Hugel's appointment among many of the professionals at the CIA. They clearly did not like the fact that an outsider was being brought into that position, especially someone without much experience in the intelligence business.

As it was, they were not happy with Casey's own appointment by President Reagan to head the agency. Cord Meyer, a former CIA agent who now writes a newspaper column, brought the displeasure over Hugel's appointment to the surface with an initial article condemning the appointment. Others quickly followed, generating momentum against Hugel. It was then that *The Washington Post* came forward with the McNell charges. Bob Woodward, who coauthored the story, dismissed the assertion that anti-Semitism played a role in the Hugel affair. In an interview with me,

Woodward said he had not come across any evidence to support such a contention during his investigation of the McNell accusations and the events leading up to Hugel's decision to leave the CIA.

Hugel also told me that he does not believe that anti-Semitism played a role. But he still pressed the CIA as well as *Washingtonian* magazine to look further into the matter in order to clarify it once and for all. After reporting the initial anti-Hugel accusations, *The Washington Post* dropped its coverage of the matter, including the disappearance of the McNell brothers.

Hugel's attorney, Paul L. Perito, wrote to James E. Taylor, the CIA's inspector general, proposing an investigation. In the letter, Hugel denied that he had passed information to the Mossad. "Moreover, our client is understandably disturbed to read the suggestion that his resignation was the result of intra-agency anti-Semitism—a suggestion he believes is totally without merit," Perito continued.

"Mr. Hugel is concerned, however, that since these charges have surfaced publicly, they will damage the integrity of and public confidence in the CIA. In addition, Mr. Hugel is concerned that these opinions will cause damage to his personal reputation and character. For these reasons, he hereby respectfully requests your office immediately to initiate an investigation of these charges to assess their truth and accuracy. Mr. Hugel is confident that a full inquiry into all of the facts will establish conclusively that these allegations are without merit or substance."

Hugel received a reply from the inspector general denying that anti-Semitism had played any role whatsoever in the incident. "There is no 'anti-Semitic old-boy network' in the agency," wrote Taylor in his reply. "No such cabal was responsible for Mr. Hugel's departure nor was there any indication of, or concern about, improper support by Mr. Hugel to Israel.

"We, no less than you, are deeply concerned that there be no damage to public confidence in the CIA. We realize, however, that from time to time, negative comments about the agency and its personnel will receive airing. My office cannot involve itself each time we read some bald assertions unaccompanied by any factual support."

Is there still some lingering anti-Semitism in the U.S. governmental bureaucracy? Probably, but the fact also remains that many American Jews today do serve in extremely sensitive national security positions involving Israel and the Middle East. Henry Kissinger, after all, was secretary of state. Sol Linowitz and Robert Strauss were special Middle East envoys.

Is there fear that American Jews are leaking information to the Mossad? Not really, because experienced U.S. intelligence officials readily acknowledge that the degree of cooperation between the CIA and the Mossad is already so close that the two organizations do not really have to spy on each other.

Despite infractions on both sides, U.S. and Israeli intelligence organizations have maintained a discreet arrangement since the 1950s, banning covert operations against each other. This was confirmed following publication in 1982 in *The Washington Post* and other publications of a secret CIA report on Israel's foreign intelligence and security services. The forty-seven-page CIA report was seized in November 1979 by Iranian militants who occupied the U.S. embassy in Teheran. It had been issued by the CIA in March of that year. U.S. intelligence sources confirmed its authenticity, although the State Department, the CIA, and the Israeli embassy in Washington refused any public comment.

Iranian revolutionaries published the CIA documents in the form of paperback books. They were made available to *The Washington Post* by three U.S. freelance journalists who had returned from Iran. The documents showed that Israeli intelligence agencies, mostly in the 1950s, had blackmailed, bugged, wire-tapped, and offered bribes to U.S. government officials in an effort to gain sensitive intelligence and technical information. What was not disclosed in the CIA report, U.S. and Israeli officials said, were several equally disturbing and largely unsuccessful incidents involving U.S. efforts to penetrate Israeli intelligence sources in the 1950s. One U.S. official described an American effort to use American Jews to obtain sensitive information about Israel. U.S. efforts to spy on Israel in the early 1950s also involved sophisticated electronic eavesdropping operations within Israel proper and against Israeli institutions abroad. Several of these were detected by Israel. In addition, U.S. officials said, there were some unsuccessful efforts to recruit Israeli army officers sent to the United States for advanced military training and other studies. Early in the 1950s, the United States also tried to penetrate the Mossad operation in Vienna, according to U.S. officials.

As a result of these and other embarrassing incidents, the United States and Israel, during the Eisenhower–Dulles administration, reached an understanding to end covert operations against each other. Angleton, the head of the Israel desk at the CIA, was said to have been largely responsible for arranging the deal.

During one particularly strained period in American–Israeli relations, while Henry Kissinger was secretary of state, there had been some high-level consideration given to reopening covert actions against Israel. But this proposal was eventually rejected, largely because of concern that it could prove politically embarrassing if detected. Generally, over the past two decades, U.S. and Israeli intelligence organizations have maintained an extremely close working relationship, although both sides continue to suspect the other may still be "occasionally snooping around," in the words of one expert in Washington.

Zbigniew Brzezinski, President Carter's national security adviser during his four years in the White House, provided some fascinating tidbits of this suspicion in his memoirs, *Power and Principle*. Brzezinski wrote that he had wanted the Israeli delegation at Camp David "bugged," but Carter had overruled him. "I had proposed such a step to the president, but he, in what I felt was an excess of chivalry, flatly forbade that. As a result, we did not have adequate intelligence on what transpired in the Egyptian or Israeli delegations—though all of them took the precaution of conducting their own business on the porches of their cabins, and not inside." Brzezinski was very suspicious that pro-Israeli U.S. officials were leaking information to Israel. "The administration," he said in a memorandum in 1978, "is permeated with those who are only too eager to share information with the Israelis."

He was always suspicious that Israel was trying to "bug" the United States. Incredibly, Brzezinski even raised the possibility that Israel had managed to eavesdrop on Carter's 1977 meeting with Syrian President Hafez Assad in Geneva. "My only concern," Brzezinski wrote, "was that some of his [Carter's] remarks, if anybody had taps at the meeting, particularly if the Israelis tapped the meeting, could be misunderstood and played against him."

Brzezinski simply assumed the Israelis were listening to Carter's private conversations in his King David Hotel suite in March 1979, when the president was trying to nail down the final issues in the Israeli–Egyptian Peace Treaty. Carter was especially harsh one night in describing Begin to White House aide Hamilton Jordan. "When Ham asked impishly whether his remarks were for the record, I laughed and said, 'The remark is already on the record,' pointing at the ceiling. I had no doubt that we were being recorded."

Israeli ambassadors in Washington often suspected that they too were being bugged. It was not very surprising, for example, to see an envoy turn on a radio and tune in some loud music during a sensitive conversation.

5

Congress and Israel

There were more than a dozen votes in congressional subcommittees, in full committees, and on the floor of the House and Senate on each of the various aspects of the required foreign aid authorization and appropriation legislation. A defeat during any one of them could have ended Israel's hopes for increases.

The long and arduous struggle wound up with President Ronald Reagan's signing of an emergency funding measure on December 21, 1982. But Israel and its American supporters did not have a lot of time to enjoy their victory. Israeli officials, pro-Israeli lobbyists, and congressmen knew that the Reagan administration was about to submit a new foreign aid bill to Congress for the 1984 fiscal year, which meant that the whole process, taking many months, had to begin anew: more hearings, followed by more roll calls. Lobbying—pro and con—would be intense.

This, then, is the story of Congress and Israel, a story that centers, for the most part, around money. Under U.S. law, Congress must authorize and appropriate all foreign aid. Israel, increasingly dependent on American economic and military assistance in recent years, has come to rely on its friends in Congress to support the necessary bills. This is not to say that Congress is important for Israel only because it controls the foreign aid package, for there are other critical roles Congress has traditionally played in support of Israel. Very often, it has provided badly needed political support in the face of a usually more critical administration stance. At other times, it has blocked or, at a minimum, scaled down large-scale U.S. arms sales to Israel's Arab enemies.

Over the years, whether Democrats or Republicans controlled the White

House, Israel has almost always been able to count on its friends in the Senate and the House of Representatives to come to its defense during periods of friction with the administration. On many occasions, when an administration's proposed foreign aid bill included too little assistance for Israel or not at the most advantageous terms, key members of the House and Senate moved to improve the package during their separate consideration of the legislation. Almost invariably, the administration was left with no choice but to go along with the pro-Israeli congressional initiatives. Congress has also protested loudly when it felt that an administration in power was either not providing necessary hardware to Israel or recommending too much advanced weaponry for Israel's Arab neighbors. When, in 1969, the Nixon administration held up Israel's request for F-4 Phantom fighters, for example, the House and Senate passed sharply worded resolutions challenging the delay. Shortly afterward, the planes started arriving in Israel. Conversely, when administrations have proposed large arms deals for various Arab countries, such as the F-15 package sale to Saudi Arabia in 1978, congressional supporters of Israel have tried to block them. In 1975, Jordan received Hawk anti-aircraft missiles only on the condition that they be fixed in sites in the eastern part of the country, far from the Israeli border. In 1978, Congress made certain that Saudi Arabia's F-15's did not include bomb racks and extra fuel tanks, although the Reagan administration later provided the fuel tanks in the 1981 AWACS deal.

The most impressive demonstration of congressional support for Israel during a confrontation with an administration came in 1975, during the six-month Ford–Kissinger "reassessment" of relations with Israel. No new U.S. arms contracts were being signed, and the administration had withheld introducing its Middle East foreign aid bill to Congress. (Israel was by then the largest individual U.S. aid recipient.) It was at that point that seventy-six senators signed a letter to President Ford calling for continued strong economic, military, and diplomatic support for Israel. On other occasions, influential senators and representatives protested what they considered to be ill-timed diplomatic initiatives, such as the October 1, 1977, U.S.–Soviet Joint Comuniqué on the Middle East, or the December 1969 Rogers Plan, which called on Israel to withdraw to the pre-1967 lines with only minor modifications. Almost all U.S. flirtations with the PLO were challenged in Congress, as were anti-Israeli votes at the UN.

Before the Yom Kippur War, Israel ranked twenty-fourth among recipients of postwar U.S. foreign aid. That meant that from 1945 to 1973, twenty-three other countries had received more total financial assistance from the United States than Israel. By 1979, however, Israel had climbed to number two on the all-time list; only South Vietnam had received more combined economic and military assistance from America since World War

II. Israel had moved ahead of South Korea, Japan, and all the West European countries that received such massive direct foreign aid under the Marshall Plan. Soon after aid was cut off to South Vietnam following the Paris Peace Treaty of 1973, Israel became America's largest individual foreign aid recipient.

A week after the surprise Egyptian–Syrian attack on October 6, 1973, and the consequent heavy losses in Israeli equipment and manpower, the United States opened a massive military airlift to Israel, depleting some U.S. stocks in Europe. During the final days of the conflict, President Nixon announced a $2.2 billion program in military credits to pay for tanks, aircrafts, missiles, and other arms sent. Until that aid package, Israel had been receiving a relatively modest amount of economic and military assistance from the United States in the annual foreign aid bills. It had never previously received any military grants—only interest-bearing military loans.

Clearly, Washington has become the single most important source of foreign assistance for Israel. In the decade after the 1973 war, the Israeli economy, badly battered by huge military expenditures, triple-digit inflation, and balance-of-payments deficits, has become very dependent (some say hooked) on U.S. financial assistance.

Even though Israel can present as a good case for receiving increased assistance every year that it is America's most reliable ally in that part of the world, foreign aid assistance does not flow easily out of Washington. All the recommendations of the relevant U.S. government agencies must be submitted to the White House, and then it is up to the president to make a recommendation to Congress. A new federal budget is unveiled by early February.

Officials in Jerusalem certainly recognize that Israel's policies with regard to sensitive diplomatic negotiations and other controversial issues, such as the settlements on the West Bank, have a direct impact on American attitudes. Thus, Israel's vulnerability to the displeasure of U.S. policymakers has become a built-in feature of the relationship between Washington and Jerusalem. But, given the influence of domestic American politics, especially as reflected in Congress, and the realities of Israel's own military power and strategic importance, their displeasure has rarely allowed American policymakers to pressure Israel as brutally as some might have liked.

Since Israel started receiving the largest individual portion of the foreign aid bill, its image and popularity on Capitol Hill have become of supreme importance to officials in Jerusalem. Visiting Israeli leaders always made a special effort to influence congressmen during their traditional briefings on the Hill. But after the 1973 war, Israel stepped up these efforts. Senators and representatives who visited Israel reported that they had been treated "royally." Nevertheless, it is taken for granted that a handful of Israel's opponents in Congress will attempt to reduce the aid figure for Israel. This attempt is strongly fought by Israel's many supporters and by administration and State Department lobbyists. Kissinger and other administration officials had to stress in late 1975, for example, that their $2.3 billion recommendation to Congress was the absolute minimum needed by the Jewish state.

The secretary pointed out that Israel had in fact sought $2.6 billion from the United States back in January, when it first presented Washington with its financial needs. That, the secretary said, was several months before the achievement of the Sinai pact, which placed additional financial burdens upon Israeli taxpayers. "We think it is terribly important," Kissinger declared, "that the American people understand that it is not the agreement that creates the need for assistance to the parties, but the long-term national interests of the United States." The whole Middle East aid program was sold by the administration to Congress as an investment in peace—an expensive proposition, but considerably less costly for America than another Arab–Israeli war.

AIPAC started its campaign early that year. It sent a detailed memorandum to all congressmen explaining why U.S. aid to Israel was in America's best national interest. "The Arab states will never make peace with a weakened Israel they feel can be defeated militarily, and Israel cannot make further concessions if her national security is endangered," said the memo, which was also mailed to AIPAC's members across the United States. It also pointed out that Israel had already gone deeply into debt to pay for her security. "Israel's defense expenditures already consume 30 percent of the country's gross national product, and Israelis are the highest taxed people in the world." These arguments, along with many others, were used by AIPAC lobbyists, friendly senators, representatives and their aides, Israeli officials, and other pro-Israeli sympathizers in seeking the final congressional stamp of approval for the aid package.

As noted, Congress has traditionally increased the administration's original aid recommendations for Israel, ever since Israel received its first $50 million economic loan from the United States in the early 1950s. During that earlier foreign aid debate, the administration did not even seek assistance for Israel, fearful of a negative reaction in the Arab world; it was Congress that initiated the aid. At times increases in aid to Israel have been made even as aid to other countries was being substantially cut. Israel was such a popular recipient among many congressmen that they would vote for the worldwide foreign aid bill only because of the allocations it provided for Israel and despite serious misgivings about allocations to other states. This was particularly true for some conservative members, like Republican Jack Kemp of New York.

As a result of the 1975 introduction of American civilian technicians into Sinai, it became almost fashionable for a few lawmakers, especially those who had never been all that supportive of Israel in the first place, to question the American–Israel relationship and the depth of the American commitment. The debate in the House and the Senate that preceded the passage of the administration's proposal to send the technicians to Sinai foreshadowed what happened in the Congress during the subsequent review of the foreign aid bill and other developments since then. There was considerable griping about the fact that American taxpayers had to pick up the tab for so much foreign assistance to Middle Eastern parties. Although these public complaints against Israel still emanated from only a handful of congressmen, there was more complaining than in the recent past. Several of those legislators were being emboldened by mail from their constituents, which was said to be running against large-scale aid packages.

Senator James Allen, Democrat from Alabama, declared that he was "deeply concerned about the escalating involvement of the U.S. in the Middle East as the guarantor of peace—and, let's face up to it—the U.S. is in effect buying the peace with billions of American taxpayers' dollars." He complained that the United States will have to "pay" Israel more than $9 billion over the next three years. Republican Senator Robert Dole of Kansas expressed concern over the large aid package to Israel. He called upon other countries to share the financial burden. "There are many countries that benefit as much as or more than we do from peace in the Middle East," he said. "It seems only fair that they should bear part of the expense."

From time to time, successive U.S. administrations have bluntly used foreign aid as leverage on Israeli policies, but most of the time the pressures have been more subtly and indirectly applied. Warnings might be made through third parties. For example, in December 1978, at a time when American–Israeli relations were badly strained over the dragging negotiations designed to nail down the Israeli–Egyptian peace treaty, Senate Majority Leader Robert Byrd, Democrat from West Virginia, warned that Congress would be reluctant to increase financial assistance to Israel so long as new settlements were being established on the West Bank and Gaza Strip. "I think the senator was speaking as Senator Byrd," said State Department spokesman Hodding Carter III on December 13, 1978, when asked if Byrd represented the Carter administration. The spokesman said he was "not aware" of any linkage between future U.S. aid to Israel and the establishment of new settlements, which the Carter administration had said were illegal under international law and "obstacles to peace."

"We have always said that Israel's security needs stand in and of themselves," the U.S. spokesman said, adding that America has met its commitments to Israel "for three decades. . . . We will not abandon that overall commitment."

Earlier, Byrd, who had just returned from a visit to the Middle East, had told a news conference that Israel should offer a "concrete demonstration of its good intentions" by freezing all new settlement activity. But, despite the official State Department disavowal, there was a widespread belief in Washington that the majority leader's tough warning to Israel had indeed been inspired, if not formally cleared, by the White House. Certainly, this was the Israeli view. In addition to the fact that Byrd had met with Carter before his statement, there were other signs to support this perception. At the news conference, Byrd had made a point of repeating that he had gone abroad as Carter's special envoy. He said he had reported on his talks to Secretary of State Cyrus Vance in London just before Vance left for Cairo. His remarks against Jewish settlements were contained in a carefully drafted statement, which he read at the start of the news conference. It did not seem likely that Byrd would take so specific an initiative on the Middle East, certainly not at such a delicate moment in the peace treaty negotiations, unless he was authorized by Carter. Finally, Byrd's remarks came at a time when the president was openly expressing his own deep concern over Israel's settlement policy. He and other U.S. officials also expressed their anger over press reports that Israel planned to try to limit severely the scope of the proposed Palestinian autonomy scheme.

Israeli officials were clearly disturbed by the senator's comments. But, at the State Department briefing, Hodding Carter tried to stress that Byrd was merely speaking on his own. "The senator is a prestigious member of the Senate," he said. "He expresses his views on a number of subjects." The administration, he continued, was then in the process of determining how much U.S. foreign assistance should be allocated to Israel in the next fiscal year. He said the United States was continuing its "internal consultations" on the Israeli aid request to pay for relocating its Sinai defense line in the Negev. "But I have nothing to add beyond that," he said. Israel, at that time, had been seeking a supplementary $3 billion as part of a special aid request to help pay for the Sinai withdrawal.

Dr. William Quandt, a Middle East staffer on the National Security Council during the Carter administration, told a fascinating story about the use of direct U.S. military pressure on Israel during a House Foreign Affairs Committee hearing on August 4, 1982. Quandt, then affiliated with the Brookings Institution in Washington, recalled that the United States learned in 1977 that some heavy American-supplied military equipment was still in place in southern Lebanon under the control of Major Sa'ad Haddad, the pro-Israeli Lebanese Christian militia commander. U.S. law barred Israel from transferring such equipment to third parties without prior American approval, and the Carter administration, through private diplomatic channels, complained to Israel. In reply, Israel denied the allegation, insisting that all U.S.-supplied equipment had been removed from southern Lebanon. U.S. intelligence, Quandt said, was then asked to take another look at the on-the-ground situation and confirmed that the heavy equipment was still in place, despite the Israeli denial. At that point, Quandt added, President Carter sent a sternly worded private letter to Prime Minister Begin, warning that unless the equipment were removed immediately, the administration would have to report to Congress that Israel had violated its arms contract agreements with the United States. Under U.S. law, that could have triggered a suspension of all U.S. military supplies to Israel. "Needless to say," Quandt told the panel, "Israel removed the equipment within forty-eight hours," and Carter never notified Congress that Israel had violated its arms commitments to the United States.

Quandt related that story to underline his contention that U.S. pressure against Israel, when properly applied, can be credible and effective. The former Carter official, however, went on to express doubt that sanctions against Israel would necessarily be useful in easing the crisis in West Beirut, which was then under way. It was probably too late in the war for such actions, he said. Instead, he proposed that the United States reserve such severe options for a later and more important stage in the broader Palestinian-related negotiations over the future of the West Bank and Gaza.

Harold Saunders, the State Department's highest-ranking Middle East expert during the Carter administration, who after leaving office became affiliated with the American Enterprise Institute, a leading think tank in Washington, took a somewhat different line. Also appearing before that same House panel, Saunders said that during the first two years of the Reagan administration the United States had lost credibility with both Israel and the Arab world. No one, he said, any longer took U.S. threats against Israel all that seriously. President Reagan should have drawn lines for acceptable Israeli behavior during his first meeting with Begin in September of 1981. If he had, Saunders added, Israel might have been less inclined later to go its own way. "It's very late in the day to ask this question about sanctions," said Saunders.

The Quandt–Saunders exchange had come as official Washington buzzed with speculation about possible Reagan administration sanctions against Israel. In the wake of Israel's shelling of the remaining PLO strongholds in West Beirut, despite Reagan's direct appeal earlier that week to visiting

Foreign Minister Yitzhak Shamir that they be stopped, U.S. officials were spreading the word privately that Washington might actually start to get tough with Jerusalem. Reagan's letter to Begin following the August 4 Israeli military actions against the PLO was blunt, containing at least two thinly veiled threats. U.S. officials said that previous Reagan letters to Begin had been warm and friendly, beginning with "Dear Menachem" and signed "Ron." But this letter, they said, was "very formal and serious." The letter, still classified, hinted at a possible U.S. military embargo against Israel. It noted that Israel's continued shelling of West Beirut had raised the question of whether Israel was using U.S.-supplied weaponry only for legitimate self-defense, as required by a 1952 American–Israeli agreement. The letter also warned of a "profound" impact on future American–Israeli relations if Israel should drive into West Beirut. Reagan had delivered the same warning to Shamir two days earlier. U.S. officials said that could include a possible U.S. willingness to support anti-Israeli resolutions at the UN. The letter went on to insist that until the latest round of Israeli shelling, special Middle East envoy Philip Habib had appeared to be on the verge of reaching an agreement with the PLO to leave West Beirut. Reagan demanded an immediate ceasefire, insisting that Israel's reaction to PLO provocations was "totally disproportionate."

Beyond the official leaks to the news media, there was other indirect pressure against Israel during those tense days of the war. House Republican Leader Robert Michel of Illinois emerged from a White House meeting with the president to tell reporters that Israel's latest military actions "certainly" do not "help the process out there." He described Reagan as "pretty distressed himself." Senate Republican Leader Howard Baker of Tennessee said: "I think the Israelis want peace and I think they'd like to neutralize the PLO threat, but I think that they are making it very, very difficult for Ambassador Habib and the U.S. to serve as an honest broker in the attempt to bring about a peaceful resoluton." Republican Senator Charles McC. Mathias of Maryland, a member of the Foreign Relations Committee, was especially bitter in lashing out against Israel. "We have to be cognizant of the fact that this has been done with American weapons, and to some extent with American money," he said. "If this continues, despite the urgent request of the president of the United States—President Reagan had made such a representation to the Israeli foreign minister— then I think we will have to look at those provisions of American law which say that this equipment was provided for the defense of Israel, and to make some judgment whether the shelling of Beirut is an act of defending Israel."

Everyone recognized that pressures were mounting on Reagan to distance Washington from Jerusalem. A year earlier, he had imposed punitive sanctions against Israel after the Iraqi nuclear reactor bombing and a subsequent aerial strike against the PLO in Beirut. F-16 fighter deliveries to Israel were suspended for some weeks. But Reagan, on the whole, was very careful before imposing additional sanctions against Israel, and many American observers suggested that they tended simply to underline U.S. impotence in trying to influence Israeli policies. As an example of administration abandonment of any thought it could pressure Israel, Vice-President George Bush assured a delegation of American Jewish leaders on August 5, 1982, that sanctions against Israel were not under consideration.

Appearing at that same time on ABC's *Nightline* program, Ambassador Moshe Arens argued that friends and allies, like the United States and Israel, should not use pressure in dealing with each other. In any case, he said, U.S. pressure against Israel would not succeed, especially when Israel's vital national security interests were at stake. Arens noted that Israel had demonstrated a willingness to sacrifice its most precious asset—its sons—to defend the northern border with Lebanon. It, therefore, would be willing to sacrifice U.S. economic assets if its security were endangered. Secretary of State George Shultz, responding to written questions from the Senate Foreign Relations Committee during his confirmation hearings, seemed to reject withholding arms from Israel as pressure. "While they may appear to have some short-term advantage," he said, "pressure and threats are not in my mind the best way to bring about stable and lasting solutions to long-term problems."

The highly influential editor of *The New York Times* editorial page, Max Frankel, caused a firestorm of protest in Israel when he reported in 1983 that Israeli opposition leaders had recommended to him privately that the United States cut its economic assistance to Israel in order to help bring down Prime Minister Begin's government. "The opposition is thus reduced to begging America to break Mr. Begin's political power," wrote Frankel after a visit to Israel. "And it now advocates means that would have been unthinkable even a few weeks ago." He described in some detail "the startling plea of many leading Israelis that the U.S. *reduce* its economic aid to their nation."

Frankel, during an interview with me, made it clear that he was referring to leaders of the opposition Labor Alignment (although he refused to reveal names) who, in their desperation to gain office, he said, were appealing to the United States for support in helping them to topple the Begin government. "And to that end," he wrote, "leading opposition figures now risk political oblivion by counseling sharp cuts in America's nonmilitary aid of $800 million a year." Labor leaders, including Shimon Peres, strongly denied the allegation.

In Washington, the idea of reducing aid was not very new. It had been debated for some time, especially during Israel's drive into Lebanon and its continuing policy of establishing new settlements. What was different this time, however, was that almost always in the past, the idea was closely associated with Israel's most vocal critics, led by former Under Secretary of State George Ball. Writing on the op-ed page of *The New York Times* in August 1982, for instance, Ball had offered this recommendation: "In the name of humanity and decency, we should provide ample help for the Lebanese people; in the name of logic and justice, we should deduct the cost of that help from our annual subsidy to Israel." Ball said the U.S. foreign aid package for Israel during the preceding four years had amounted to "one-fourth of our total foreign aid—which, for a country with a population less than that of Detroit, and only one-tenth of 1 percent of the world's population, suggests some distortion of values."

Within the Reagan administration's foreign policy bureaucracy, some voices proposed that the United States reduce its economic assistance to Israel by the approximate amount budgeted by Israel for developing Jewish settlements and suburban housing projects on the West Bank. In the U.S. government, the "low" estimate for settlement activities in 1982 came to $100 million; the "high" estimate was $200 million. But both President Reagan and Secretary of State Shultz rejected that advice. Reagan told a White House news conference on November 11, 1982, that economic sanctions against Israel would not be "helpful in the situation we're in today. I don't think to start talking about whether I should or should not make threats of some kind or other is going to be fruitful at all." Shultz, at a State Department news conference on November 18, was asked whether economic aid to Israel should be linked to the settlement policy. "There hasn't been any link made," he replied, although he went on to deplore the settlements. "We have been very clear, I think, from the beginning that we think the settlements and the expansion of them are not constructive at all, not a contribution to the peace process."

Ambassador Arens told me at that time that no U.S. official had ever in his presence threatened, even remotely, to use economic assistance to Israel as pressure to stop the settlements. My interviews with key U.S. officials confirmed that the dominant view within the administration was strongly against the use of direct economic pressure against Israel. In short, they said, the Reagan leadership had accepted the opinion of U.S. Ambassador Samuel Lewis, who in his cables to Washington argued strongly that such pressure tactics would merely play into Begin's hands and strengthen his coalition government. (Referring to the recommendation to reduce aid to Israel in order to topple Begin's government, Max Frankel, in his controversial article, wrote: "American diplomats in Israel resist the anguished counsel; they fear that Mr. Begin would exploit American coercion to rally still greater public support.")

But there were other reasons why the Reagan administration did not accept Ball's advice. Henry Kissinger, in an interview with the *Economist*, reflected a widely held view within the administration when he warned that such economic pressure would prove counterproductive to the overall peace process. "Yes," he said, "we should encourage Israel to negotiate. Israel is more likely to do so, paradoxically, if it feels compassion on our side, maybe even affection, rather than unremitting pressure. Where we disagree with Israel on substantive points, we must be prepared to express this— strongly if necessary. But it is a very difficult maneuver to bring off, to press Israel on individual points, as we must do with perseverance, and yet not cumulatively to harass it into emotional and psychic collapse." Too great pressure, Kissinger went on to note, would also confuse the Arabs into concluding that the United States would do all their dirty work for them. "In other words," he said, "I feel that pressure on Israel should be exerted retail rather than wholesale, if one can put it in such crude terms." Asked about the formal use of broad economic sanctions against Israel, Kissinger replied, "I would hope such a point will never be reached."

Influential people close to Ronald Reagan agreed. There was, to be sure, a vocal minority in the State Department, the Pentagon, and the White House that agreed with George Ball's get-tough approach, but the prevailing view was that other less blunt forms of pressure would be considerably more effective in changing Israeli policies. As Kissinger said in the *Economist* interview, "The most effective one is for King Hussein to step forward with whatever Arab acquiescence he needs as the Arab negotiator for the West Bank. This would pose for all Israelis the concrete necessity for decisions. So long as the Arab participation in the process remains only hypothetical, the debate [in Israel] will be sterile and bitter."

The Reagan administration did impose a series of less publicized but still concrete punitive sanctions against Israel. These took several disparate forms, including:

- A refusal to support congressional initiatives to improve the terms of pending economic and military assistance to Israel by converting loans to outright grants.
- The continued delay in submitting to Congress a proposal to sell seventy-five additional F-16's to Israel.
- A go-slow in approving Israel's requests for vital technology transfers needed for the development of Israel's new-generation fighter, the Lavi.
- The continued suspension of the 1981 memorandum of understanding regarding American–Israeli strategic cooperation.
- The delay in concluding an agreement to permit Israel to use some of its annual U.S. military sales credits for purchases within Israel itself.

Normally, Israel is supposed to spend all of that military aid in the United States, but an administration can waive that regulation.

- The delay in the earlier signed "offshore procurement" agreement, whereby the U.S. military would be permitted to make purchases within Israel. One deal then on hold would have enabled U.S. phantoms in the Mediterranean to be serviced in Israel rather than in Greece or West Germany.
- The delay in permitting third countries receiving U.S. military credits to use some of that money for purchases from Israel. There had been speculation that the Philippines would purchase U.S. patrol boats with Israeli-made missiles, all financed by the United States.

On top of all those sanctions, the Reagan administration, of course, had many other ways—short of a direct cut in economic assistance—to make its views known in Jerusalem. Probably the most formidable was the direct public condemnation. Since Reagan's September 1, 1982, Arab–Israeli peace initiative, the administration had not been bashful in speaking out publicly against those Israeli decisions that were upsetting to Washington, especially the settlements. In short, during those many months of the war, the administration did not use the sledgehammer against Israel. There were more subtle and effective ways to get the job done, as earlier administrations had also come to learn.

Prime Minister Begin's unprecedented verbal blast against the United States, which followed the December 1981 U.S. suspension of the strategic cooperation agreement with Israel, clearly resulted in a wave of negative publicity for Israel. Columnist James Reston of *The New York Times,* for example, said that "seldom, if ever, has an allied leader made such a vicious charge against a president or administration of the United States." Reston, said U.S. officials "feel that Mr. Begin is a certified disaster for Israel and the rest of the world. Officials here are waiting and wondering how long it will take for the Israeli people to decide how to tolerate the declining economic, political, and strategic problems in Jerusalem." Lars-Erik Nelson, the Washington bureau chief of the *New York Daily News,* underscored Israel's enormous dependence on U.S. economic and military assistance by calculating that the roughly $2.2 billion in annual U.S. governmental assistance for Israel came to some $6 million a day, more than the Soviet Union "provides its puppet, Cuba, which has three times as many people."

There was a wave of news media coverage focusing on the disturbing aid aspect because Begin himself had raised it in his lengthy statement delivered to U.S. Ambassador Samuel Lewis and later officially released by the Israeli cabinet. Indeed, the Begin statement had the unintended but clear impact of highlighting for the American public just how financially dependent Israel had become on the United States.

The roughly $2 billion in grants and loans provided annually since the 1973 war came at a time of severe domestic budget cutting in America, intensified after the Reagan administration took office. While Washington was cutting back on school lunch programs, social security payments, and all sorts of other welfare subsidies, and some 9 million Americans were unemployed, the executive and legislative branches of the U.S. government continued to support massive aid packages for Israel. "This is a case of overreaction by Mr. Begin," said Democratic Senator Henry Jackson of Washington, one of Israel's most devoted friends on Capitol Hill.

Begin obviously would have been in a much stronger and completely different moral position from which to attack the United States if Israel were not so financially hooked on Washington. But the facts were otherwise. Even a modest reduction in aid would cause serious economic and social dislocations in Israel: even higher taxes, more unemployment, heightened ethnic tensions between the have's and the have-not's, and increased emigration.

When Begin asked, "Are we a vassal of yours?" *The New York Times* had this reply: "The answer is no, but Israel depends upon more American aid and weapons than are available to any other nation. This support sustains not only a vital military superiority but also a standard of living that emboldens a talented people to struggle on against great odds." *The Washington Post* commented that Begin's intensity "betrays an awareness of what is for Israel a reality terrible to contemplate. Zionism is the Jewish people's assertion of control over their own destiny. Yet some of Israel's policies, and especially some of Mr. Begin's, have worked to make Israel ever more dependent on the outside power, the United States."

There was no denying that the United States had provided such enormous financial aid to Israel over the years because successive administrations and congresses have also come to recognize it as an investment in peace and in America's own national security interest. As President Reagan has pointed out, it's not just a one-way street, with the United States doing all the giving and Israel all the taking. Israel does provide important strategic benefits for the United States. In a rather unstable part of the world, Israel is the only democratic, reliable ally, with a military ability proven to be capable of helping America and the West. At the same time, it is foolhardy for Israel's leaders to lose sight of the fact that their country remains very dependent on America, and that American taxpayers, therefore, could not be expected to react well to anti-American outbursts.

Begin himself knew only too well exactly how painfully dependent Israel had become, especially since the 1973 war. It was first underscored to him shortly after Israel and Egypt signed the Camp David accords in 1978. He blundered badly when, in a gush of national pride, he shot from the hip and informed Secretary of State Cyrus Vance that Israel wanted the United States to provide Israel with loans, rather than outright grants, to help pay for the construction of new airbases in the Negev and for other expenses resulting from the Sinai withdrawal. Israel would pay back every dollar "with interest," Begin said. Israel did not want charity. But when his stunned economic advisers later pointed out to him exactly how costly this would be—how great would be its impact on the Israeli economy and society—he quickly backed down from his noble stance. His pride was hurt, but, painful as it must have been for Begin to accept, the realities of Israel's pocketbook came first.

The traditional base of American support for Israel—namely, the Senate and House of Representatives—had shown signs of cracking in the wake of Israel's move into Lebanon. Israel's friends on Capitol Hill acknowledged the damage. The angry mood erupted during Begin's ninety-minute meeting with some thirty-six senators on June 22, 1982, just a few hours before he returned to Israel. It was reflective of the deep concern in Washington over the extent of civilian death and injury that followed Israel's move into Lebanon.

On the one hand, of course, there was admiration for the way Israel handled the operation, especially from the military point of view. But on the other hand, many senators had been deeply distressed by what they saw as an excess of force used by Israel during the operation. These senators, moreover, had been greatly influenced by the U.S. news media's graphic reportage of the agony and suffering in Lebanon and the physical destruction of the country. As Israel's image suffered, so did its political clout on Capitol Hill. Pro-Israeli legislators complained that Israel was tortuously slow in providing its own figures on the casualties. What was especially distressing to pro-Israeli lobbyists was the fact that so many senators were willing to go public in rebuking Begin. To these senators, the perceived arrogance of Begin had become the issue, despite their long-standing support for the state of Israel.

Begin was certainly a match for anyone in his one-on-one verbal exchanges. The prime minister was tough, consistent, and proud, even defiant. Those admirable characteristics came through very dramatically during all of his meetings in Washington. He was also charming, especially during small, private meetings. But during larger gatherings, he had a tendency to become somewhat condescending, which is a common tendency among political leaders. This helped explain why Begin was rather successful in impressing Reagan during their one-on-one meeting in the Oval Office on June 21, 1982, but why he failed rather miserably in his closed-door exchange with the senators a day later. As an orator, Begin could be very effective before large audiences, especially when they consisted of his supporters in Israel and the American Jewish community. But he showed his worst side during an appearance before a committee of senators, who are themselves accustomed to being accorded an almost imperial respect by all who appear before them. *New York Times* diplomatic correspondent Bernard Gwertzman said that Begin "tends to be didactic and brooks no criticism."

According to several sources who were present, Begin got off on the wrong foot by repeatedly "lecturing" the senators rather than simply responding to their questions. Several senators later charged that Begin's lecturing had bordered on arrogance. "I think it is fair to say that in my eight years in Washington I've never seen such an angry session with a foreign head of state," said Democrat Paul Tsongas of Massachusetts. Democrat Daniel Moynihan of New York, one of the few senators who defended Israel during the meeting, concurred: "It was the most difficult meeting with a head of state, certainly in my experience." And Republican Larry Pressler of South Dakota later told reporters, "It was the first time I've seen such a confrontation between the prime minister of Israel and senators—head to head."

The night before, Begin had met in his hotel suite with seven other senators. By all accounts, that meeting went well. The senators emerged with a better understanding of Israel's positions, and Begin had gained some insight into the thinking of a broad spectrum of Republicans and Democrats on Capitol Hill. Even Begin's separate session with members of the House Foreign Affairs Committee had gone well, according to sources present. But all of that success in Congress evaporated during the formal meeting with the senators.

Israel's Ambassador Moshe Arens later tended to blame the "group dynamics" established when Democratic Senator Joseph Biden of Delaware lashed out against Israel's policy of establishing settlements on the West Bank. Biden is a well-known friend of Israel, but he clearly touched a sensitive nerve in the prime minister. And whenever a known pro-Israeli senator criticizes Israel, other lesser friends are emboldened to jump aboard the anti-Israel bandwagon. Biden, an outspoken lawmaker with an oratorical streak not unlike that of Begin, did not criticize the Israeli assault against the PLO in Lebanon. Indeed, he had expressed support for it. But he was rather forceful in complaining about the settlements. And he also rejected Begin's earlier assertion, in response to a comment by Republican Charles Mathias of Maryland, that support for Israel among the American public was not eroding. Begin had insisted that support for Israel was never higher. Other senators, challenging Begin's upbeat assessment, came out of the meeting to say that U.S. public support for Israel had reached an all-time low. "I think there is a lot of concern among those of us who are supporters of Israel that their politics are in excess," said Tsongas, "and support for Israel in this country is eroding." Like others, Tsongas differentiated between his support for Israel as opposed to his response to Begin. This had been a constant Tsongas theme since Israel's bombing of the Iraqi nuclear reactor a year earlier.

The end result clearly spelled a disappointing conclusion to what earlier had appeared to be a rather successful Begin visit to Washington. For a time there was even a flipflop in the traditional executive–legislative roles in Washington. For one of the few times in history, an Israeli prime minister seemed to find more support and understanding in the administration than in Congress, Israel's more usual and expected base of support in Washington. For the first time in memory, a substantial number of senators complained that an administration was not being tough enough with an Israeli prime minister. Because the session with the senators received such extensive publicity in the U.S. news media, Israel's bargaining position with Washington was automatically weakened. The Reagan administration pointed to this perceived slippage of support for Israel in pressing for more concessions.

But the depth of congressional support for Israel ensured that this period of severe strain would not last very long. Things started to pick up on Capitol Hill long before Israel signed its May 1983 troop withdrawal agreement with Lebanon. By February 1983, key congressmen were lining up to demonstrate their support for Israel. They foreshadowed the administration's more favorable attitude toward Israel by several months. A February 28, 1983, hearing before the House Foreign Affairs Subcommittee on Europe and the Middle East underlined this trend.

In his opening statement, Assistant Secretary of State for Near Eastern and South Asian Affairs Nicholas Veliotes said: "Support for Israel's security and economic well-being is a basic, firm principle of American foreign policy. Our support for Israel grows out of a long-standing commitment to a free nation which has been a haven for immigrants from all over the world and which shares many of our own social and democratic traditions. Our security assistance programs are designed to assist Israel in continuing to maintain its qualitative and technological superiority over any potential combination of regional forces. Our economic assistance helps Israel to finance balance-of-payments deficits. Taken in combination, our programs are the material manifestation of our traditional commitment to Israel."

Democrat Mervyn Dymally of California, who is black, and fellow Democrat Mel Levine, a Jew whose district borders Dymally's in Los Angeles, discovered that their constituents had fundamentally opposing views on U.S. economic and military assistance to Israel. Dymally told the subcommittee that 95 percent of his largely black district could not justify the large aid package to Israel at a time of high unemployment and budget cuts in America. Making matters worse, he said, was that Israel had received more U.S. loans and grants since the 1973 Yom Kippur War than all the nations of Black Africa combined. Levine, on the other hand, said his constituents, who included many Jews, wanted the administration to improve the terms of its proposed 1984 fiscal year $2.485 billion package for Israel, meaning more outright grants instead of loans. A third Democrat on the panel, Robert Torricelli of New Jersey, joked that *his* constituents were interested mostly in current policy toward Italy. But he, like Levine, then went on to press the administration's witness to improve the aid terms for Israel. He wanted to make sure that Israel did not misread the administration's proposed levels, less than Congress had approved the year before, as signaling any weakening of U.S. support. Assistant Secretary Veliotes replied that the recommended level for Israel could be seen as "a strong vote of confidence in our relationship" with Israel, even though it contained $200 million less in grants than the Congress had appropriated in the 1983 fiscal year legislation. The overall level for Israel, he said, again "would be the largest U.S. bilateral assistance program."

But other congressmen flatly told Veliotes that the recommendation for Israel was not enough. Subcommittee Chairman Lee Hamilton of Indiana made it clear that an effort was going to be made on Capitol Hill once again to convert more of the loans to grants. Democrats Tom Lantos of California, Larry Smith of Florida, and Steve Solarz of New York joined in the pro-Israel chorus. They—like Hamilton, Torricelli, and Levine— asked Veliotes extremely pointed questions designed to underscore America's own strategic interest in a strong Israel. Smith, for example, managed to win from Veliotes an admission that all of the economic and military assistance for Israel actually remains in the United States to pay for military hardware and other goods and services. This, Smith said, creates more jobs for Americans. But, even in the face of that pressure, Veliotes held firmly to the administration's position that the requested aid "should be more than sufficient to meet the objectives of our program." He also cited "our budgetary constraints." He opposed additional aid to Israel beyond the recommended level, only to change that position four months later.

Once again, the pro-Israeli attitude of Congress was underlined. It has been a fundamental aspect of generating U.S. support for Israel since 1948. Of course, congressional support for Israel has not been on a straight-line increase since that time.

There have been congressional critics of Israel, some quite surprising.

What happens, for example, when a Jewish senator takes a position that undermines policies of the Israeli government? For one thing, it makes it a lot easier for the non-Jews in the Senate to abandon pro-Israel positions. In June 1976, Democratic Senator Abraham Ribicoff of Connecticut accepted an invitation from Democratic Senator James Abourezk of South Dakota to a luncheon for PLO official Shafik al-Hout, who was making the rounds in Congress. When Democrat Thomas Eagleton of Missouri was later asked why he had also attended the luncheon, Eagleton explained that when he came into the room, "I saw Abe Ribicoff there." It was for this reason that Israeli officials and pro-Israeli activists in Washington were so upset by the 1978 decision of Ribicoff to assail publicly Prime Minister Begin and those American Jews who backed him. Senators concerned about their image as strong supporters of Israel might now point to Ribicoff's position when they explained that they wanted to continue to be counted among the firm friends of Israel, while taking positions inimical to its interests. And that was exactly what happened in the wake of Ribicoff's interview in *The Wall Street Journal* on March 13, 1978. He said the "overwhelming" majority of Americans were against Begin, "and that's the way it should be." Ribicoff also lashed out against AIPAC. By taking such an active pro-Israeli stance, AIPAC was doing a "great disservice" to the United States, Israel, and the Jewish community, Ribicoff said.

Many Americans, Jews and non-Jews alike, were naturally shocked to see Ribicoff go public against the Israeli government. After entering the Senate in 1961, Ribicoff had developed a reputation as one of Israel's best friends in Congress—not only because of his Jewishness but because of the strong positions he often took in support of Israel. But most Washington insiders in Congress, at the White House, at the State Department, at the Israeli embassy, and among the press corps, were not all that surprised. Starting in 1976, they had become aware of a gradual change in the senator's position toward Israel.

Ribicoff denied that his support for Israel had weakened. It remained as strong as ever, he said in *The Wall Street Journal* interview. The only thing that had changed, he said, was his willingness to go public against Israel. But, for the reasons mentioned above, that alone was a significant development.

Ribicoff consistenty supported Carter's Middle East policies. He was one of only three senators who publicly defended Carter's decision to issue the October 1977 joint statement with the Soviet Union on the Middle East. That statement spoke for the first time of American recognition of "the legitimate rights" of the Palestinians.

The Ribicoff "defection" was part of a broader coalition of American Jews who were willing to dissent publicly from the Israeli view. This was reflected in April 1978 in a letter from thirty-seven prominent American Jewish intellectuals expressing support for the Peace Now movement in Israel.

Even before Ribicoff spoke out, he had largely been written off by the Israeli government as one of Israel's best friends in Congress. For example, when Begin came to Washington in December 1977 to present Carter with his peace plan, the prime minister also arranged a private briefing at Blair House with Israel's best friends in the Senate. Ribicoff was not invited.

Indeed, for two years, visiting Israeli leaders, from both the Rabin and Begin governments, emerged from closed-door sessions with the Senate Foreign Relations Committee upset by the fact that Ribicoff had taken the lead in criticizing various Israeli positions. Ribicoff was not a member of that committee, but he was often invited to briefings with visiting Middle East leaders. By asking obviously hostile questions, said Israeli officials, he was encouraging his colleagues to take critical views of the Israeli position.

One of the ironies of Ribicoff's decision to lash out against AIPAC was the fact that the organization's executive director was then Morris J. Amitay, who had served for five years as Ribicoff's chief foreign policy assistant before joining AIPAC at the end of 1974.

In denying that his support for Israel had weakened, Ribicoff said that he supported the positions of former Prime Minister Golda Meir and Foreign Minister Abba Eban, who had also criticized the Israeli government. Obviously sensitive to the criticism leveled against him following his statement, Ribicoff inserted into the *Congressional Record* of April 13, 1978, a statement applauding the vocal debate in Israel over Begin's policies. "In spite of wars, troubles, and adversity, Israel has remained true to democratic principles," he said. "Freedom of speech and discussion is a basic tenet of Israel's existence and faith, whether in the Knesset, in the press, in the home, on the street. . . . It is, therefore, disturbing that there are those in this country who by pressure seek to throttle freedom of discussion in the United States. There can be no greater disservice to Israel, the United States, or the people of Jewish faith everywhere than to deny any American the freedom to speak out on any issue, a freedom so meaningful to Israelis and Americans alike. In the quest for a real peace in the Middle East, it is essential that there be full discussion on basic issues, so that when peace comes, it can be permanent."

Earlier, on March 9, he had inserted into the *Congressional Record* Abba Eban's article in *The Jerusalem Post* criticizing the Begin government's interpretation of UN Security Council Resolution 242. In his introductory remarks, Ribicoff said: "Some of Israel's most prominent and respected leaders have reminded us that dissent and disagreement are as much a part of politicial life in the Israeli democracy as in our own. Two outstanding and heroic figures in the life of the Israeli nation are former Prime Minister Golda Meir and former Foreign Minister Abba Eban. Their dedication and devotion to the state of Israel and strong and harmonious relationship with the U.S. is known throughout the world and to the Jewish people everywhere." Ribicoff went on to point out that former Prime Minister Yitzhak Rabin and former Foreign Minister Yigal Allon also disagreed with Begin. His point was obvious: if these great Israeli leaders can dissent publicly from the views of the present Israeli government, why can't an American senator? The same point was being made by other senators in explaining their criticism of Israel.

The Carter White House was enormously pleased by Ribicoff's dissenting view, just as it was by the positions of the American Jewish Committee, the letter signed by the thirty-seven Jewish intellectuals, the debate over Begin's policies in Israel, and the Peace Now movement. Carter had spoken often about the impact of public opinion, including Jewish public opinion, on the positions of the Israeli government. He regarded this as more effective than brutal economic, political, or military pressure in persuading Israel to change its stance.

Pro-Israeli activists in Washington then considered these free expressions of criticism inappropriate, coming as they did in the midst of difficult negotiations between Egypt and Israel. In the end, all these pressures automatically tended to strengthen Egypt's negotiating posture, allowing Anwar Sadat and his government the luxury of sitting back and waiting for Israeli concessions. Israeli officials and American supporters of Israel contended that these pressures represented another attempt to impose a settlement on Israel rather than allowing Israel and Egypt to try to reach a fair settlement between themselves.

Despite these occasional exceptions, most Jewish members of Congress accepted their special responsibilities. Thus, Republican Senator Rudy Boschwitz of Minnesota, chairman of the Senate Foreign Relations Subcommittee on the Middle East, was always fully aware of his special responsibility as a Jew and as someone who had escaped the Holocaust. Born in Berlin in 1930, he recalls: "My father had foresight. He had so much foresight that he came home on the day that Hitler came into power on January 30, 1933, and told my mother that we would leave Germany. We left Germany in July 1933."

The Boschwitz family, like so many other Jewish refugees in Europe, roamed from country to country before receiving entry visas to the United States in 1935. "My father always felt that he hadn't gotten far enough away from Germany, from the Nazis. So we just kept coming this way." The senator, who grew up in and around New York before moving to

Minnesota in 1963, where he established a successful retail building-ma-
terial business, acknowledged that the Holocaust has had a tremendous
impact on his life. "It has given me more of that so-called Holocaust
mentality than most people would otherwise have had," he said. "I have
a great sense of the dangers facing Jews and Israel."

Democratic Representative Sam Gejdenson of Connecticut, a member
of the House Foreign Affairs Committee, also learned to cope with his
special role in dealing with the Holocaust. He is the first and, so far, only
"child of the Holocaust" to be elected to the U.S. Congress; he was born
in a displaced-persons' camp in West Germany in 1948. He and his parents
came to America two years later.

Gejdenson, an articulate and intelligent public official who also speaks
with quite a bit of emotion on this subject, has tried to make certain that
the world does not forget the Holocaust and its lingering effects today.
"Whether you're talking about a boatload of Jews off the coast of Cuba
during the war looking for a place to live, or Vietnamese in the South
China Sea today, it doesn't take a great imagination to see the similarities.
And we are still arguing the same lessons."

While most American Jewish public officials did not have such direct
connections to the Holocaust, few had to look far among their relatives to
find someone who had been personally affected. As a consequence of this
connection, as well as the mutuality of interests between the United States
and Israel, most American Jewish congressmen and senators have led
congressional support of Israel.

6

American Jews
and Politics   I

"We are an immigrant and second-generation ethnic community," the
election guide said. "We have attachments and feelings about the lands of
our origins, and, in many instances, we are concerned about the welfare
of family and friends who live 'back home.' We demand that our heritage
be respected and that our ethnicity and traditions not be subjected to
defamation."

That sounds like it could have been prepared by an American Jewish
organization. It was not. It was included in a 1982 document written by
the American–Arab Anti-Discrimination Committee, a relatively new organization in Washington openly patterned on the model of the B'nai B'rith
Anti-Defamation League. It was founded by former Democratic Senator
James Abourezk of South Dakota, a Lebanese-American and an outspoken
supporter of the Palestinians.

"We have prepared this little guide book in order to encourage ADC
members to take an active part in the 1982 elections and debates and in
the postelection process. We want all ADC members to challenge those
who seek to represent them in Washington," the book said in its introduction. "A generation of blind and blank-check U.S. support for Israel
has resulted in a massacre of devastating proportions in Lebanon. Continuing to send Israel $9 million a day is too costly a practice to go unchal-
lenged. It costs the U.S. too much—not just economically and politically,
but morally as well."

The book then went on to appeal to Arab–Americans to get involved
in the political process. "Most candidates would prefer to avoid discussing
the Middle East and U.S. aid to Israel altogether, so it is up to us to keep

119

these issues alive in the minds of the candidates and voters. We must voice our concerns frequently and publicly—in letters, petitions, debates, talk shows, and public events." The ADC offered several "organizing tips" for its members, many of which have also been actively promoted by Jewish political activists over the years. "Isolated in Washington and subject to constant pressure from the Israel lobby—they [congressmen] have never before felt pressure from our side. We need to begin making that pressure felt."

American Jewish leaders fully recognize that "the other side" is becoming increasingly active and effective in pushing its case and that those Americans who want to see close American–Israeli relations maintained and even strengthened have to redouble their own efforts in the political marketplace. The main focus of activity, naturally, has been Washington.

Since the 1973 Yom Kippur War, in fact, the American Israel Public Affairs Committee (AIPAC) has emerged as the new glamour organization of the American Jewish community. Once a quiet, largely insider (but always effective) group lobbying Capitol Hill, AIPAC is today a much more highly visible operation. One respected Washington observer, Ken Wollack, coeditor of the *Middle East Policy Survey* and himself a former legislative director of AIPAC, has called it "the sexy Jewish organization."

Whereas well-to-do and politically active Jews flocked to the United Jewish Appeal, Israel Bonds, or the American Jewish Committee as their first priority in the 1950s and 1960s, an increasingly large number of key Jewish leaders around the country began to concentrate their efforts on AIPAC in the 1970s. "I remember when I first started to work for AIPAC before the 1973 war," Wollack recalled. "I used to go to some metropolitan areas, and very few, if any, of the people in the audience even heard of AIPAC. That's very different today."

Wollack and others in Washington have praise for I. L. "Si" Kenen, the man who founded AIPAC in 1954 and served as its executive director until December 1974. Kenen's success in winning friends for Israel during that period was impressive; even Israel's opponents in Washington came away with a grudging admiration for him. Through his direct lobbying with influential members, his lectures and radio and television appearances, and his polished editorials in the *Near East Report*, the weekly Washington newsletter which AIPAC continues to mail to all its members, Kenen was a powerful political asset for the Jewish community in Congress.

But AIPAC has changed in many ways since then, largely because Israel's needs have changed. In one example, before the 1973 war, the burning issue for AIPAC was trying to increase the economic assistance portion of the U.S. foreign aid package for Israel from $25 million to $50 million. Since the war, Israel has been receiving more than $2 billion annually in various forms of economic and military grants and loans.

According to State Department figures, Israel received some $86.5 million in economic grants between 1948 and 1952. Another $518 million ($249 million in loans and $269 million in grants) was approved through 1961. That relatively modest level of U.S. assistance was maintained until the Yom Kippur War. The emergency U.S. airlift of military supplies to Israel after the first week of that war and the Nixon administration's subsequent request for $2.2 billion in military credits designed to pay the bill for much of the war dramatically changed the level and type of aid. Until then, all the military portion of the annual U.S. foreign aid bills for Israel was in the form of interest-bearing loans. It was not until the $2.2 billion package that Israel started to receive outright military grants. Indeed, that historical aid package was significant in many other ways, including the fact that it set a trend for forgiving repayment of much of the total package. In 1984, the Reagan administration, with congressional backing, made the entire aid package for Israel an outright grant.

Since 1948, total U.S. economic and military grants and loans for Israel have exceeded $27 billion; this includes the 1985 fiscal year program. The need to keep up with an escalating arms race in the Middle East guarantees that Israel's foreign aid requests from the United States are going to continue to be high through the foreseeable future, and that money proposed by the executive branch of the U.S. government and appropriated by the legislative branch will remain an indispensable part of the Israeli budget.

Thus, AIPAC's higher profile can be viewed as resulting largely from the heightened increase in U.S. government assistance to Israel. Before the 1973 war, direct cash contributions to the United Jewish Appeal, loans through the purchase of Israel Bonds, and West German war reparations were the most significant sources of external financial assistance for Israel's fledgling economy. But in recent years these sources of income, while still critically important for Israel, have become a much smaller portion of total foreign financial aid. The approximately $300 million in annual UJA cash transfers to Israel in recent years is about one-tenth of what Congress appropriates. Another $500 million is purchased each year in Israel Bonds, though these must be repaid with interest, albeit at low rates and over a long term.

AIPAC plays a unique role in the organized American Jewish community. It is the only Jewish organization officially registered with the U.S. Congress to lobby on behalf of legislation affecting Israel. Because it is a domestic political lobby, its money must be raised the hard way; contributions to AIPAC are not tax-deductible. In addition, it cannot accept any funds from the government of Israel, since doing so would require AIPAC to register with the U.S Justice Department as a foreign agent. But, despite those built-in difficulties, AIPAC's budget has expanded rapidly since 1973. Before the war, AIPAC managed to get by with a budget approximating $300,000. Its 1985 budget was over $5 million.

"Obviously, the name of the game, if you want to help Israel, is political action," said Morris J. Amitay, who succeeded Kenen as AIPAC's executive director. Amitay, a former legislative assistant to Democratic Senator Abraham Ribicoff of Connecticut and a State Department foreign service officer, worked for AIPAC for six years. In December 1980, he went into private consulting and law work (he is a graduate of Harvard Law School) and was replaced by Tom Dine, a former legislative assistant to several Democratic senators, including Edward Kennedy, Edmund Muskie, and Frank Church. Dine, too, had earlier served in the State Department.

Given Israel's increasing needs and the recognition that one legislative slip-up on a subcommittee vote or a parliamentary maneuver can cost Israel hundreds of millions of dollars, AIPAC has expanded its staff and its nationwide grass-roots level of support. Kenen had been AIPAC's only registered lobbyist until 1973. Before the war, he hired Wollack to join him as a lobbyist. By 1983, Dine had six registered lobbyists on his staff, each specializing in different areas—the House or Senate, Democrats or Republicans, liberals or conservatives. In total AIPAC now has more than eighty people on its payroll as opposed to only twelve in 1973.

AIPAC's growth started during the final years of Kenen's tenure but really jumped during Amitay's six-year period. America's front pages may have focused on the Cold War during the 1950s and on Vietnam during the 1960s, but the Middle East became the hot issue after the Arab oil embargo and during the Kissinger shuttles, and the Middle East dominated foreign affairs coverage in the 1970s. During that decade, the Arabs and their political supporters also started to step up their activity, generating even greater support for AIPAC in the Jewish community.

On the eve of the 1973 war, a Standard Oil of California letter to its stockholders and a Mobil advertisement in major U.S. newspapers urged a more pro-Arab policy. Americans of Arab ancestry became more politically active, establishing the National Association of Arab–Americans in Washington on the AIPAC model. Some twenty Arab embassies in Washington began to hire top Washington public relations experts, lobbyists, and lawyers to promote their cause.

Very much in response to this competition, AIPAC moved to larger, more modern offices on Capitol Hill, just two blocks from the Senate office buildings. Its list of key local political contacts around the country was expanded and computerized. Its fund-raising operations went into high gear. That development continued under Dine.

Making Jews more politically active has been another major item on the national Jewish agenda for many years. Indeed, as far as Israel is concerned, Jewish political activism is seen as critical. AIPAC's Arthur Chotin, in an interview with me, hailed direct mail and its impact on AIPAC. "I think the potential for direct mail in the Jewish community is unlimited. And one of the most critical things, I think, is that our mail is not designed simply to get money for AIPAC and new members. It's educational. We have never done a mailing that wasn't educational about what's happening in Washington. That's another purpose."

Direct mail clearly has been a tremendous success for AIPAC. According to Chotin, AIPAC had 8000 members in January 1981. At the time of the Reagan administration's Saudi AWACS sale, AIPAC for the first time began a massive campaign of direct mail. Its first mailing, involving some 400,000 pieces of mail, generated 10,000 new members, an unusually successful return. By the middle of 1983, AIPAC's membership had increased to nearly 45,000, largely the result of direct mail.

In recent years, there was also an overhaul of AIPAC's Executive Committee and National Council, the lay leadership that supported the professional staff. Several heavy hitters very active in local Jewish federations and community relations councils began to focus their attention on AIPAC. Edward Sanders of Los Angeles became president. (He later resigned to work for candidate Jimmy Carter in the 1976 election, eventually joining the White House staff as a senior liaison to the Jewish community and an adviser to Secretary of State Cyrus Vance.) While most of the presidents of major American Jewish organizations have always been involved in AIPAC to varying degrees, many dynamic young Jewish leaders now see AIPAC as holding the key to Jewish political power in America. Larry Weinberg of Los Angeles succeeded Sanders. New faces moved to the forefront of AIPAC's lay leadership, including Mort Silberman of Miami, Bob Asher of Chicago, Don Diamond of Tucson, Gordon Zacks of Columbus, Irwin Levy of Palm Beach, Robert Riesman of Providence, Charles Shusterman of Tulsa, Jesse Cohen of Pittsburgh, and Robert Loup of Denver.

Amitay also assembled an informal advisory group of Washington lawyers, former Hill aides, and other professional political experts to help. Jews and non-Jews were involved, including John Lehman, later secretary of the Navy in the Reagan administration; Elliot Abrams, later assistant secretary of state for human rights; Max Kampelman, the chief U.S. arms control negotiator; Ben Wattenberg of the American Enterprise Institute; and such respected former legislative aides to senators as Jay Berman and Ken Davis.

AIPAC, of course, also worked very closely with the Washington representatives of the other Jewish organizations, including Hyman Bookbinder of the American Jewish Committee and David Brody of the

Anti-Defamation League. They met weekly, and during crises even more often, to plan political strategy for pushing legislation through Congress or countering anti-Israeli propaganda.

But AIPAC and its professional staff were allowed unusual autonomy in making decisions and taking actions, an exceptional freedom both from the AIPAC lay leadership and from other American Jewish organizations, very much because so few leaders without daily contact with the inner sanctum of Capitol Hill have the necessary knowledge of the complicated legislative process to secure passage of a favorable foreign aid bill without risking the addition of some crippling amendment. Unless AIPAC's staff is free to act, a large cut in aid to Israel could get through within minutes.

Further, there is the possibility of a simple mistake during the lengthy and often complicated review of the foreign aid bill costing Israel millions. Few people without direct experience in the American legislative forum have instant command of the distinction between budget "authority" and "obligation," between legislative "appropriation" and "authorization," or between budget "outlays" and "line items." That's why, under Kenen, Amitay, and Dine, AIPAC's professional team has received a mandate from the organized Jewish leadership to operate with such independence, certainly more than that given any other American Jewish organization. According to Richard Straus of the *Middle East Policy Survey,* "Dine has power that comes from knowledge. AIPAC is just too plugged in to be stepped on." Dine says of AIPAC, "I like to use the phrase that we are a small elite professional organization without being elitist."

Dine demonstrated considerable political savvy by generating early and strong opposition to the Saudi AWACS sale, though AIPAC did eventually lose this fight. He has a long-range vision of the future, one that already has started to revolve around the direct mail campaign practices so successfully established by conservative political operations. That first mailing, dated September 8, 1981, focused on the dangers of the AWACS sale. From there, it made its pitch for membership ("35 nondeductible dollars") and even larger financial contributions by quoting from some of the newspaper comments recently made about the organization.

The most powerful, best-run and effective foreign policy interest group in Washington.

The New York Times

A power to be reckoned with at the White House, State and Defense Departments, and on Capitol Hill.

The Washington Post

AIPAC's direct mail campaign was merely a further refinement of traditionally successful Jewish fund raising. Yehuda Hellman, executive vice-chairman of the Conference of Presidents of Major American Jewish Organizations, remembers very vividly his first United Jewish Appeal fund-raising speech in the United States in 1948. In an interview with me, he recalled what a prominent leader in the New York Jewish community had told him: "I'll give but my son is not interested. We are the last generation of supporters of the UJA." Thirty-five years later, Hellman ran into the man's son at another UJA meeting. "The son was the chairman of the dinner," he said. "He told me, 'My father was never a good giver. He loved Israel greatly but he was never a good giver.' "

Hellman's point, of course, is that American Jews over the years have managed to maintain their traditional commitment to the worldwide Jewish community. "The difference is this," he said. "In 1948, the guy spoke with a Yiddish accent. Today, you have a modern American boy."

Jews, of course, have a well-earned reputation for being charitable. They have become the envy of many other American organizations involved in fund raising. *The Wall Street Journal* reported on April 1, 1983, that the 1982 national UJA budget of some $567 million was about a third the size of that of the nationwide United Way, even though the nearly 6 million Jews in this country represent less than 3 percent of the total population. "The UJA raises more each year than the American Cancer Society, American Heart Association, Muscular Dystrophy Association, March of Dimes, and National Easter Seal Society combined," the newspaper reported.

That is truly impressive. What is even more remarkable is the fact that Jews are actually giving very generously to many other Jewish causes besides the UJA—to their local synagogues, Jewish schools and colleges, Jewish hospitals, and all sorts of other Jewish organizations that operate separate budgets as well as to secular charities.

Still, the American Jewish leadership is not satisfied. A lot of American Jews, they believe, do not give a penny to any Jewish cause. According to some nationwide estimates, this may include as many as 50 percent of the Jewish population. These are not just poor Jews, who will often find a way to make a contribution, no matter how modest, to a Jewish cause. In many large communities, there are wealthy Jews who may be generous givers to the children's hospital and other non-Jewish causes but will not give to the local Jewish federation.

In the largest Jewish communities, such as New York and Los Angeles, the percentage of givers to Jewish organizations is relatively low; according to Los Angeles federation officials only around 10 percent of the 500,000 Jews in the Los Angeles area give to the local federation. In the smaller communities, the percentages increase, largely because greater social pressure can be exerted. In the approximately 12,000-member Jewish community of Columbus, Ohio, some 60 or 70 percent give to the local federation, a former executive director, Charles Schiffman, told me. In the tiny Jewish communities scattered around southern Illinois, the local federation reaches out to around 90 percent of the Jews, according to Elliot Gershenson, the local federation executive director.

Among the various ethnic groups in America, the Jewish community has a reputation for being extremely organized in politics. Indeed, a notion has emerged of a supposedly all-powerful Jewish lobby on Capitol Hill, especially as far as winning support for Israel is concerned. But as Delaware's Democratic Senator Joseph Biden reminded some 1400 Jews who converged on Washington from all parts of the United States on May 10, 1982, to attend AIPAC's policy conference, the pro-Israeli lobby has lost two major battles in recent years. First, there was the original 1978 F-15 package sale to Saudi Arabia, which the Carter administration managed to push through the Senate by a vote of fifty-four to forty-four. And later, President Reagan used all of his own powers of personal political persuasion to get the Senate to approve the controversial 1981 Saudi AWACS/F-15 enhancement package. That vote was fifty-two to forty-eight. Those two highly publicized defeats have had a major impact on many influential Jewish political activists. They have learned their lessons well.

Recognizing that the pro-Arab opposition has become increasingly effective in forging a new petrodollar-financed political coalition against Israel, Jews from coast to coast, as well as in Alaska and Hawaii, have begun to fight back. They have involved themselves in the political process in an even more energetic fashion. Dine spoke of a "virtual explosion of Jewish political activity" throughout the United States.

If the Jewish community did not know it before, they certainly learned it after the AWACS defeat: victory is no longer automatic when it comes to maintaining U.S. support for Israel. They also know that to have influence with a senator or a representative on specific issues, you first have to help that person get elected. That was Dine's central message during the AIPAC conference in 1982. "We, you and I, must step up our level of political action," he told the delegates. "The other guys may have the money, but we've got the people—committed people whose motive is not profit but principle. Our supporters are energetic people who act from the heart, American people who don't need Saudi princes to speak for them so they can make petrodollar profits." The registered AIPAC lobbyist urged the Jewish community to get involved "at a level and intensity never before performed." He warned that "the stakes are very high" because "the Saudi connection does not wish us well."

Beyond the more traditional methods of political organization, Jews all over the United States also have come to establish separate political action committees, or PACs. This probably has been the single most fascinating aspect of the Jewish community's involvement in politics in recent years. Because federal campaign financing laws passed in the 1970s have sharply limited individual campaign contributions to candidates, all kinds of PACs have been created to skirt the new regulations. They represent virtually every ethnic and special-interest group in the country, including Jews. The New Right groups, so far, may have been more highly visible in using their PACs to promote conservative candidates, but others on the American political spectrum have also jumped aboard the PAC train.

Compared to the giants, the various individual Jewish PACs, whether in Chicago, Los Angeles, New York, or smaller cities, are still rather modest in terms of their actual numbers and the overall amount of money they have raised for pro-Israel candidates. But, make no mistake about it, taken together they have already started to make an impressive dent in influencing congressional races.

Determining exactly how much money has been raised by Jewish PACs is very difficult, since these groups do not have to identify themselves as Jewish or Israel-oriented in their required reporting to the Federal Election Commission. Like most special-interest and ethnic PACs, the Jewish ones simply list "good government" or something equally innocuous as their groups' basic objective. That is not the case, however, when the checks are actually handed over to candidates, all of whom are very well aware of the Jewish PACs' specific conerns.

The Wall Street Journal reported on February 26, 1985, that more than seventy Jewish PACs contributed a total of $3.6 million in the 1984 congressional campaigns. "American Jews have organized new financial muscle to back up their already powerful lobby for aid to Israel," the newspaper said. Unless new campaign regulations further restrict political fund raising, PACs are clearly the wave of the future in American politics. Like other Americans with causes to advance, Jews will use that avenue to try to influence the course of U.S. policy toward Israel. It has become part of the democratic landscape. "Let us heed in this election year the words of Senator Jesse Helms," Dine told the 1982 AIPAC gathering. "If you are going to win on issues, you've got to help elect the candidates who will vote your way."

For politically active Jews, therefore, learning to operate through the legally intricate PAC process has become a high priority. "Not surprisingly," said Morris Amitay, the former AIPAC executive director, "in communities around the country, PACs with a Jewish orientation have sprung up—particularly in the last two years." (The *PAC* in AIPAC, it should be noted, is misleading since it is not a political action committee.

AIPAC, a domestic American Jewish organization registered with Congress to lobby on behalf of legislation affecting Israel, does not distribute funds to candidates.)

Amitay explained that the Jewish PACs which have been established in local communities around the country "serve as a focal point for politically active Jews to support candidates who are sensitive to the concerns of the American Jewish community." There were some sixty local Jewish PACs in business by 1983. Most of them were small, although they clearly have been effective in helping pro-Israel candidates. Since leaving AIPAC, Amitay has opened his own legal and consulting office in Washington and has organized a PAC of his own. In 1982, he became embroiled in a controversy surrounding the National Political Action Committee, or NatPAC, the first nationally based pro-Israeli PAC. Why would a pro-Israeli political activist like Amitay criticize an organization whose goal is to support America's long-standing commitment to Israel? The issue here was means, not ends.

NatPAC's treasurer, Marvin Josephson, the prominent New York talent agent and businessman, explained the purpose of his group: "Mobil Oil has a PAC, Bechtel has a PAC, Fluor has a PAC, Boeing and Amoco and Grumman all have PACs. But those of us who believe deeply in this country's long-term stake in Israel's survival have not had a nationwide PAC. By participating in NatPAC, we can stand against the petrodollar lobby in Washington and its flood of campaign contributions."

Filmmaker Woody Allen, one of Josephson's clients, joined the long and impressive list of personalities supporting NatPAC and signed a mass mailing to 200,000 Americans, urging them to join. "I believe very strongly that this country's strategic interests in the Middle East are best served by maintaining our traditional commitment to the security of Israel," Allen wrote. "But not everyone believes that. The profits of many large multinational corporations are closely tied to petrodollar interests. A long-range effort is under way to discredit Israel in the eyes of Congress, to convert a disagreement over tactics into a weakening of ties between our two democracies. And though some of us might not always agree with Israel's policies on all matters, still the benefits of close ties between our two democracies outweigh the points of disagreement."

NatPAC made a big splash trying to raise money. It placed full-page ads in major newspapers. One featured a large photo of PLO chairman Yasser Arafat. The caption read: "Next year in Jerusalem?" Another declared in big bold type: "Supporting candidates who believe in Israel isn't just good for Jews, it's good for Americans." Noting Israel's strategic advantages to the United States, the NatPAC ad went on to say: "Charitable organizations, like the UJA or the ADL, cannot make political contributions.

According to federal election law, the only organizations that can fund these candidates are political action committees."

During the 1982 campaign, NatPAC gave the maximum $5000 contribution to candidates in thirty-one Senate and seventy-three House races. Twenty-eight of their Senate candidates and fifty-seven in the House were elected. In 1984, NatPAC distributed $784,000 to candidates. That would seem to be an impressive achievement. So the question remains: Why would Amitay and several other influential Jewish political analysts in Washington oppose such an operation?

The answer lies in visibility. They believe that the high profile struck by a nationwide PAC simply strengthens the impression that Jews give heavily to politicians, that the Jewish lobby tries to buy Congress. They prefer Jewish political activity to be more subtle and behind the scenes. Local Jewish PACs, Amitay said, are low-key and noncontroversial. They attract "scant attention." But the creation of a national PAC, in his view, was a mistake. "What American Jews don't need is a high-profile target for detractors who will seize upon this as another example of Jewish influence on the Congress," Amitay said. "Think of the expectations that will be raised and unfulfilled by such an organization. Almost every member of Congress considers himself or herself a friend of the Jewish community and of Israel. Who will make judgments for this super PAC in the 'book of political life'?" Amitay went on to say that the political strength of the Jewish community lies in its geographic distribution and in strong, cohesive community ties. "One large New York-based PAC cannot substitute for scores of smaller groups working to accomplish the same goals," he said.

David Weinstein, the former executive director of NatPAC, disagreed. He argued strongly for more concerted Jewish involvement in politics at all levels. "Today," he told me, "the possibility that American support for Israel can be extinguished, not simply eroded or deteriorated, but extinguished, is very real. I view this as a threat to America as well as to Israel, and frankly I sense a personal threat as well." That was why he got involved with NatPAC. "A new and powerful pro-Israel voice has been added to the Washington scene and in electoral districts throughout the nation to complement the efforts of previously existing entities—both individual and collective," he said.

Despite tactical differences, for activists like Weinstein, Amitay, and many others around the country, politics, simply put, is the name of the game.

What is clear is that American Jews over the years have learned to use the political process effectively. And today Jews have come to recognize that PACs are one important tool that is going to be around for some time.

There can be no denying that Jewish money and organizational skill were very much involved in the defeat of Congressman Paul Findley, Republican of Illinois, in 1982. Findley, the PLO's strongest supporter on Capitol Hill, was upset by Democrat Richard Durbin, who was assisted financially by many Jews around the country. Jewish PACs pumped more than $104,000 into his campaign. Findley, for his part, received contributions from pro-Arab Americans and corporate PACs.

For some influential Jewish political activists, getting involved has meant not only national politics but state and local politics as well. For them, it's never too early to establish contacts with budding politicians who may be going places. "One of the major mistakes made by the American Jewish community is its failure to establish relations with politicians early in their careers," said Richard Krieger, a former Jewish federation director in Michigan and New Jersey who later went to work for the Republican National Committee. "By the time a politician comes to Washington," he said, "it may be too late."

A new generation of lawmakers has taken charge in Washington. These senators and representatives—unlike Henry Jackson, Hubert Humphrey, and Jacob Javits—do not have the personal, firsthand experiences of living through World War II, the Holocaust, and the birth of Israel. For many of this new crowd, Israel is simply another country in the world. The challenge for American Jewish leadership has been to educate these people about Israel. That means, first and foremost, getting them to visit Israel. Taking politicians to Israel, Jewish leaders and Israeli officials agree, is probably the single most important and effective way to generate pro-Israeli feelings in them. A high priority of AIPAC and the supporting Jewish groups around the country is to arrange trips to Israel. It can be extremely beneficial to have local Jewish constituents accompany the lawmakers there, constantly providing a ready source of positive feedback. The Israeli Foreign Ministry's North American desk has been charged with taking care of these official visitors. The Israelis, after some silly but costly mistakes several years ago, now take these visits very seriously.

This line of thinking convinced Krieger to organize several visits to Israel for local and state officials who showed some promise in their careers. In the mid-1970s, Krieger organized a trip to Israel by local district attorneys. One of those who joined him was a young Democrat from Tucson, Dennis DeConcini. He later became a U.S. senator from Arizona.

It naturally makes sense that a large percentage of the senators and representatives in Washington were once local and state officials. Moving up the political ladder is one of the most common aspects of American politics. Nearly half of the eighty freshmen in the 98th Congress, which took office in 1983, were former state legislators. These included several of the new Jewish members—Republican Senator Chic Hecht of Nevada, a former state senator; Democratic Representatives Mel Levine and Howard Berman of California, who had served together in the state assembly; and Democrat Larry Smith of Florida, who had served in his state house. These three representatives, by the way, joined the House Foreign Affairs Committee.

The pro-Israeli community in the United States is limited in its ability to influence policy toward the Middle East. It has to carefully and practically select key target areas, aware of financial, political, and other factors which may, perhaps, restrict activity. Thus, it always makes more sense to establish good relations with a key member of the U.S. Senate and House of Representatives than with a local official. But that does not mean that regional political powers are ignored, according to AIPAC's Dine. One particularly crucial area, he said, involves Jewish state legislators around the country. It is from this group that many of the next generation of Washington politicians can be expected to come. That was why Dine addressed the National Association of Jewish Legislators at its meeting in Atlanta in 1981. "The Jewish community in the United States is under attack," he declared. "We are accused of possessing too much power, of having parochial interests and dual loyalties." The AIPAC official went on to urge the Jewish state legislators to get more actively involved in the pro-Israeli battle. "Political activity," he said, "is survival, and one does not choose to survive—it is a feeling that is levied on us by nature."

Al Abrams, the retired secretary of the New York State Senate, was the driving force in the original establishment of the National Association of Jewish Legislators in 1978. Since then, that organization has expanded rapidly. By 1983, according to Abrams, there were some 250 Jewish state legislators in about thirty-five states. This, he said, comprised about 3 percent of all state legislators, or roughly the same precentage of Jews to the overall American population.

In the early days of the organization, Barney Frank, a Democratic Massachusetts state lawmaker, was actively involved in helping Abrams. Frank was elected to Congress in 1980 and quickly emerged as a power on Capitol Hill.

What exactly can Jewish state legislators do to help promote closer American–Israeli ties? According to Abrams, there are several important areas. For one thing, he told me, they can introduce resolutions into the state houses in order to "educate" their colleagues, many of whom may not be aware of Israel's concerns. These resolutions tend to get picked up in the local news media, and that "always can be beneficial" in improving public opinion.

Conducting U.S. foreign policy, of course, is the responsibility of the federal government in Washington. There is a clear limit regarding the involvement of local and state officials in such foreign affairs. But over the years there has been some spillover. Thus, Steve Sklar, a former member of the Maryland House of Delegates and active in the National Association of Jewish Legislators, recalled that he was personally behind a drive to make illegal U.S. business cooperation with the Arab economic boycott against Israel. In fact, it was the state legislatures that initially set the pace for persuading Congress to fight the Arab boycott. Several other state legislatures followed the Maryland lead and clearly helped to create a climate of opinion in the United States that eventually resulted in the strong anti-boycott legislation enacted during the Carter administration.

Some Jewish members of Congress established their initial contacts with their non-Jewish colleagues back home in their state legislatures. Democratic Representative John LaFalce of western New York does not represent a particularly large Jewish district. Still, he has been a consistent supporter of Israel since entering Congress in 1975. He has always voted in favor of economic and military assistance packages for Israel. He has opposed large-scale arms sales to Arab states. When he first came to Washington, he said he had become close friends with Democratic Representative Steve Solarz when they both served in the New York State Assembly in Albany. LaFalce said he would look to Solarz, one of Israel's best friends on Capitol Hill, for guidance on Israel-related issues. That was the type of impact a good pro-Israeli politician can have among his colleagues. It explains why AIPAC has looked to the Jewish legislators and other local officials around the country as key contacts in reaching influential lawmakers in Washington.

AIPAC's strength over the years has also been the result of its bipartisan support. Wanting to help Israel cuts across the U.S. political spectrum. Top Democrats and Republicans work with AIPAC closely. Of the thirty-eight Republican Jewish activists who signed a 1981 letter to Reagan opposing the AWACS sale, all but two or three were aligned with AIPAC. Dine may have come to AIPAC from Democratic Senate offices, but he quickly made a point of establishing close ties with top Republican leaders, especially with a Republican administration in power. He worked closely with Max Fisher of Detroit, who has long been the most influential Jew in the Republican Party. Fisher, while always active in AIPAC, has stepped up his involvement in recent years.

But those American Jewish political activists who are most successful in supporting AIPAC are those who are Zionists first, Democrats or Republicans second. Dine said he hoped to work over the next few years to broaden Jewish political activity around the country in both parties. "What is critical is that Jews get involved seven days a week, fifty-two weeks a year, and not just during presidential election years," he said. AIPAC, therefore, has sought out younger Jewish political activists in local city councils, state legislatures, and the better law firms. It has done so with the usually generous support of local Jewish federations and community relations councils. Many local leaders are very politically astute, and whenever they cooperate with AIPAC, the end results for both the Jewish lobby on Capitol Hill and the local Jewish organizations benefit. "We can reach deeper into a local Jewish community, both financially and politically, when they work with us," said Dine. For the most part, he had only praise for the organizational structure of Jewish communities around the country. They are constantly approaching their representatives and senators. They stay on top of the issues. By doing so, they become politically persuasive.

As politics has become more important for generating U.S. support for Israel, being politically active has become the most attractive way for Jews to become involved in helping Israel. Many of the key Jewish leaders around the country are no longer so much interested in giving money to various Jewish causes as they are in being engaged in lobbying for congressional action. Meeting with lawmakers and administration officials is exciting. There is a new cachet to being a politically active Jew in America. For many, that means AIPAC.

This is most dramatically demonstrated at the annual AIPAC policy conference in Washington. In recent years, nearly 1000 AIPAC members from around the country have spent three rather full days listening to senators, representatives, State Department officials, and other senior administration staff members discuss a wide range of issues affecting American–Israeli relations. Local Jewish community activists can compare notes with their colleagues from other parts of the United States. There is a clear sense of comradeship among the delegates. It is rewarding to other devoted supporters of Israel from other parts of the country to come to Washington, hear America's top political leadership declare their everlasting love for Israel, and eventually return home with a strong sense of accomplishment. At every AIPAC conference, several hours are set aside for constituents to go to their respective lawmakers' offices and talk about Israel—in other words, to lobby. This not only has an important impact on the senators and representatives, but it also recharges the batteries of the AIPAC members.

In addition, as American Jews have risen in the political and economic structure of the country, they have begun to feel more comfortable with lobbying openly. No longer is Jewish political power a function of solely-relying on an old-boy network of personal acquaintances. A sophisticated grass-roots approach to politics has sprung up in the country, with AIPAC as its focus.

As AIPAC's visibility has grown, of course, so have its critics. Former Republican Congressman Paul McCloskey of California, writing in *The Los Angeles Times*, and Republican Senator Charles McC. Mathias, writing in *Foreign Affairs*, were only two of several politicans going public in their criticism of AIPAC. "This is not just lobbying persuasion of Congress," charged McCloskey. "It is lobbying *control* of a Congress all too willing to abdicate its responsibility. If the United States is to work effectively toward peace in the Mideast, the power of this lobby must be recognized and countered in open and fair debate."

An influential member of the Foreign Relations Committee, Senator Mathias was reelected to the Senate in 1980 with overwhelming support from Jews in Baltimore and the Maryland suburbs of Washington. These facts merely added to the distress he caused among American Jewry by expressing the opinion in *Foreign Affairs* that their strong partisan support for Israel may at times go against the national interest. "Lest these pages be read as criticism of our country's ethnic groups," he said, "the distinction must be drawn between ethnicity, which enriches American life and culture, and organized ethnic interest groups, which sometimes press causes that derogate from the national interest." Mathias maintained that over the years senators and congressmen "have been subjected to recurrent pressures from what has come to be known as the Israel lobby."

His twenty-four-page article, which also reviewed the influence of Americans of Irish, Greek, Eastern European, Arab, and other ancestries, concluded that the Jewish lobby was by far the most effective. In part, he explained, this was because of the "substantial merit" of its case. "For the most part," he said, "they [the Jewish lobby] have been responsive, and for reasons not always related either to personal conviction or careful reflection of the national interest. The Arabs are unequal competitors with an aid-dependent Israel for influence on American policy, not for lack of resources but for lack of an Arab–American community comparable in size and unity of motivation to the Jewish community in the United States."

The article again raised the specter of a supposedly powerful Jewish lobby undermining American foreign policy toward the Middle East. There have been, especially since the 1973 Yom Kippur War, many similar accusations, including the well-known charge in 1974 by the chairman of the U.S. Joint Chiefs of Staff, General George Brown, that Jews controlled American newspapers, banks, and other influential institutions. Mathias did not go nearly as far as Brown in criticizing the Jewish lobby, but his article still caused an uproar.

In criticizing the Israel lobby, and most specifically AIPAC, Mathias used as an example the 1978 fight between the Carter administration and Congress over the package sale of F-15 fighters to Saudi Arabia. The Senate approved it after a lengthy debate. Mathias, who earlier had been considered "friendly" toward Israel, voted for approval. "Although it was interpreted at the time as a defeat for the Israel lobby, a more sober and objective interpretation is that the Senate withstood countervailing pressures to recognize the *variety* of American interests in the Middle East and the necessity of a policy aimed at *reconciling* these interests, as distinguished from choosing one and sacrificing others."

His article appeared just as a similar battle over arms sales to Saudi Arabia was shaping up between the Reagan administration and Israel's supporters in Congress. AIPAC and other American Jewish organizations were already lobbying hard against the AWACS sale to the Saudis. Mathias said immediately after his *Foreign Affairs* article was published that he would vote against the AWACS sale "if the vote were held today." But he later voted for it.

Mathias was by no means anti-Israel, even though some Baltimore Jews were recalling that after a 1976 visit to the Middle East, which included a meeting with Yasser Arafat, he called the PLO leader "a moderate and reasonable man." He was then quoted as having said that Arafat was "seeking a peaceful solution to the world's most difficult problem."

Amitay and others have pointed out that those criticizing AIPAC for being overly aggressive are almost always on the other side of the line as far as a particular issue involving Israel is concerned. Thus, he said, both McCloskey and Mathias wanted the Israeli government to take a more pro-Arab stance on the Palestinian question.

Amitay did have some critics in the American Jewish leadership who charged that he, on a personal level, was too pushy. To these critics Dine was seen as more softspoken and discreet, along the lines of Kenen. But, during the AWACS fight, several administration officials came to resent what they also charged was Dine's overly aggressive lobbying tactics. There can be no denying that Dine, like Amitay, is a tough fighter, a trait that comes after years of Capitol Hill experience battling over legislation. In the world of Washington politics, Amitay said, one is better off with a reputation as "hard driving and aggressive" rather than "easygoing and nice." He added: "It's nice to be liked in certain circumstances, but to be an effective lobbyist you have to be more than liked. My personal relationships with people on the Hill tended to be very good. I tended to stick to the issues and to try and get a commitment, if I could."

Occasionally, American Jews have been accused of maintaining a dual loyalty, one to the United States and the other to Israel. When there have been serious strains in the American–Israeli relationship, for instance, this allegation has been revived most frequently. When President Reagan told a nationally televised news conference on October 1, 1981, that "an ob-

jective assessment of U.S. national interests must favor" the proposed
Saudi AWACS sale, he may not have realized that he was coming very
close to hitting an extremely sensitive nerve in the American Jewish community. Coupled with Reagan's earlier warning to Israel to stay out of the
AWACS fight, this was widely seen as a suggestion, at least indirectly,
that those Americans who opposed the sale was more concerned about
Israeli interests than those of America. "While we must always take into
account the vital interests of our allies," Reagan said, "American security
interests must remain our internal responsibility. It is not the business of
other nations to make American foreign policy." In addition, by flatly
asserting that the AWACS sale "poses no threat to Israel now or in the
future," the president was directly challenging the repeated statements by
Prime Minister Begin and virtually all of Israel's military experts that the
sale did indeed represent a threat to Israel's security. In Israel, the opposition Labor Party had been even more concerned about the sale than
the Likud-led coalition government. When Begin, for example, merely
hinted at a reduced level of Israeli opposition shortly following his summit
with Reagan in early September of that year, Shimon Peres and other
Labor leaders were quick to criticize him. For the president later to suggest
that the Israeli assessment was simply wrong was, for many Israelis, merely
a revised version of the old George Ball school of thought that the United
States knows best what is in Israel's national interest.

Throughout the AWACS debate, other administration officials as well
as their supporters on Capitol Hill raised some ugly innuendos about a
dual loyalty to the United States and Israel. Defense Secretary Caspar
Weinberger went even further than the president in discounting Israeli
protestations against the sale. Answering questions on October 1, 1981,
before the Senate Foreign Relations Committee, Weinberger insisted that
the sale posed no threat to Israel. "I don't think there is any basis for that
opposition. They could shoot down this plane in less than a minute and a
half. It's not an armed plane. There isn't even a BB gun on that plane."

"Whose policy do you support: Reagan's or Begin's?" was a question
often heard during the hectic lobbying undertaken by administration officials. The implication was clear.

Five months later, on March 15, 1982, Vice-President George Bush
sought to erase the administration's earlier insinuation that American Jews
have a dual loyalty. Addressing some 2000 delegates at the third biennial
Young Leadership Conference of the United Jewish Appeal, Bush said he
wanted "to clear the air of some misconceptions."

"During the debate over the sale of AWACS to Saudi Arabia," he said,
"the American Jewish community was charged by some with having two
loyalties. People in certain quarters grabbed the opportunity during that

emotionally heated time to accuse American Jews of being more loyal to Israel than to the United States. This was a scurrilous charge. It was an outrageous charge. It never should have been made. And those who did it did a profound injustice to all Americans, whose birthright it is to dissent." Bush did not say who specifically had made that allegation, although he flatly denied that "this charge came out of the White House or out of our president." Bush said Americans have a constitutionally guaranteed right to disagree. "It's exercised—Lord knows—every day and in every single way."

He continued "We're all citizens of the United States. If our blood is Irish, African, Jewish, Italian, or Polish, it doesn't make us one iota less American. To say that someone is disloyal to America because he or she has an abiding affection for another country is an insult. It's offensive, and it's just basically un-American."

The dual loyalty accusation has been around for some time, although in the past it was most often associated with a tiny right-wing fringe of the U.S. political spectrum, such as the Liberty Lobby. In recent years, particularly during times of strain between Washington and Jerusalem, it has become more politically acceptable. George Ball raised the specter on many occasions. On July 30, 1981, he wrote in *The Washington Post* that "Europeans are disturbed that America, having preempted Middle East diplomacy, seems disabled by domestic constraints from effectively promoting peace or restraining Israeli adventurism." At the October 1, 1981, news conference, Reagan himself seemed to accept this line of thinking when he was asked to elaborate on his AWACS warning to Israel. After insisting that he was not "deprecating" anyone, he said: "I suppose what really is the most serious thing is that other countries must not get a perception that we are being unduly influenced one way or the other with regard to foreign policy."

Probably the best and most passionate response to the dual loyalty charge was made by Senator Hubert H. Humphrey before AIPAC's 17th Annual Policy Conference on May 3, 1976:

> I've noticed a comment or two in some columns . . . about the appropriateness of the kind of work that you're engaged in. In other words, questions have sort of been raised. Should you be here? Much of the talk, frankly, as I see it, has been downright ridiculous and silly. Columnists, editorial writers have warned us about ethnic lobbies. We've been hearing a lot about 'ethnic' lately. They've been warning us about ethnic lobbying, especially in foreign affairs. We've heard careless and, I think, reckless things being said about the powerful Jewish lobby, the Greek lobby, the Turkish lobby, the Baltic states lobby—you mention it—as if somehow or another, it was against the law in this country to speak up for what you believe in.

Now, let me just lay it on the line. What a privilege it is to be both a good Jew and a good American at the same time. Let no one contest the patriotic dedication of the Jewish community in the United States. From the first days of our Republic, from the days George Washington needed help in the battle for independence, people of the Jewish faith have been in the front lines doing their job for freedom, for justice. The whole theme of justice and the priceless nature of the human spirit comes from Jewish philosophy and Jewish religion. I'm very proud to be with an audience such as this, and I want you to know that I approve of what you are doing. . . . It is good for the basic democratic process that people who have convictions about what American public policy should be take time to get their fellow Americans and their public officials to understand what they believe and to urge their support. That's what we mean by free speech in this country.

We have some people in this government who think that if they make a statement, everybody is supposed to agree with them. I thought we had gotten over that nonsense. I say it will be a sad day for this country when its citizenship stops using the precious guarantee of the first amendment to petition their government. Let's never forget it. And let us remember that even in the Declaration of Independence, the people were petitioning, they were stating their grievances, and they were petitioning then the King of England.

Now, if oil producers can spend millions of dollars in their lobbying efforts, and much of it tax-deductible, as they put full-page ads in the paper to get special consideration, to influence legislation, to get special tax breaks; if sugar companies and shoe companies and clothing manufacturers can seek trade and tariff and quota policies that they think will benefit them; if workers can seek favorable labor legislation; and doctors can work against national health insurance, why can't Americans be concerned about the cultural or physical genocide of their coreligionists and relatives in the Soviet Union and in the Middle East? I think it speaks for itself. Thank God there are voices in America that speak up against injustice, and I don't care where that injustice may be. . . .

So I say there is nothing new about lobbying on behalf of causes in foreign places. It's as American as a hot dog or apple pie, spaghetti, gefilte fish, or Polish sausage. We are a nation of immigrants, even into our two hundredth year. We are concerned about the land of our fathers, be it Poland or Italy or Russia or Norway or England or Ireland or Africa. And we have every right to urge the Congress and the president to pursue policies that we deem to be correct. We are never assured that those policies will be followed. We may not win. We may not be able to gain the majority, but we surely have the right to state our case. . . .

Every once in a while I hear people say, 'Well, the real trouble is these people—the Jewish people—they're just thinking about Israel.' That's just a log of hogwash. I want to tell you that the Jewish people in America, the people of the Jewish faith, have been thinking about the poor in this country, they've been thinking about the education of our people, they've been thinking about how to make our cities better, they've been thinking about immigration laws, they've been thinking about civil rights and civil liberties and the Bill of Rights and the Constitution of the United States. And I would think that you should be terribly proud, all of you that represent these great organizations, for what you stand for. I, for one, as a member of Congress, applaud you. I only wish to God there were thousands more like you. We need you.

Clearly, one reason why AIPAC has become so much of a force in the American Jewish community in recent years is the fact that the Israeli government itself has come to rely on AIPAC for advice in understanding what, to Israelis, is an unusually complicated U.S. legislative process. "The Jewish lobby" has come to be a well-known phenomenon in Israel since the 1973 war. As Israelis concentrate more of their foreign policy attention on relations with the United States, they come to understand the critical role played by AIPAC and other supporting Jewish organizations in winning friends and influencing people, on behalf of closer American—Israeli relations. The Israeli ambassador in Washington and the political counselors assigned to focus attention solely on Capitol Hill can never hope to have AIPAC's contacts with or understanding of American politicians. Indeed, that's why Kenen came to Washington in the early 1950s in the first place.

A strong case could be made that the Begin government's eventual decision to hang tough on the AWACS fight, instead of reaching some sort of accommodation with the administration, was strongly influenced by AIPAC. Dine and other AIPAC leaders had warned the prime minister that any easing of Israel's position would have damaged Israel's credibility on Capitol Hill, where many members had gone out on a limb against the sale largely because of their concern over the potential threat to Israeli security. Back in February of 1981, Begin and the Israeli cabinet had agreed to swallow the F-15 enhancement package (minus the AWACS) in exchange for an additional $600 million in military loans spread out over the following two years, permission to export the Kfir fighter to Ecuador and other Latin American states, and other U.S. political benefits. But when the administration announced in April its decision to include the AWACS in the overall $8.5 billion package, Israel publicly attacked the sale. Later, when some foreign ministry officials were recommending that Israel avoid an all-out fight with a president considered generally sympathetic toward Israel, AIPAC and other American Jewish leaders and congressional opponents of the sale conveyed their high level of concern to the Israeli government. They did not want to see the rug pulled out from under their feet. In the end, Begin remained firm in his opposition. The prime minister was also constrained by the sharply critical stance of the Labor opposition. Begin could not afford to be accused of taking a weak attitude toward such an issue of national security. Thus, between Israel's best friends in Washington and the domestic Israeli political constraints, Begin's hands were effectively tied.

AIPAC is often accused of simply following the lead of the Israeli government, as are so many other American Jewish organizations. But here was a case where the Israeli government appeared to follow AIPAC's lead. AIPAC was clearly out in front on this issue.

Pro-Israeli lobbying in Washington has become a big operation. Like other lobbies in town, whether the National Rifle Association or the AFL–CIO, AIPAC has come to play hardball. It has taken on all the trappings of a major Washington lobby. *Washingtonian* magazine included Amitay in its 1980 listing of nineteen Washington "movers and shakers/heavy hitters/insiders." Two years later, Dine's name was listed. That in itself is a sign of political maturation for the American Jewish political establishment, since the others named were mostly lobbyists for major *Fortune* 500 corporate giants. But AIPAC still represents, in the end, a cause. And that is still its secret weapon.

7

American Jews
and Politics   II

The Conference of Presidents of Major American Jewish Organizations has served a very useful function over the years, very often as a complement to AIPAC. An umbrella group representing more than thirty of the most important national Jewish organizations, it has come to be viewed as the authoritative voice of the mainstream Jewish leadership, especially in its contacts with the White House and the State Department. Instead of having to deal with a myriad of separate Jewish organizations, an administration in Washington simply can call in the Presidents' Conference. It makes life somewhat easier for everyone.

Since the 1973 war, the prestige of the Presidents' Conference has been significantly enhanced by the talents of its chairmen—Rabbi Israel Miller, who is Orthodox; Rabbi Alexander Schindler, who is Reform; Theodore Mann, a Philadelphia lawyer; and Howard Squadron, Julius Berman, and Ken Bialkin, all New York lawyers. This group has demonstrated an impressive behind-the-scenes ability to unite the Jewish leadership behind a firmly based consensus over some rather difficult periods. This was especially true for Schindler, who was in charge in 1977 when Menachem Begin first became prime minister. Probably more than any other American Jewish leader, Schindler was instrumental in establishing Begin's legitimacy and popularity in the United States. In addition, all have been extremely effective in articulating the concerns of the Jewish community for the U.S. news media. The chairmanship of the President's Conference is probably the most prestigious leadership post in the American Jewish community.

Because the President's Conference, like AIPAC, can almost always be found in support of the official Israeli position, U.S. officials in all recent administrations have come to view it largely as a de facto arm of the Israeli government. There can be no denying that while the President's Conference (and most other American Jewish organizations) does criticize U.S. government policy when it moves against Israel, it almost never dissents publicly from the Israeli line, even when Jewish leaders privately express dissatisfaction or concern about decisions and statements made in Jerusalem. With notable exceptions, such as the American Jewish Committee, members of the organized Jewish community tend to remain silent when they feel uncomfortable with an Israeli action. This quickly came to be the American Jewish tradition in the years following the establishment of Israel, although after Begin took office and well-known and respected opposition Labor leaders in Israel like Shimon Peres, Abba Eban, and Yitzhak Rabin went public in their own attacks against the Likud-led coalition, the tradition has not been as rigidly followed as it once was.

Reagan administration officials initially deluded themselves into believing, as their predecessors in the Carter White House had believed for a while, that they might be able to split American Jewry away from Israel. But the ties that bind American Jews and Israel are just too strong. All U.S. administrations have had to deal with the influential Jewish leadership, and in the process the direction of U.S. policy toward Israel and the Middle East has been affected.

Dissent in the American Jewish community, from the right and from the left, has gone through several stages in recent years. The tiny but well-publicized Breira organization of the late 1970s is no longer around, but other dovish groups have come to replace it, including the New Jewish Agenda. Leonard Fein, the editor of *Moment* magazine, rankled Prime Minister Begin during the summer of 1980 by organizing a public letter signed by several well-known American Jews supporting an earlier statement released by the Peace Now movement in Israel. A few Jewish organizations on the right, such as Americans for a Safe Israel, have backed the hardliners in Israel. For years, the tiny Jewish Defense League has accused all Israeli governments of virtually selling out the Jewish people.

A handful of respected "establishment" Jewish leaders have publicly broken ranks with the official Israeli position, including Rabbi Arthur Hertzberg, a past president of the American Jewish Congress, and Philip Klutznick, a past president of the World Jewish Congress and B'nai B'rith International. During meetings late in 1977 with Secretary of State Cyrus Vance, National Security Adviser Zbigniew Brzezinski, and White House aide Mark Siegel, Dr. Nahum Goldmann called the Conference of Presidents of Major American Jewish Organizations a "disruptive force" and a "major obstacle" to Middle East peace negotiations. Goldmann, who had long opposed Begin's foreign policies, pleaded with the U.S. leaders not to back off from confrontation with the American Jewish community. He said Carter would even stand to gain politically if he thus managed to achieve a peace settlement. The president would become "the hero of the Jews," Goldmann said. These appeals were first reported in an article in *New York* magazine by freelance writer Sol Stern.

It was not the first time that Goldmann had sought to influence the direction of U.S. policy away from the government of Israel. The former president of the World Jewish Congress told the State Department as early as 1950 that he would try to be helpful in stopping American Jews concerned over U.S. policy toward Israel from pressuring the U.S. government. This was revealed in top-secret 1950 State Department documents released on July 13, 1978. The documents, contained in a 1889-page book entitled *Foreign Relations of the U.S. 1950, Volume Five, the Near East, South Asia and Africa,* included a memorandum of a conversation between Secretary of State Dean Acheson and Goldmann on March 28, 1950. The memorandum was prepared by Acheson, who noted that Goldmann, then the head of the American section of the Jewish Agency, had requested the meeting.

Referring to the earlier criticism of U.S. policy by the American Jewish leadership, Acheson wrote: "Dr. Goldman began the conversation by saying that he thought the situation in the various American Jewish organizations was now well in hand." Specifically, Goldmann noted that the situation had improved because his rival, Rabbi Abba Hillel Silver, "was out of the picture and likely to continue so."

The Acheson memorandum went on to say: "Dr. Goldmann thought that he could, therefore, devote more time to relations between the American Jewish community and the State Department. He said that in the past he had been successful in stopping pressure on the department by various Jewish organizations concerned over developments affecting the Palestine situation" and that "he believed that he could be useful in conveying to the department the feelings of the American Jewish community, and in transmitting to American Jews the thinking of department officials. Dr. Goldmann said that he thought it was a waste of time for [Jewish] delegations to call upon the department, that perhaps individuals would be much more useful. He inquired whether I thought it might be helpful if he were to keep in regular touch with the department's Near Eastern experts."

Acheson recorded his reply as follows: "I said that I knew Dr. Goldmann had always been discreet in the past and that I would be delighted to have him keep in touch with the Near Eastern division." Goldmann later went on to become the first chairman of the Conference of Presidents of Major American Jewish Organizations and the president of the World Jewish Congress.

Despite such exceptions, American Jewish leaders until recently tended to present a united front of support for Israel in dealing with the United States. Now there has been change, subtle though substantive. For example, the former White House liaison to the Jewish community during the first year of the Reagan administration, Jacob Stein, called for greater debate in the Jewish community by lashing out against the American Jewish press as "intellectually shallow" and "politically naive." Israeli newspapers, he said, are "much more open to dissenting opinions." Stein is a past chairman of the Conference of Presidents of Major American Jewish Organizations.

This is not to say that on the whole mainstream national Jewish groups have not remained steadfast in trying to project a united front supporting Israel; they have, even during the extremely difficult times of the changing American perception of Israel from besieged underdog to the area's dominant military power. Howard Squadron, chairman of the Presidents' Conference, had this to say during a January 15, 1982, interview with National Public Radio: "If you're asking me whether I approve [of] everything that Prime Minister Begin says and does and every bit of rhetoric and every bit of action that he takes that sometimes, I think, is unnecessary and sometimes is provocative, the answer is no. I do not. And I convey that to him in just exactly the kind of direct language I am now using. But that, in my view, is not undermining policy. One of the things that must be understood is that this particular prime minister of Israel is a man who, on the basis of his life history, will not be pushed without pushing back. And we do not advance the cause of peace one bit by falling all over with penalties [for] our small friends while we step very gingerly with respect to that other superpower that supposedly is our principal opponent in the world."

Even such mild irritation had earlier been avoided.

American Jews have been very sensitive to the political fact of life that much of their political clout in Washington has come from their unity. In addressing the White House and the U.S. Congress, the Jewish leadership has spoken, for the most part, with one firm and loud voice. This is critical if a minority is to be successful in pushing a cause. Just as the overall strength of any ethnic or interest group in the United States would be diminished by a chorus of different positions coming from their representative organizations on various crucial issues, so too would the power of the Jewish community be reduced in promoting close American–Israeli ties. There is no denying that U.S. support for Israel would be weakened if there developed a widespread sense—in the government and among the public at large—that Israel's best friends in the United States, namely the Jewish community, were themselves divided on many of the gut issues. That, of course, is the fear of too public a debate emerging over these issues in the Jewish community. Politicians are sensitive to the nuances of division within various constituent groups. Israel's enemies, as a result, would move quickly to exploit that debate.

Over the years, Israel's best friends in the United States, especially the organized American Jewish leadership, naturally have spent a lot of time worrying about various Israeli policies. Very often, this concern has been directly conveyed to the Israeli government, although almost always quietly and without much fanfare. This was certainly the case during the six years of Begin's tenure in office. His vision of a greater Land of Israel, including an aggressive scheme to advance settlement construction on the West Bank, clashed with the personal views of many leaders in the American Jewish community.

But it would be a mistake to assume that Jewish leaders always agreed with every policy taken in earlier years by other governments in Israel. There were plenty of headaches in the Israeli–American Jewish relationship long before Begin assumed office, although, again, they were not allowed very often to surface with much publicity. In 1975, for example, many American Jews reacted negatively and even fearfully to the initial Israeli desire for an American presence in Sinai following the signing of the interim agrement with Egypt on September 1 of that year. The number of Americans involved may have been small, but in the wake of the Vietnam experience, the political precedent was a source of considerable misgivings. In the past, Israel had always maintained that it did not need any Americans to defend Israel, that it simply needed the tools from the United States to get the job done by itself. Yet, in the complex negotiations leading to the Sinai II accord, Israel pressed hard for the introduction of U.S. civilian technicians to operate the early warning stations near the Mitla and Gidi passes. With hindsight, of course, those approximately 200 Americans turned out to be the precursor to the much larger number of U.S. soldiers who later joined the multinational peacekeeping force in Sinai in the aftermath of the 1979 Israeli–Egyptian Peace Treaty and, ultimately, the 1200 marines dispatched to Lebanon in 1982. "The failure in Lebanon disproves the old Israeli saw about never needing the help of a single American soldier," editorialized *The New York Times* on August 31, 1983.

In the mid-1970s, many Jewish leaders had also been made increasingly uneasy by Israel's growing dependence on American economic and military assistance. Although the Jewish leadership did not by any means come out publicly against either this greater financial dependence or the use of American personnel in Sinai, there was a disquieting uneasiness brewing among them, and they were wondering among themselves whether the Rabin government was moving in the right direction.

Rabbi Israel Miller, Chairman of the Conference of Presidents of Major American Jewish Organizations in 1974–75, repeatedly made the point to Secretary of State Henry Kissinger that although there are many shades of opinion among 6 million Jews in America, the mainstream has traditionally supported the policies of an Israeli government in office. Julius Berman, the chairman in 1983, made that same point to Secretary of State George Shultz. It is assumed by most Jewish leaders that the democratically elected government in Jerusalem has a direct mandate to define Israel's priorities and to formulate policies that will protect its national interests. It is considered inappropriate for Jews living in the Diaspora to tell Israelis how best to ensure the survival of Israel. American Jews, after all, are not being asked to risk their own children's lives.

Still, that has not stopped authoritative Jewish leaders from worrying and, occasionally, even speaking out on sensitive matters. During the first few years after the 1973 Yom Kippur War, there was concern expressed about the growing donor–recipient relationship developing between Washington and Jerusalem. Concerned Jews were asking how much longer Israel would be able to conduct a truly independent foreign policy if it continued in that direction. They were fearful that Israel's $2-billion-plus aid requests from the United States, at a time of economic turmoil and rising unemployment in America, would undermine Israel's base of support in Congress and among the public at large. Many American Jews, and some Israeli officials as well, believed then and continue to believe today that Israel would be better off instituting such additional economic austerity measures as would reduce rather than increase the nation's dependence on U.S. aid. But the makeup of most recent Israeli governments makes the imposition of more economic hardships on the Israeli public political suicide. It is certainly politically safer for such coalition governments to seek more financial assistance from Washington than to force a lower standard of living back home.

During the Begin administration the reservations about the stationing of Americans in Sinai and the continued dependence on massive American aid were eventually overshadowed as areas of concern to U.S. Jewish leaders by the Likud-led coalition government's clear desire to hold on to the West Bank and Gaza, even in the face of some potential long-term demographic and political problems facing Israel. Yes, there was extensive support in the United States for Israel's legitimate security concerns in retaining various strategically important parts of those territories. Yes, there ought to be some changes in the vulnerable pre-1967 lines. And yes,

Jerusalem could never again be divided. But after Begin took his hard line, many Jews started asking whether it was really necessary for Israel to rule out any territorial partition of the West Bank.

Curiously, the politically contentious American Jewish community for the most part has demonstrated a remarkable ability to adjust its thinking to the views expressed by the Israeli government, no matter how controversial. After an Israeli government—Labor or Likud—formally adopted a stance, the Jewish community in America was quickly brought into line. Earlier vocal reservations were quickly muted. This occurred in the wake of the stationing of the Americans in Sinai, the annual Israeli increases in aid requests, and the promotion of new settlement activity on the West Bank.

"There is a feeling of guilt as to whether Jews should double-check the Israeli government," said Hyman Bookbinder, the Washington representative of the American Jewish Committee. "They automatically fall into line for that very reason. There isn't anything very profound about explaining or understanding why Jews would be supportive of Israel."

On occasion, Bookbinder and the organization he represents have disagreed with Israeli policies, especially regarding the settlements on the West Bank. But those have been the exceptions rather than the rule. "We're unembarrassed fans, devotees of Israel," he said.

There is also the legacy of the Holocaust. The Jewish community in America in the 1930s and 1940s has been accused of not doing enough to publicize what was going on in Europe during Nazi rule. Could additional American Jewish political activity have forced President Franklin D. Roosevelt to order the bombing of the railroad lines to Auschwitz and the other death camps? That question will be hotly debated for many years to come. In 1983, it was revived with the publication of a study chaired by former U.S. Supreme Court Justice Arthur Goldberg. Whatever the ultimate verdict, a new generation of Jewish leaders does not want to be accused of doing anything now that might contribute to the weakening of Israel. This is why there has been relatively little open criticism of Israel on security-related issues, even from American Jews with reputations as doves in most military matters. On the other hand, there have been many complaints heard about the lack of religious freedom for non-Orthodox Jews in Israel and in other nonsecurity areas. Bookbinder and a handful of other "establishment" Jewish leaders are willing to criticize Israel on some matters in which they claim Israel's security interests have been poorly defined, such as the settlements. "It doesn't weaken Israel," Bookbinder said. "It can strengthen Israel. If you help shape what you think is a better policy. But relatively few are willing to go that far yet."

He went on to explain why there continues to be a reluctance to quarrel with Israel publicly. "Israel cannot exist without American support, and therefore we are always driven to make Israel's case as approvable and acceptable to the average American as possible. You don't do that by saying that Israel is wrong. Basically you want to make the case that Israel is making. Otherwise, you might lose American support. And you just can't be casual about that. Unless something is terribly pressing, really critical or fundamental, you parrot Israel's line in order to retain American support. As American Jews, we don't go around saying that Israel is wrong about its policies. We'd rather say it's right."

Bookbinder made another good point in explaining the built-in tensions affecting the degree of American Jewish dissent from the official Israeli position. "Most American Jews," he noted, "have never toyed with the idea of making *aliyah* [emigrating to Israel]. They are American. Still, there has developed over the years a very close kinship and friendship with Israel. In a sense, we're sort of vicarious members of the Israeli society. We have lots of friends there, and we know internal party intrigues. We have relatives there as well. In a sense—and this is a delicate matter because it can be taken out of context and used to embarrass the Jewish community—the fact is that, and I'll put it crudely, many Jews feel that Israel is their other country. And those of us who don't think in those terms are every now and then rudely reminded that the rest of America does think of Israel as our other country. We even have top American officials, journalists talking to a Jew like me and saying, 'Your ambassador has said,' referring to the Israeli ambassador."

Aaron Rosenbaum, a former AIPAC director of research and now a private Washington consultant, denied that the Jewish community would always be a rubber stamp for the Israeli government. "I don't think the Jewish community is quite as plastic as some might suggest," he said in an interview with me. "Consider the very real criticisms that were voiced in the Jewish community during the Lebanese War."

But he agreed that the mainstream of American Jews were basically anxious to support Israel. "There's a recognition," Rosenbaum noted, "that we're supporting the country, and secondarily the government. One of the problems that Begin had and that many people had when he came to power was to recognize that the Labor party was not synonymous with Israel—something they had never had to confront before. And that was certainly a challenge to people. Since then, people have come around to accept it. Begin came in, and people felt uncomfortable with him, but they also had begun to feel uncomfortable with the Labor party because some of its leaders were corrupt and incompetent."

American Jews, Rosenbaum said, have learned to support even unpleasant Israeli moves because Israel's enemies are so threatening. Thus, the move into Lebanon in 1982 was understood, even if not always totally supported, because it was aimed at the PLO. "People were willing to find a reasonable rationale for supporting an Israeli action that at first they had viewed with some concern," he said. The same was true with Israel's annexation of the Golan Heights in December 1981. "People thought that the Golan decision was counterproductive, but they also recognized that the Syrians had created this situation for themselves. Similarly in the West Bank. A lot of people have concerns about settlements, but again, there's a push–pull in what they say. 'Look, the Palestinians refuse to negotiate and recognize Israel's right to exist, so they are bringing this upon themselves.' "

Very often, Jews and other pro-Israeli supporters, especially in the Congress, will simply remain silent when they actually do come across policies of an Israeli government with which they disagree. "Israel's friends are generally out front," said Rosenbaum, "but when it becomes difficult to be out front, what they do is to become quiet. People who are critical are the ones who are hostile to Israel. That's the minority. But for the majority of supporters the choices are not 'support' or 'criticize'—but rather to support or to remain silent. And that's the distinction you have to make.

"The Jewish community has a strong historical sense that you don't abandon other Jews because this threatens all Jews. And they also are not going to strike an unrealistically moral stand in an immoral world. They're not going to posture in a world that doesn't care. In addition, the adversaries of Israel don't play fair. What happens is that you occasionally get a loving critic of Israel. But the problem is that the adversaries of Israel never have a sense of restraint. And this is something that many Jews are aware of, and thus they restrain themselves. The Jews recognize that the people in a position to judge are not treating Israel with real fairness. So why should they join in?"

So, in the post-Begin era in Israel, it is unreasonable to expect any real split to develop between Israel and the Jewish community in the United States, no matter what positions are eventually adopted in Jerusalem. The American Jewish leadership quickly learned to accept the vagaries of earlier Labor governments as well as those of Begin himself. That ability to bend will continue, given the nature of the overall relationship.

If there was still any lingering doubt, the November 2, 1982, midterm congressional elections demonstrated very clearly that the American Jew has come of full age in American politics. What was very obvious in the respective House and Senate contests around the country was that a large number of Jews were actively seeking political office. It was not so long ago that American Jews preferred to stay in the background of American politics. Usually, they were the organizers, the campaign managers, and the fund raisers for non-Jewish candidates. But, in recent years, talented Jewish activists from coast to coast have decided to step out in front of the crowd and plunge directly into the political arena. First they did so in heavily Jewish-populated areas, such as in New York City. But now there are Jews running for office in states with very small Jewish populations. As Jews have come to feel more at home in America, they have started to seek out elected office for themselves in large numbers.

A persuasive argument can be made that Jews have been involved in the political process since the days of the founding of the republic. For example, Haym Solomon was George Washington's major financial backer during the Revolutionary War, and Judah P. Benjamin was vice-president of the Confederacy. From the time of Louis D. Brandeis's appointment to the Supreme Court in 1916, through the terms of Benjamin Cardozo, Felix Frankfurter, and Arthur Goldberg, until the resignation of Abe Fortas in 1969, there was what politicians called a Jewish seat on the country's highest court (during two brief periods, two of the nine sitting justices were Jewish). There have also been several prominent Jews elected to high political office in this century, especially in those states having substantial Jewish populations. In New York, for instance, Herbert H. Lehman was elected governor in 1939 and U.S. senator in 1949, Louis Lefkowitz had a long career as the state's attorney general, and Jacob Javits served as congressman, attorney general, and U.S. senator. But, until recent years, a decision to place a Jew on a slate of either political party required that the nomination serve and not offend ticket-balancing concerns. It has only been in recent years that Jews have come out of the closet and have sought political office based on their own qualifications and with little regard for whether a larger vote would be gained or lost because of their Jewishness.

Underlining this trend was the fact that the 1983–84 Senate included a record eight Jews, as opposed to the previous six. (Jews make up only about 3 percent of the overall American population.) In the House, there were thirty-one Jews, also a record; the previous session of the House included twenty-five Jews. If all the Jews seeking Senate and House seats had won their respective contests in 1982, there would have been twelve Jewish senators and nearly fifty Jewish congressman. Some House races in the New York city area pitted Jew against Jew.

Most of the Jews running for national political office, moreover, were clearly recognized, practicing Jews, many having earlier been active in their own Jewish communities. In the Senate, Republican Rudy Boschwitz of Minnesota and Democrat Howard Metzenbaum of Ohio were deeply involved in local Jewish affairs long before they ran for public office. The same, of course, could be said of the Democratic senator from New Jersey, Frank Lautenberg, a former national chairman of the United Jewish Appeal.

Underscoring the trend of Jews coming to Capitol Hill from the smaller states where there are virtually negligible Jewish populations was the election of Chic Hecht, the Republican senatorial challenger in Nevada. He defeated Howard Cannon, a five-term incumbent. Similarly, Edward Zorinsky, the Democratic senator from Nebraska, was reelected.

But, as pro-Israeli political activists have come to point out, a senator's being Jewish does not necessarily ensure that he or she will always support Israel. During the Saudi AWACS vote in the Senate (the final outcome was fifty-two to forty-eight in favor of the sale), two Jews actually voted with the Reagan administration in support of the package: Zorinsky and Republican Warren Rudman of New Hampshire. In the House over the years, moreover, several Jewish members have often voted against the annual foreign aid package, of which Israel is the largest single recipient. (In Washington, the saying goes, you can't be pro-Israel and vote against the foreign aid bill.)

In both chambers, the Jewish members have organized but only informally. Unlike black and women members in the House, for example, the Jews have not established any formal Jewish caucus. They do meet informally, in recent years under the chairmanship of Democrat Sidney Yates of Illinois, the dean of Jewish congressmen. When they meet, usually to discuss legislative strategy in support of Israel, several non-Jewish friends have often been invited. More appropriately, the group could be called the pro-Israel caucus. Recognizing the importance of the Jewish members, Prime Minister Begin made a point of meeting with them as a group when he visited Washington in 1982. The Jewish members, for the most part, understand the special role they play. Among their non-Jewish colleagues, they are regarded as bellwether supporters of Israel. If a Jewish congressman or senator is critical of Israel, his non-Jewish friends are more likely to feel free to express their own criticisms.

Large numbers of American Jews may have run during the 1982 congressional campaigns, and a record number may actually have been elected in the Senate and House of Representatives, but several of those contests were accompanied by ugly incidents of anti-Semitism. Some of the most vicious slurs came up in Iowa, where Democratic challenger Lynn Cutler faced Republican Representative Cooper Evans. Cutler did not accuse Evans of any anti-Semitic tactics, although some of his supporters were crude in attacking the Democratic nominee. "Worth County voters of Manly will stage a barbecue on the upcoming election day and all gentiles are invited to attend," read a note typed and circulated in one of Cutler's own brochures. "They will cook Lynn Cutler's goose kosher style. You can also get Las Vegas odds that Cooper Evans will whip the pants off this Chicago Jew transplant dame to Iowa come November 2."

Cutler had lived in Iowa for more than twenty-five years. At forty-four years old, she was vice-chairman of the Democratic National Committee. She had been defeated by Evans in the 1980 race as well. She did not believe that anti-Semitism was the reason for her defeat, although she also did not want to ignore the incidents. In the second election, she lost by some ten percentage points. There are only a few hundred Jewish families in her district. On the Sunday before the election, a group called "Christian Voice/Moral Government" circulated what it described as a "Christian Voters Guide." It was distributed, she said, in more than 200 local churches. It noted Evans's virtually down-the-line support for such "moral" issues as prayers in public schools and Christian schools.

While in Marshalltown, Iowa, for an address before a civic group, the editor of the local newspaper asked Cutler, "Mrs. Cutler, there's a whispering campaign in the town that because you are a Jewess, you will blindly support Israel despite its intractable, bellicose behavior." In reply, Cutler said she supports Israel as an American. She went on to explain why such support was in America's own best interest.

When Cutler first went public in referring to the anti-Semitic incidents, many people in Iowa and around the country were upset. They would have preferred, she told me, that the issue be ignored, by Jews and non-Jews alike. "I was amazed at the response I got when I went public," she said. "A lot of people were angry. They just didn't want to hear about it. I had thought about it for two solid days before I raised it. And I was very careful about how I did it. I am proud of my religion, and I am sorry that this happened in Iowa."

There were other scattered incidents around the country—some crude, others more subtle. In California, for example, Democratic Congressman Tom Lantos, a survivor of the Holocaust, was reelected although his Republican challenger, Bill Royer, used a slogan that said: "Vote for Royer—He's One of Us." In Birmingham, Alabama, Democratic candidate Ben Erdreich, a Jew, faced incumbent Republican Albert Lee Smith. "Do you want a Jew representing the Christians of Birmingham?" was one slogan heard during the campaign, though it was not expressed by Smith. Erdreich won the contest despite the smear.

David Brody, the Washington representative of the B'nai B'rith Anti-Defamation League, dismissed the importance of these "isolated" incidents of anti-Semitism. In his monitoring of the various campaigns, he said, such talk did "crop up but almost outside the mainstream of the American political system." Like other Jewish political activists in Washington, Brody was especially pleased by the record number of Jews elected to the House and Senate, a fact that tended to confirm his impression that the anti-Semitism that did surface was not widespread.

Still, other political activists around the country were more concerned. Carol Boron was the director of research of the Joint Action Committee, a large women's political action committee that supports pro-Israel national candidates and is based in Chicago. "There was anti-Semitism in virtually every campaign where a Jew was running," she said. Fortunately, she added, most of these incidents were of only marginal importance. She cited especially disturbing slurs that surfaced against Democratic Congressman Sidney Yates of Chicago and an unsuccessful Democratic House candidate from New Jersey, Adam Levin. (Yates was reelected.)

According to Boron, not all of the incidents even involved Jewish candidates. In Houston, for example, Democratic Congressman Mickey Leland, who is black, was bitterly attacked because of his support for a special program to send underprivileged local children to spend their summer months on kibbutzim in Israel. The implication made was that he was sponsoring the special program because he had accepted political contributions from local Houston Jews.

Nearly everyone recognizes that the political clout of American Jewry would suffer a serious setback if the electoral college system of electing U.S. presidents were abolished. Yet several Jewish senators have come out in favor of doing exactly that. And this raises some fundamental questions, even though few observers actually believe that a proposed constitutional amendment to abolish the traditional system of selecting presidents could possibly win the necessary votes in the foreseeable future, with or without Jewish support.

For many years, leading the fight to remove the electoral college was former Democratic Senator Birch Bayh of Indiana, who often introduced a proposal to have the president and vice-president elected by popular vote. Bayh was defeated in his bid for reelection in 1980.

As it now stands, the president and vice-president are put into office by the electoral college, a system established by the nation's founding fathers two centuries ago and codified in the Constitution. Under this system, a president is not elected directly by the American people. Those nationwide elections are legally permitted to do no more than enable states to select representatives to the electoral college, whose members eventually name the new president.

States are granted representation at the electoral college roughly in proportion to their populations. California, the most populous, has the most electors; Alaska, the state with the smallest population, has the fewest. One must say roughly in proportion rather than in proportion, because according to the Constitution the number of electors from each state is determined by the number of seats that state has in the House of Representatives (these assigned in direct proportion to the population of the states) plus the number of the state's senators (directed by the Constitution to be two from each state, no matter what the state's population). Indeed, this disproportionate representation in the Senate is not only required by the Constitution but is the only provision of that document excluded from the amending process. Article V, which describes how the Constitution may be amended, includes this wording: "Provided that no State, without its Consent, shall be deprived of equal Suffrage in the Senate."

This weighting toward the smaller states works against Jews and other ethnic groups that tend to cluster in the more densely populated urban areas. However, alongside this offense to the one-person one-vote principle, the electoral college system works in another, more decisive way to favor urban groups that tend to vote as blocs. Though the power to determine just how each state shall choose its electors was originally left to the states, case law and tradition have established that virtually all states use a unit rule; that is, the presidential candidate getting the most votes in each state wins all of that state's electoral votes. Because of this winner-take-all method of awarding electors, it is possible that a candidate could be elected president without having won a majority or even a plurality of the popular vote. For example, a candidate could do so by winning the eight most populous states by only the narrowest of margins while losing the remaining forty-two states by wide margins. That a candidate could win the presidency while losing the popular vote is the most often expressed fear of opponents of the electoral college system.

But there are other political consequences of sticking with this system. Because the winner-take-all method makes it possible for the enormous numbers of electoral votes in the largest states to be won by the movement of a handful of votes, groups that hold the balance of power in these states exert inordinate power over who will be elected president. Indeed, the need to carry these large states influences virtually every presidential campaign decision—where the candidate will campaign, what issues will be engaged, what positions will be taken on these issues, and even at what level the campaign will be waged.

Among the many urban liberals in the American Jewish community, the two arguments against the electoral college—that the college itself gives disproportionate voting power to the smaller rural states and that nondirect election of presidents invites the political disaster of a candidate winning the presidency while earning fewer votes than an opponent—have a natural appeal, despite the fact that abolishing the present system would diminish their own political influence, which is considerably enhanced by the current system. Though American Jews constitute only 3 percent or so of the total American population, most of America's Jews are concentrated in the eight largest states, those with the largest electoral prizes. In these states, Jews represent much more than 3 percent of the population. In New York, for example, there are more than 2 million Jews, about 15 percent of the state's population. But that 15 percent is translated into about 25 percent of the actual voters because of the extraordinarily high turnout rate of Jews on election day. Thus, in New York—and several of the other largest states—Jews are considered a critical swing vote, on which the final outcome of an election could turn.

Because candidates obviously want to win the large states, they have had to take the interests of the Jewish community into very serious consideration. It was no accident, for example, that Jimmy Carter and Gerald Ford tried to surpass each other in making pro-Israel statements during the 1976 campaign, or that Carter and Ronald Reagan followed suit in 1980. The same was, of course, true in the 1984 Reagan–Mondale contest.

Without the electoral college, the Jewish vote would lose much of its importance to politicians. This happens to be a political fact of life. Yet many Jews have a hard time justifying their support for the electoral college on such a narrow, parochial level. In fact, several Jewish senators over the years supported the Bayh amendment to abolish the system. They were Jacob Javits (Republican from New York), Abraham Ribicoff (Democrat from Connecticut), Edward Zorinsky (Democrat from Nebraska), Carl Levin (Democrat from Michigan), and Howard Metzenbaum (Democrat from Ohio).

Many American Jewish leaders prefer not to get involved in the controversy because many of them doubt it will ever get off the ground. They see it as a strictly liberal–conservative battle. Jewish involvement as such, they fear, would be counterproductive.

But others are concerned. They fear possible developments later and want the move stopped before its appeal broadens. One such organization is the American Jewish Congress, which has now gone on record against this type of election reform. Howard Squadron, a past president of the organization, testified against the measure on April 3, 1979, before the Senate Judiciary Committee. But interestingly, even Squadron did not refer directly in his prepared statement to the impact that the elimination of the electoral college would have on the political influence of the American Jewish community; instead, he came up with the standard reasons against the amendment—that any move to abolish the electoral college would upset the "network of balances and accommodations which insures a concern for all groups and a genuinely representative government." Without referring specifically to the American Jewish community, he said that the presidency must be responsive to "urban and ethnic interests" as a counterweight to Congress.

Former Israeli Prime Minister Yitzhak Rabin offered some advice in late 1979 to the Likud-led coalition about the impact of American presidential elections on Israel's foreign policy. Writing in the London *Jewish Chronicle*, Rabin said that 1980 should prove to be an "easy" year for Israel: "It is inconceivable that during an election year the administration in Washington will find time for the kind of diplomatic move that could be considered damaging to Israel. Moreover, during an election year, there is customarily much greater receptiveness in Washington to new ideas. The challenge by Teddy Kennedy to President Carter, plus the galaxy of candidates in the Republican camp, could augment Israel's position in both a direct and indirect way."

Rabin wrote with some authority about American elections, since he served as Israel's ambassador in Washington during the 1972 campaign. At that time, he caused somewhat of a stir by virtually endorsing President Richard Nixon over the Democratic challenger, Senator George McGovern of South Dakota. Rabin did not hide the fact that he felt more comfortable with a Republican in the White House and a Democratic majority in the Congress. The Democrats in the House of Representatives and the Senate, most of whom are pro-Israel, would be likely to be more willing to come to Israel's defense during a confrontation between Jerusalem and the White House if the president were a member of the opposite party. To this day, Rabin sticks to this theory.

Rabin's analysis, however, was not accepted by Israeli Defense Minister Ezer Weizman and other Israelis in and out of the government. Weizman, during talks with Carter in Washington late in December 1979, virtually endorsed the president for another four years. "I like that man," Weizman told me. He echoed the view of former Foreign Minister Moshe Dayan, who had said in September that Carter, by achieving the Israeli–Egyptian peace treaty, had done more for Israel than any other American president. Weizman accompanied Carter on a highly publicized campaign flight to Cleveland.

A review of Israel's relationships with the various American presidents and their campaign challengers indicates that Israel has always favored the incumbent, with one exception. In 1956, Dwight Eisenhower failed to support the combined Israeli–British–French attack on Egypt. Israelis clearly favored Adlai Stevenson.

That Israelis in power would be more comfortable with incumbent presidents makes sense. Officials in Washington and Jerusalem spend a considerable amount of time together. They become friends. Even if they disagree on certain issues, their adversaries are at least known quantities.

In politics, as in life, fear of the unknown is greater than fear of the known.

This helps to explain why the Begin government seemed to be signaling its support for Carter despite the supposedly "brutal" pressure exerted by the administration during the months leading up to the peace treaty and the administration's continuous flirtation with the PLO. Carter, while not perfect, had demonstrated his support by providing billions of dollars in economic and military assistance, some $10 billion during his four years in office.

But what was perhaps most surprising about the Israeli tilt toward Carter, even while he was dismally low in the public opinion polls, was the conventional wisdom among political observers in Washington that second-term presidents have more flexibility to pressure Israel, since they don't have to worry about getting reelected. Carter supporters in the American Jewish community and in Israel recognized the dangers. But they countered by pointing out that Vice-President Walter Mondale, a strong and consistent friend of Israel, had already made it clear that he wanted to succeed Carter in 1984. Mondale would supposedly serve as a pro-Israel force, as indeed he had been during the first four years.

Running parallel to all these considerations was the more general question of whether Israel was better off with Republicans or Democrats in the White House. The American Jewish community traditionally has been a pillar of the Democratic Party since the days of Franklin D. Roosevelt. In recent years, however, many Jews have crossed over to the Republican side; some have become active in party politics. Max Fisher of Detroit, Albert Spiegel of Los Angeles, Gordon Zacks of Columbus, Richard Fox of Philadelphia, and George Klein of New York are prime examples. Their involvement in Republican affairs has made an impact. Together with many local Republican Jewish leaders around the country, they have sensitized the Republican national leadership to the concerns of the American Jewish community.

In 1979, Republican presidential candidate John Connally angered most friends of Israel by issuing a tough Middle East policy statement calling for an Israeli withdrawal practically to the 1967 lines and Palestinian self-determination, including the right to an independent entity. He later backtracked, trying to shore up his ties with Republican Jewish leaders.

But if we were to count sheer numbers, the Democratic Party has been much more the party of American Jews. Among the party leadership on a national and local level, Jews are present and in visible positions. Robert Strauss, the director of Carter's campaign, was a most obvious example. An examination of the major fund raisers and key professional staffers confirms that Jews play a critical role in all areas of party affairs.

Democratic politicians argue that Israel was always better off with a confirms that Jews play a critical role in all areas of party affairs.

Democratic politicians argue that Israel was always better off with a Democratic president because of the tremendous influence the Jewish community has within the party. After Carter's election, in fact, there had been no problem for Jewish leaders in conveying their views directly to the highest officials in the administration. That did not necessarily mean that the White House always heeded the Jewish advice. But Jewish leaders certainly could not complain that they had no one to talk to during the Carter administration.

"Familiarity breeds contempt," is the response of Michael Gale, a Republican activist. He suggested that, ironically, Israel was better served by Republican presidents, precisely because they generally were not all that close with Jewish leaders. They had to be more sensitive to the views of the Jewish community. Since Democrats have dealt with Jews during most of their political careers, they can more easily reject their recommendations, Gale said in an interview with me.

An axiom of American–Israeli relations has it that all first years of administrations generally have been more difficult for Israel. The president, feeling confident after the election, aware that the next election is four years off, usually decides that the time is ripe for some new peace initiative in the Middle East. Translated, that often means pressure on Israel to make concessions. The Rogers Plan was unleashed in 1969 by a Republican administration. Carter's Palestinian homeland proposal came in 1977. There can be no denying that 1981 also turned out to be a difficult year for Israel, especially because of the Saudi AWACS battle.

The safe assumption today is that Israel is going to have a rougher time during first years of administrations no matter who is elected the previous November. Responsible Israeli leaders accept the fact. They have no great illusions about campaign rhetoric.

8

The News Media and the Think Tanks

Israel's honeymoon with the American news media, if there ever really was one, is clearly over. This was dramatically demonstrated following Israel's June 7, 1981, aerial strike against the Iraqi nuclear reactor and the subsequent bombing of PLO targets in Beirut, when criticism of Israel was open and sharp. But long before, since the 1973 Yom Kippur War, various Israeli decisions, especially the establishment of new settlements on the West Bank, have been thoroughly examined by the American press. Indeed, nearly every facet of Israeli life and government policy has come to be fair play for the American press. American radio and television networks, news magazines, wire services, and newspapers probably report more about events in Israel than in any other country, with the possible exceptions of only Britain and France.

There has developed a troubling perception among many Israelis and pro-Israeli supporters in the United States in recent years that the U.S. news media are turning increasingly against Israel. Anti-Israeli biases have been leveled against such prestigious news organizations as *The Washington Post*, *The New York Times*, *Time* magazine, and many others. Nationally syndicated columnists, including Carl T. Rowan, Anthony Lewis, Rowland Evans, and Robert Novak, have regularly been charged with maintaining anti-Israel slants. They, of course, deny any such feelings, differentiating between their overall support for the country of Israel and their right to criticize the decisions of any particular government in power, such as Begin's Likud-led coalition. In support of their position, they can point to the number of influential Israelis and Israeli newspapers that also freely criticize the Israeli government.

This, in fact, may be one of the reasons why coverage of Israel in recent years has become more harsh. Israel is an open society, a thriving democracy, where dissent is extensive. As in all democratic countries, opposition parties are free to say what they want—and they do. But this openness contrasts sharply with the generally closed societies of the Arab world, where news is controlled by the government in power. In Israel, a foreign journalist can roam around the country, interviewing virtually anyone. There are ample communication facilities designed to make access to diverse opinions simple for a correspondent. In most of the Arab world, on the other hand, journalists, who often have to be accompanied by government officials, are blocked from going anywhere that the local regime considers off limits. That makes candid questioning of people quite difficult. Thus, members of the press usually see only what the regime wants them to see. There is very little, if any, free coverage from Libya, Syria, Iraq, Saudi Arabia, and most other Arab states. Press restrictions in Egypt have eased in recent years, but there, too, obstacles remain.

Naturally, the many positions heard within Israel on crucial issues have an immediate tendency to spill over to the outside world. When former Prime Minister Yitzhak Rabin, as a member of the Labor opposition, challenged Begin's version of the Beirut bombing, for example, there was an almost automatic echo of the criticism outside Israel. This is one of the prices Israel has to pay for being a democracy—having the world watch over the shoulder of its decision-making process. But to almost all Israelis, it is a price worth paying. Freedom of speech in Israel is a cherished tradition.

At the same time, the Arabs themselves have improved their public relations campaign. They are now more sophisticated in their propaganda. No longer do we very often hear blatant Arab declarations calling for the destruction of Israel, as we heard on the eve of the 1967 Six-Day War. Instead of "let's throw the Jews into the sea," there are now subtle code words to express virtually the same intent. Thus, the PLO calls for the establishment of a "democratic, secular state in Palestine." Only the more attuned listener recognizes that, in effect, that calls for the end of the state of Israel.

To help bolster the Arab image, some of the best Madison Avenue public relations and advertising firms have been retained. Their efforts are two-pronged: to highlight the positive aspects of the Arab cause and at the same time to launder as much of Israel's dirty linen in public as possible. A case in point was a slick, sixteen-page all-color brochure prepared by Fred Dutton, a former White House speechwriter for President John F. Kennedy, who now heads one of the most respected and highly paid Washington lobbying offices. The brochure was commissioned by one of Dutton's best clients, the embassy of Saudi Arabia. Dutton, who has registered as a Saudi foreign agent with the U.S. Justice Department, made the case in the document for the Reagan administration's sale of AWACS radar planes to Saudi Arabia. He, of course, stressed Saudi support for the United States and other positive aspects of the Saudi case. But he also tried to score points for his clients by suggesting that Israel was not all that friendly to the United States. He recalled for those who might have forgotten, for instance, the tragic Israeli attack against the *USS Liberty* during the early hours of the 1967 war.

But even more important in the increasingly dramatic improvement of the Arab image in America was Egyptian President Sadat's decision to travel to Jerusalem in November 1977 and to make peace with Israel. Before Sadat's steps, there was a general recognition in the United States that Israel wanted peace with its Arab neighbors; it was the Arabs who wanted to destroy Israel. Sadat managed to change that perception. What was once almost black and white is today widely regarded as gray. The U.S. news media, for the most part, now see merit on both sides. As a result, there is today a new willingness to try to bend over to hear the Arab point of view because of the assumption that Israel had a free ride over the years.

To a very large degree, U.S. news media coverage of Israel is also affected by decisions taken in Washington. When an American president is arguing with an Israeli prime minister, it is to be expected that many U.S. newspaper editorials will side with the White House. This is especially true when the president is popular; if he plays his cards right, he can virtually call the shots as far as public opinion toward Israel (or any foreign country, for that matter) is concerned. The corollary is also true: When American–Israeli governmental relations are running smoothly, the press can be expected to be friendly toward Jerusalem.

Partially because so many diplomatic correspondents and foreign affairs editors look to Washington for guidance, the U.S. news media's coverage of the Arab–Israeli peace process since the 1973 war has been rather weak. This was especially the case during the sixteen months between President Sadat's trip to Jerusalem and the signing of the Israeli–Egyptian peace treaty in Washington in March 1979. When it comes to the Arab–Israeli conflict, an even more serious flaw in the media's news-gathering process comes into play. Too many reporters rely almost exclusively on the Middle East "experts" at the State Department, who themselves don't always display a good grasp of the significance of developments and trends in that part of the world. These are the same people, it should be recalled, who did not foresee the consequences of the shah's downfall in Iran or the Soviet invasion of Afghanistan. Journalists only too willing to accept their analysis as divinely inspired truth cannot help but sometimes confuse the American public about the Middle East.

Because many top Washington journalists and columnists depend solely on administration officials for their understanding of the Middle East, it's no wonder they often lose patience with the slow pace of negotiations. This was apparent after Sadat's journey to Jerusalem, which, incredible as it may sound, was not initially well received by many U.S. "experts" because it forced the United States to abandon the then popular all-or-nothing "comprehensive" approach in favor of a step-by-step formula. The fact is that a significant number of careerists at the State Department, both then and now, still happen to agree with George Ball's disparaging view of the Israeli–Egyptian Peace Treaty. Privately, these officials will tell you that American sponsorship of the treaty may have been a mistake. By splitting the Arab world, the treaty was said to have made it more difficult for the United States to rally support against the Soviet Union.

Manipulating the news media has been a tradition of statecraft for many years. Administration officials often have a clear interest in evoking the most dire scenarios to advance their goals. For tactical purposes, widespread dissemination of such dark predictions works to put increased pressure on the other side's negotiators to become more tractable. This is exactly what happened just before President Carter managed to wrap up the final details of the peace treaty during his swing through Israel and Egypt in March 1979.

The forecasts in the press of a possible breakdown in negotiations caused by one side or the other forced that side to make greater concessions. Israel and Egypt are very interested in maintaining a positive image in the United States, given their heavy dependence on U.S. economic and military support. Neither wants to be accused of intransigence.

Shortly after takeoff from Cairo's international airport en route back to Andrews Air Force Base outside Washington in March 1979, White House press secretary Jody Powell got up from his front-row seat and casually began to walk toward the rear of the cabin to chat with the traveling press corps. Most of the reporters were clearly exhausted by the physical and emotional strain of just having written and filed lengthy dispatches describing President Carter's dramatic tarmac announcement of the Israeli–Egyptian peace treaty breakthrough. Most were also furious at Powell, believing he had deliberately misled them the night before in Jerusalem about the prospects for a successful outcome. Based on Powell's gloomy background briefings that night, nearly all of the regular White House correspondents had forecast almost certain failure for Carter's first venture into the world of Middle East peacemaking. They were not alone. The superstars of network television news, who were also accompanying the president and had been briefed by Powell, painted a similarly bleak picture.

As the spokesman moved down the aisle, he was confronted with sharp accusations, some very ugly. The press corps had been burned badly that day. They had informed their audience (and their editors) only hours earlier that Carter would be returning home empty-handed. Yet now, to their embarrassment, the opposite was true.

The subsequent explanation developed into a full-scale controversy. Helen Thomas, the veteran White House correspondent for *United Press International*, for example, wrote in a commentary only a few hours after Carter had triumphantly returned home: "Did President Carter pull off a last-minute miracle of peace between Arab and Jew? Or was the defeat-turned-victory a public relations coup?"

Powell strongly and convincingly denied that he had deliberately tried to mislead the press. Aboard the aircraft, he defended those briefings, arguing that he had presented an accurate picture of the situation as it had then stood. Things had, in fact, appeared to be on the verge of collapse, he said, even though he knew that another session between President Carter and Prime Minister Begin had been scheduled for the next morning. He also knew that Secretary of State Cyrus Vance and Foreign Minister Moshe Dayan were meeting that evening at Jerusalem's King David Hotel, as were Defense Secretary Harold Brown and Defense Minister Ezer Weizman a few doors down the hall on the sixth floor. Why all the activity if the negotiations were so close to collapse?

After the "surprise" reversal the next day, reporters began to look for a scapegoat. Since reporters don't like to fault themselves for failure to anticipate events, Powell became the instant culprit. Some charged the spokesman with trying to manipulate the news media to make the eventual Carter success so much more dramatic. How much sweeter a victory if it were to appear to have been snatched from the jaws of certain failure.

There were other benefits to be gained for the president by offering a dark scenario that night. The White House, naturally, did not want to be blamed for a failure, so why not set up Israel as the fall guy? The precedent was there—former Secretary of State Henry Kissinger's March 1975 sling of accusations against Israeli "shortsightedness" following the collapse of the Sinai II negotiations, a collapse that led to the famous "reassessment" of U.S. policy toward Israel.

But reporters could have avoided falling into this trap if they had taken Powell's remarks with at least some skepticism and a little common sense in trying to assess precisely where the negotiations stood at that point. Very few, if any, of the White House correspondents asked the fundamental question: Why was it in Powell's interest to say what he did? Did he have an angle?

By the time of that round of briefings, it was public knowledge to everyone covering the negotiations that all of the critical issues had already been
resolved, including the extremely sensitive matters of "linkage" between
the treaty and the proposed Palestinian autonomy scheme on the West
Bank and Gaza Strip and the "priority of obligations" clause involving the
relationship between the treaty and Egypt's earlier defense pacts with other
Arab countries. Powell himself acknowledged that these obstacles had been
bridged. The two points, it must be stressed, had been the core of the
delay in signing the treaty ever since the ill-fated Blair House negotiations
in Washington the previous October. Yet, in a flurry of diplomatic activity
beginning with Begin's visit to the White House in early March 1979, the
points had been successfully compromised. Both sides had moved away
from their earlier positions, a development that should have convinced
everyone with even a modest understanding of the Middle East and the
geopolitical relationships between Washington and these two countries that
a treaty was at hand.

Yes, there were still some issues that had to be dealt with, but everyone
agreed that they were marginal and relatively easy to overcome. Though
each involved symbols more than substance, they still proved to be quite
stubborn during Carter's first two days in Israel. The Israelis dug in their
heels and refused to budge. Begin asked the president, "Why should you
force us to make these final concessions? Why not pressure Sadat?" The
Americans explained that Sadat had already gone as far as possible, given
the hostile reactions in the Arab world. "We can't squeeze him anymore,"
they said.

So on that Monday evening in March, Israel and the United States found
themselves in a tough round of bargaining, with Carter pressing for concessions from the Israelis so that there could be a quick treaty signing.

Two hours before Powell's first public briefing at the Jerusalem Hilton
hotel, where the visiting press corps was staying, the Israeli government's
spokesman, Dan Pattir, briefed reporters at the Jerusalem Theater, which
had been converted into a giant press center. Pattir was upbeat in his
assessment, insisting that great progress had already been achieved with
only a few remaining differences unresolved. He clearly left the impression
that things were not so bad. Indeed, a solution was still very much possible.
Yet only a handful of the hundred or so visiting Washington-based correspondents on the trip had bothered to take the shuttle bus for the ten-
minute ride to the theater for Pattir's briefing; the rest were happy to leave
it to their colleagues normally stationed in Israel to cover Pattir.

When Powell and the U.S. delegation heard the bottom line of Pattir's
message, they were upset. They thought the Israelis were deliberately
painting an overly rosy picture in order to throw the burden back on

Egyptian shoulders. The American team did not want the news media to accept this optimistic assessment, since such a development would ease the pressures on Israel to make the remaining concessions during the scheduled Carter–Begin meeting the next morning. It was then that Powell decided to brief the reporters. If his strategy was to neutralize Pattir, he succeeded. All of the television networks, and the wire services, plus the major national newspapers the next morning, ignored Pattir's assessment in favor of Powell's, leaving Israel largely to blame for the imminent setback. The Israeli embassy in Washington, meanwhile, immediately sent back word to the foreign ministry in Jerusalem describing the nightly television news programs, all of which, concluded the cable, had damaged Israel's reputation. The Carter administration had successfully countered the Israeli gambit. This was the background that must be understood in trying to determine why Powell presented his doom-and-gloom forecast the night before triumph.

None of this was especially surprising to the Israelis, despite Begin's television assertions the next night, after the treaty breakthrough had been announced, that the U.S. media were involved in a squeeze play. Begin said that "the American commentators should perhaps admit now that they were wrong, that they should apologize to the American people whom they misled." But Begin then went on to note that "perhaps it is not the commentators who have to apologize but those who briefed them in this way. And they ought to apologize because I heard that they [the American briefers] said Israel is to blame and that the prime minister is bogged down in small items."

In Israel, reporters as well as the general public know they have to take everything they hear from official government sources with more than a grain of salt; these people are seldom impartial dispensers of factual information. In fact, all government officials, as part of their job, are always trying to induce others to see events in a special light. This is especially the case when it comes to press coverage of ongoing diplomacy. The Israelis recalled Kissinger's thirty-one-day shuttle in 1974 between Damascus and Jerusalem, during which the secretary's "senior American official" always manipulated the press in such a way that they would help his efforts by putting pressure either on Israel or on Syria to make more concessions. The only trouble with that, however, is that an imbalance was inevitable because Israel is much more sensitive to its image in the United States than is Syria, and the press, with the same effort, could be more effective in squeezing Jerusalem than Damascus. With this recent history, those reporters hearing Powell's briefings should have considered that they were being used to exert some additional pressures on the Israelis. The almost universally consistent tone of the stories that ran suggest that few did.

Despite all his publicity, Sadat remained an enigma to U.S. journalists. His initial decision to make peace with Israel, as well as his subsequent performance in the negotiations with Israel, were not well understood. He staked his entire political fortune, and eventually his life, on the peace initiative. There was no reason for him to court defeat by demanding concessions from Israel which he knew it would not make and which he, in fact, would not want it to make. He had already won his significant victory: the return of Sinai and the freeing of Egyptian society from a painfully costly thirty-year war. He also won some concessions for the Arabs of the West Bank.

Israel has had other special problems in the US. news media. "There is a double standard by which Israel is judged," *The Washington Post* editorialized on September 24, 1982, "and it is turning out to be Israel's pride." The angry reaction within Israel itself to the Beirut massacres of Palestinian refugees that month, and the deep anguish expressed by so many Israelis over their government's indirect responsibility, underlined dramatically the vitality of Israel's democracy. Indeed, it was none other than Republican Representative Paul Findley of Illinois, then the PLO's best friend on Capitol Hill, who drove that same point home during a hearing of the House Foreign Affairs Subcommittee on Europe and the Middle East on September 22. Assistant Secretary of State for Near Eastern and South Asian Affairs Nicholas Veliotes was scheduled to appear before the panel in open session. On the agenda were the latest developments in Lebanon. Given the extreme sensitivity of the situation, Veliotes told the members, the State Department was insisting that the hearing go into secret session. Findley, like the other congressmen present, was clearly upset. He wanted the meeting to remain open to the press and to the public. Israel's parliament, he said, had earlier that day reviewed the circumstances leading to the Beirut massacres in open session, and those deliberations were "of great sensitivity to their nation." He welcomed the "frank and candid discussion" in the Knesset. Why, he asked, was the administration in Washington not willing to follow the Israeli example? Veliotes, of course, stood his ground, promising the members that he would return to their committee in the near future to discuss the situation publicly. A roll call was taken, and the doors were closed.

Israel's very aggressive newspapers were unrelenting in their own investigations of the massacres. Vice-President George Bush, addressing the Washington Press Club on September 23, expressed full confidence that all of the facts surrounding the tragedy would emerge from within Israel itself. "There are more investigative reporters there than you had in *The Washington Post* in Watergate times," he said.

Indeed, if there was any silver lining for Israel, it was that Israel's image as a country that cherishes a free press and an open debate had been underscored in the aftermath of this slaughter. U.S. newspapers quoted extensively from stinging Israeli editorials. Israeli reporters were the first to break new and damaging relevations surrounding the incident. After interviewing two Israeli editors who challenged Prime Minister Begin to come forward with all of the facts, ABC's Ted Koppel referred to Israel's free press.

"The Lebanese may be unable to address the question of responsibility, but Israel is throwing itself into it in a way that defines its essence," commented *The Washington Post*.

"When a crime of this magnitude is committed during one's watch, one is honor-bound to resign," added *The New Republic*. "That is not only our view, it is the view of a large segment of a shocked, outraged, and remorseful Israeli society. It is also the view of many leading Israeli newspapers, including some on the political right normally sympathetic to the Begin movement. This week we write not in praise of Israel, but in praise of its shame."

The torment within Israel over responsibility was in sharp contrast to the reaction in the rest of the world to Lebanese responsibility. After all, the actual murderers were Lebanese Christians, not Jews. "In a morally sane climate," wrote *Commentary* editor Norman Podhoretz, "responsibility would have been assigned to the thugs who initiated this particular cycle of murderous horrors and their opposite numbers who responded in barbarous kind. . . . But something more was implicit in the fact that, when Christians murdered Moslems for having murdered Christians, the world immediately began denouncing the Jews, who were, at the very worst, indirectly involved." He added: "Here again the old double standard made another ugly appearance. And with this new failure to distinguish among relative weights of responsibility, our public discourse has taken another great slide down the slippery slope to moral idiocy."

Writing in *The New York Times*, Jerusalem correspondent David Shipler explained the Israeli perspective this way: "Who are the Americans to attack Israel, when their own troops slaughtered innocent Vietnamese women and children at My Lai? Who are the Europeans to deplore this massacre, when they barely took notice of the massacres in which thousands of other Lebanese Christians and Moslems were murdered by one another through years of civil strife? How could Pope John Paul II, a personification of high morality, receive Yasser Arafat, head of the Palestine Liberation Organization, who ordered guerrillas to take over a school and gun down children in Maalot, to take children hostage at the kibbutz Misgav Am, to commandeer a bus and shoot their way down the coastal road?"

Which American newspaper in recent years has been the most pro-Israel on its editorial page? You might be amazed to learn that the consensus among almost all Israeli officials and their most active Jewish supporters in Washington is *The Wall Street Journal*. Given the newspaper's focus on big business, that might indeed be surprising. America's major banks and corporations do a hefty business in the petrodollar-rich Arab world, while links with Israel are more modest. But that has not stopped *The Wall Street Journal* from regularly coming to Israel's defense on a host of issues. This was evident, for example, on October 3, 1983, when the newspaper lashed out against Egypt for refusing to return its ambassador to Tel Aviv. "The U.S. now gives the Egyptians some $2 billion a year in aid, and the State Department wants more," the editorial said. "President Mubarak is now paying a pleasure visit to our shores, and there is little evidence that anyone, from President Reagan on down, has put any real pressure on him to shape up. Instead, U.S. foreign policy smiles its willfully ignorant smile, content to oversee this erosion of American plans and interests in the Mideast."

Earlier, the *Journal* had repeatedly criticized the Reagan administration for undermining Israeli policy in Lebanon. Before that, it opposed the sale of AWACS to Saudi Arabia. When Washington held back arms supplies to Israel, the newspaper came down hard against such embargoes. On almost every controversial Israeli decision, including the bombing of the Iraqi nuclear reactor, the Knesset law declaring Jerusalem Israel's eternal capital, the creation of additional West Bank settlements, and the annexation of the Golan Heights, it has come to Israel's defense.

Why all this support? Basically, the *Journal* views Israel as one of America's few pro-Western, democratically elected, and strategically reliable friends in an otherwise hostile world.

The United States, it believes, should treat friends like friends and enemies like enemies. When you disagree with a close ally, you don't publicly embarrass or scold it as you would your adversaries. You cooperate with your friends and consult with them privately. You don't wash their dirty linen before the eyes of the entire world. In short, you do not undermine your friends, even when there are serious differences of opinion.

When it comes to the Middle East, the editorial opinions of *The Wall Street Journal* these past years have been very similar to those expressed by syndicated columnists William Safire and George Will, both of whom are Republican and conservative in their political orientation. They are, by the way, probably Israel's two best friends among the nationally read commentators. *The New Republic*, edited by Martin Peretz, also fits into this solid pro-Israel pattern, although its basic ideological bent is clearly liberal and Democratic. That only goes to underline a fundamental fact involving U.S. support for Israel as it has developed over the years: Israel has both friends and enemies among Democrats and Republicans, as well as among liberals and conservatives. Support for Israel spans the political and ideological spectrum of thought in the United States. This also has been very evident in the many congressional roll calls involving Israel and the Arabs. Safire and Will may be card-carrying conservatives, but so is Republican senator Barry Goldwater of Arizona, one of Israel's most consistent foes on Capitol Hill.

If Israeli officials have nothing but praise for *The Wall Street Journal*, the opposite is the case when it comes to *The Washington Post*, a newspaper that has consistently challenged many Israeli policies. The criticism of Israel by *The Washington Post* intensified after the election of Prime Minister Begin in 1977, but it was also very much a part of the Washington scene even during the Labor-led governments of Golda Meir and Yitzhak Rabin. Why? Unlike the *Journal*'s basically global, pro-Western strategic outlook, the *Post* sees the Middle East and the Arab–Israeli conflict in more narrowly humanitarian terms. For it, the core of the problem is the Palestinian question. That means leaning on Israel to withdraw to roughly the pre-1967 lines. External sources of tension, such as Soviet adventurism, are secondary. This explains why editorials in the *Post* have repeatedly condemned almost all the same controversial Israeli decisions that *The Wall Street Journal* defended.

In 1982–83, the *Journal* filled its editorial columns with praise for Israel's destruction of the PLO's military infrastructure in Lebanon and the consequent loss by the PLO of political clout. It even lamented the fact that the United States did not let Israel finish the job in West Beirut. The weakening of the PLO, it commented, has been a great benefit for the free world because the PLO mini-state within Lebanon had become the training ground for international terrorism. If there had been a decline in international terror, it was the result of Israel's deeds in Lebanon. Such praise for Israel is missing from the editorial page of *The Washington Post*.

There is, according to senior Israeli officials who carefully monitor the U.S. news media, another important difference between the two newspapers. They charge that the editorial opinions of the *Post* have clearly been allowed to spill over into its hard news coverage. In recent years, they said, there has been enormous coverage of the plight of the Palestinians living under Israeli military occupation, probably more so than in any other U.S. newspaper, with the possible exception of *The Christian Science Monitor*. Apparently, the foreign desk of the *Post* has roughly the same mind set as the newspaper's editorial page editors. That is not the case with the *Journal*, whose diplomatic and Middle East reporters often have a clearly different attitude toward the Arab–Israeli conflict—meaning less pro-Israel—than that newspaper's editorial page staff.

Where does the most important American newspaper, *The New York*

Times, stand on these matters? Somewhere in the middle, according to Israeli officials. They say that many, although by no means all, of the *Times* editorials are generally favorable toward Israel. A few have been quite harsh. Where the *Times* in recent years has really stood out is in its experienced team of journalists actually covering the Middle East, including Bernard Gwertzman, Thomas Friedman, and David Shipler. That trio developed a well-earned reputation as being by far the best informed and most reliable when it comes to understanding the nuances of the region.

Beyond the news media, there's a whole network of nongovernmental, Washington-based think tanks, research centers, and other related academic institutions that have a significant impact on the shaping of U.S. policy toward the Middle East. They also influence domestic American public opinion, largely through the news media.

Everyone recognizes that there are several external factors seeking to influence the direction of U.S. policy toward the Arab–Israeli conflict. Any administration in power, for example, begins with the built-in views of the government's foreign policy bureaucracy at the State Department, the Pentagon, the various intelligence agencies, and elsewhere. Members of Congress, especially those serving on the Senate Foreign Relations and House Foreign Affairs Committees, are always trying to play a role. There are, of course, Israel and the Arab states, represented through their Washington embassies, and, in the case of the Arabs, through highly paid consultants registered with the Justice Department as "foreign agents." Finally, there are the domestic, highly partisan supporters of the two competing sides, largely the organized American Jewish leadership and the Arab–American or pro-Palestinian groups. But often overlooked are the supposedly "neutral" or "objective" scholarly institutions scattered throughout the city. Given the traditional power and respect for intellectual persuasion in America, they occasionally have played significant roles in putting forward ideas for the policymakers to consider. Sometimes, their proposals are officially inspired "trial balloons," too sensitive or controversial to come directly from the government. Other times, they represent a new, independent approach to an old problem. Winding one's way through this organizational maze is an absolutely essential ingredient in understanding the foreign policy decision-making process in Washington.

In terms of the Arab–Israeli conflict, perhaps the best known of these groups is the Brookings Institution. "No long lines of tourists wait outside 1775 Massachusetts Avenue, the home of the Brookings Institution," wrote *The New York Times* a few years ago. "It represents not raw power, as the White House does, but the genteel influence of a university without students." Brookings was put on the Middle East map by its December 1975 report, *Toward Peace in the Middle East*. President Gerald Ford and Secretary of State Henry Kissinger were still in office. At that time, none of the sixteen members of the Brookings Middle East Study Group was in government. But after President Carter entered the White House in January 1977, four Brookings panelists joined him: Zbigniew Brzezinski as the national security adviser, William Quandt as the Middle East staffer on the National Security Council, Robert R. Bowie as deputy director of the CIA, and later Philip Klutznick as secretary of commerce. Brzezinski and Quandt were especially active in advocating recommendations of their Brookings study as a guide to the Carter administration's Middle East policies. This was clearly evident during the first year of the new administration.

Thus, Brookings supported an end to Kissinger's step-by-step approach in favor of a "comprehensive settlement." It said the United States "should work with the USSR . . . to play a constructive role." It called for Palestinian "self-determination," noting that "this might take the form either of an independent Palestine state accepting the obligations and commitments of the peace agreement or of a Palestine entity voluntarily federated with Jordan but exercising extensive political autonomy." Israel, it added, should withdraw to "the June 5, 1967, lines with only such modifications as are mutually accepted."

Carter, during that first year in office, advocated the "comprehensive" approach to resolving the conflict. He called for a Palestinian "homeland or entity." In March 1977, he said Israel would have to withdraw from all the territories captured during the 1967 war except for some "minor modifications." On October 1, 1977, the United States and the Soviet Union signed a joint communiqué supporting a reconvened Geneva Peace Conference, where both superpowers would serve as equal cochairmen.

Thanks largely to the key roles played by Brzezinski and Quandt and the general support for the Brookings Report at the State Department, the carefully drafted document had an impact in shaping U.S. policy. It dramatically underscored the power of the Washington think tanks.

The Brookings experience also demonstrated the revolving door between government and the Washington-based research centers. Quandt, for instance, returned to Brookings in 1978, shortly after Israel and Egypt had signed the Camp David framework agreement. The fact that so many influential policymakers go through this revolving door (not necessarily from or to Brookings, but between the government and other research centers as well) ensures close cooperation between the two. After leaving office, officials often will be interested in pursuing related academic careers, writing and researching, as they wait patiently to return to power. The academic institutions offer them a good base from which to advance their careers.

The Atlantic Council of the United States, established in 1961, describes itself as "a unique nongovernmental, bipartisan, tax-exempt, educational, citizens' organizations." It consists of the Who's Who in the Washington foreign policy establishment, with Honorary Directors including former secretaries of state Dean Rusk and William P. Rogers.

In November 1979, following the Brookings model of almost exactly four years earlier, the Atlantic Council released its own study on the Middle East. The report was prepared by a group of experts, including ten former U.S. ambassadors to countries in the Middle East. It was chaired by Lieutenant General Brent Scowcroft (retired), President Ford's National Security Adviser who later emerged as a foreign policy aide to Republican presidential nominee Ronald Reagan, and Lieutenant General Andrew J. Goodpaster, commandant of the U.S. Military Academy at West Point. Among those signing the report were George W. Ball; Walter J. Levy, the noted oil economist; Winston Lord, president of the Council on Foreign Relations; and Charles W. Yost, former U.S. ambassador to the UN under President Nixon. Two members of the panel, Professor Eugene V. Rostow of Yale and Dr. Joseph Sisco, both former under secretaries of state, later disassociated themselves from some of the report's conclusions.

The report, following closely the prevailing views of the State Department, noted that "the question of Palestinian self-determination in the West Bank and the Gaza Strip is crucial to the process of negotiation and to the prospects of a political settlement." It noted that the United States is the only power "with influence over Israel," adding that the United States "should make clear its conviction that Israel's security will be better served by real, firmly based peace with the Arabs, including the Palestinians of the West Bank and Gaza, than by continued war and terrorism." The report said that "while this is not the moment to bring the Palestine Liberation Organization into active negotiations, the U.S. should maintain informal contact with the PLO."

The Atlantic Council report did not exactly become a household name. But within the top circles of the State Department and among knowledgeable Middle East specialists in and out of government, it was well read and studied. Because it tended to confirm so much of the widely held stance of the State Department—that resolving the Arab–Israeli conflict is "a key factor" in maintaining good relations with the Arabs, ensuring the availability of oil, and preventing the extension of Soviet control in the region—the report's recommendations made an impact.

The Carnegie Endowment for International Peace tries to influence policy through a different approach. In recent years, it has published various books on the Middle East; hosted several "off-the-record" dinners, where experts meet and discuss problems with Washington officials, journalists, and scholars; and organized breakfast press conferences for visiting foreign leaders through its prestigious quarterly, *Foreign Policy*. It produced a television program on Israel and the Palestinians, which featured Terence Smith, formerly *The New York Times* correspondent in Jerusalem, and Rita Hauser, a New York attorney who had served as a member of the U.S. delegation to the UN.

On a much smaller scale, such has also been the approach of the Woodrow Wilson International Center for Scholars at the Smithsonian Institution. The center, which invites experts to spend a year researching a specific problem, has arranged occasional conferences, such as the one on "Security in the Middle East and Persian Gulf Region in the 1980s," where Hebrew University Professor Moshe Ma'oz and Georgetown University Professor Hisham Sharabi led seminars.

The American Enterprise Institute, often described as the conservative Brookings Institution on economic issues, is also active on the Middle East. It has tried to be very "evenhanded" in its approach, although pro-Israeli activists in Washington traditionally have viewed it as pro-Arab, perhaps because its former president, the late William J. Baroody, was a leader in the Arab–American community. Harold Saunders, the influential assistant secretary of state for the Middle East during the Carter administration, joined AEI after leaving the government. Studies by Robert J. Pranger and Dale Tahtinen at the institute were regarded by Israeli officials and their Washington supporters as overly pro-Arab. As an institution, however, it included some very respected pro-Israeli voices, including Ben Wattenberg, Irving Kristol, Michael Novak, and Jeane Kirkpatrick. Two scholars associated with AEI, Richard Scammon and Howard Penniman, both experts on elections, were asked by former special Middle East Ambassador Robert Strauss to draft some guidelines on holding elections for the proposed Palestinian self-governing authority on the West Bank and Gaza Strip.

The Middle East Institute has pretensions of being a strictly academic research center with a special interest in the Middle East. But Israeli officials and others are in general agreement that its makeup and sponsorship—largely the major oil companies and other U.S. corporations with extensive business dealings in the Arab world—have combined to give it a built-in slant in favor of the Arabs. Its board of governors includes many of the State Department's most prominent Arabists, who often associate with the institute after leaving office. The institute's most important event is its annual conference, which brings several hundred Middle East specialists from around the country to Washington to focus on a specific issue. Sensitive to accusations that it is anti-Israel, the institute has tried to reach out to other traditionally more pro-Israeli academics and experts on the Middle East in recent years. The *Middle East Journal*, its quarterly publication, occasionally will publish something about Israel, although the major attention is on the Arabs.

The Center for Contemporary Arab Studies at Georgetown University, on the other hand, is considerably more blatant in its pro-Arab approach. It has accepted large financial contributions from Libya, Kuwait, and other Arab states. Its director, Professor Michael Hudson, is an outspoken supporter of the Palestinian cause. Its board of advisers has included Mansur R. Kikhia, Libya's former ambassador to the UN; J. William Fulbright, a Washington lawyer who was a leading Israeli critic as chairman of the Senate Foreign Relations Committee; and Issa Al Kawari, Qatar's minister of information.

As if to balance off the Center for Contemporary Arab Studies, Georgetown also has the Center for Strategic and International Studies. Among those affiliated with CSIS are former Secretary of State Henry Kissinger and defense specialist Edward Luttwak (also a Reagan adviser). Dr. Joyce Starr, a former White House liaison to the American Jewish community during the first two years of the Carter administration, has served as the center's "Coordinator of the Study Mission to Israel and Egypt." She arranged conferences in Washington in conjunction with Tel Aviv University's Center for Strategic Studies, led by former Chief of Military Intelligence Aharon Yariv. One of the most respected scholars associated with the center in Washington is Professor Walter Laqueur, whose works on the Middle East in *Commentary* magazine and elsewhere are carefully read.

There are, of course, several research centers with specific political leanings. The leftist Institute for Policy Studies, for example, has not been very active in the Arab–Israeli conflict, but most of its associates are extremely pro-Palestinian. Former Senator James Abourezk has lectured at the institute's "Washington School." James Zogby, the former director of the American–Arab Anti-Discrimination Committee, has also taught at the school.

On the other side of the political spectrum is the Heritage Foundation, which lately has become increasingly more involved in dealing with the Middle East and is quite pro-Israel. Dr. Joseph Churba's Center for International Security highlights Israel's strategic value to the United States. Churba, a former Middle East intelligence staffer at the U.S. Air Force, made that case in his book, *The Politics of Defeat: America's Decline in the Middle East.*

A pro-Israeli think tank, the Washington Institute for Near East Policy, was formed in 1985 by activists associated with AIPAC.

As long as government officials and members of Congress continue to rely on these institutions and organizations for information and new thinking, and the revolving door principle remains in effect, we can expect Brookings, AEI, Heritage, Carnegie, and the others to play important roles in formulating U.S. policy.

9

Trade, Labor, Blacks, and Christians

Secretary of Agriculture John Block, a successful Illinois pig farmer, was the guest of honor at the Israeli embassy in Washington on the eve of his January 1984 departure for Europe and the Middle East, which would include a stopover in Israel. There were several reasons for including Israel besides the fact that it is one of America's closest friends in the region, he told me. For one thing, Block noted, Israel happens to be America's second largest trading partner in the Middle East, following Saudi Arabia. Israel, he added, is a major purchaser of U.S. farm products, some $400 million worth in 1983 alone. "I have to stay in touch with our customers," Block said.

His point underlined a little-known but very significant trend which has developed in American–Israeli trade relations over the years, namely that business deals between Washington and Jerusalem have become significant for *both* sides, not just for Israel. There are many jobs at stake in Israel as well as in America, although there is no denying that the American market for Israeli exports is certainly much more important than the Israeli market for U.S. exports.

In 1983, the United States exported more $1.7 billion worth of nonmilitary products to Israel. (U.S. military sales to Israel in recent years have averaged between $1 billion and $2 billion annually.) Israeli exports to the United States in 1983 came to about $1.2 billion. Israel's military sales to the United States are modest, although there are efforts under way to try to increase them. Israel is also moving ahead with some service contracts for U.S. military equipment, including fighter aircraft, attached to the Sixth Fleet. In 1984, the U.S. Navy leased twelve Israeli-made Kfir fighters to simulate Soviet MiGs in training exercises. Israel Aircraft Industries, in the process, won a $68 million contract to service the Kfirs.

Thus, the trade between the two countries represents significant sums for both countries, but, of course, especially for Israel. The United States is Israel's largest individual trading partner, with 23 percent of its exports going to the United States. In addition, 25 percent of Israel's imports come from the United States.

But there are some very real benefits for Washington as well. Based on the traditional U.S. Department of Commerce rule of thumb that each $1 billion in exports translates into 30,000 jobs, that American export traffic to Israel means roughly 50,000 U.S. jobs. Using the same principle, another 50,000 Americans are employed in various U.S. defense-related industries as a result of fighter aircraft and other sophisticated military sales to Israel.

It has been estimated that over the next twenty years, the production of Israel's new Lavi jet fighter will provide at least 37,000 jobs in the United States, since much of the production for that plane will have to be subcontracted to American firms. These subcontracts will represent an infusion of an additional $1.5 billion for the U.S. companies involved.

There is clearly room for increased trade between the United States and Israel. Remember, Israel's total imports in 1983 were in excess of $8 billion. That means that American exporters can still capture a greater share of the Israeli market. And Israeli exporters believe that they, too, can do better in the United States with some additional help from their friends.

This can help to explain President Reagan's decision at the end of his November 1983 summit with Prime Minister Yitzhak Shamir to authorize the start of formal negotiations between the two countries, leading toward the creation of a free trade area (FTA), which would go a long way toward totally eliminating all existing trade barriers between the United States and Israel. Israel had been pressing the Reagan administration for over two years to open such talks, but it was only following the improved American–Israeli strategic relationship that the president finally agreed. There are economic as well as political benefits for both countries. "It is good trade policy and sound foreign policy for the United States," said Tom Dine, AIPAC's executive director. The agreement was successfully completed in early 1985.

These matters are extremely complicated, given U.S. and Israeli compliance with other international trade agreements, especially the General Agreement on Tariffs and Trade (GATT). Although Israel has entered into a free trade area on many products with the European Economic Community, it will go considerably further in eliminating all trade barriers with the United States. For the United States, moreover, this represents the first time it has ever accepted any such sweeping free trade arrangement with another country, although some aspects have been accepted with Canada and some of the friendly Caribbean island nations.

Earlier, the United States had merely sought to achieve most favored nation (MFN) trade status with other countries. In short, all friendly countries were treated equally. But with Israel, the Reagan administration was prepared to go beyond that traditional principle, with far-reaching implications for other countries as well. U.S. officials confirmed that they are prepared to follow the Israeli example with others.

But not everyone in the United States was thrilled with the prospect of greater competition. Several U.S. manufacturing and agricultural lobbying organizations expressed opposition to the establishment of the free trade area with Israel. They were by no means anti-Israel. In fact, when they appeared before the Senate Finance Committee, they went out of their way to make this point. But what worried them was the potential loss of sales to Israeli imports and, even more important, the precedent set by an agreement of this sort with Israel. What happens when Spain, Greece, or Portugal seeks such special trade status? they asked.

Among those understandably concerned about their industries were the American Farm Bureau, the California Olive Growers, the California Tomato Growers, the American Onion and Garlic Association, the Bromine Coalition, the Textile and Fiber Coalition, and the Jewelers' Association. They had seen less expensive imports cripple other U.S. industries over the years, and they wanted to continue to prevent foreign competition from challenging their hold over the U.S. market.

But Reagan administration officials strongly argued that the overall health of the U.S. economy and the individual American consumer was best served by free trade. Let the marketplace lower the cost for everyone, they suggested, even if some U.S. companies may be hurt in the short run. In the process, moreover, U.S. products had a better chance of capturing additional foreign markets, thereby creating more jobs in America.

There are, of course, some very special reasons for trying to help Israel's beleaguered economy. Israel faces enormous external debt obligations, over $23 billion at last count, the highest per capita in the western world. Thus, it has to try to improve its negative trade balance. In the long run, the only way Israel can overcome these problems is by increasing exports. That is the real hope of the economy. That is why the free trade area was so vital to Israel's future health.

In taking a careful look at its competitive edge, Israeli economists have concluded that their best long-range hope is to develop Israel's export capabilities in specialized areas involving high technology. This, of course, would take advantage of Israel's expertise in state-of-the-art technology in a host of areas—science, computers, medicine, and so on. Already, some of these newer Israeli companies have demonstrated spectacular growth. Their stock values, including those sold in the United States, have soared. It is in these areas where the real growth in Israeli exports will develop, although the bread and butter, Israeli officials acknowledged, will continue to be in the more traditional citrus products and polished diamonds for several years to come.

Reagan administration officials have recognized that a strong and healthy Israeli economy is an important American interest, given Israel's strategic and political importance to the United States. That helps to explain why the administration, backed by bipartisan majorities in both the House and the Senate, is prepared to provide extensive economic and military assistance to Israel every year. It also explains why the administration and Congress were prepared to accept a free trade area with Israel.

Thus, when Deputy Assistant Secretary of State for Near Eastern Affairs Robert Pelletreau testified before the House Foreign Affairs Subcommittee on Europe and the Middle East on February 1, 1984, he spoke of the extensive U.S. dialogue with Israel on its economic problems. "Throughout these consultations, we have proceeded from one basic premise: our own interests and those of the state of Israel require a strong Israel, not just for today but over the long haul. That presupposes a strong Israeli economy. We want and need to help make that a reality."

Pelletreau conceded the recent economic difficulties in Israel, but he made it clear that the situation was by no means hopeless. "While Israel's economic circumstances have deteriorated in the last year and a considerable effort will be required on its part to overcome the impact of past Israeli policies and international adversities," Pelletreau said, "there is no question about the fundamental firmness of Israel's resolve or the sound base of its economy. We know and the Israelis know that the sort of program required cannot be accomplished without some cost. But the Israeli people are the strength of that nation. And they have, time and again, shown their capability and willingness to confront difficult circumstances."

That same theme was picked up by AIPAC's Dine when he testified in favor of the free trade area. He sought to put Israel's economic problems into their historical perspective. "A nation of impoverished immigrants returned to the land almost barren of natural resources," he recalled. "Within a few years, Israelis built agricultural, industrial, and service sectors comparable in their level of development to many in Europe. This is reflected in the statistics of per capita production and in the visible evidence you witness when you travel throughout the country."

He added: "This remarkable development in a few short decades was achieved primarily by the hard work and entrepreneurial spirit of the people themselves, in an economy that rewards free and intelligent enterprise. It is also an example of what people can accomplish in a free and unfettered market."

But Israel's enormous defense burden, more than 25 percent of its gross national product as opposed to 7 percent in the United States, forced the country to accept huge external debts, mostly to the United States to pay for weaponry since the 1973 Yom Kippur War. This has been the single greatest cause of Israel's economic woes today.

For several years, Elmer Winter, a successful Milwaukee businessman, has worked to promote private U.S. investment in Israel. A former president of the American Jewish Committee, Winter established the Committee for Economic Growth of Israel to achieve this objective. He has carefully monitored all of the many success stories, major U.S. firms that established operations in Israel and are making money as a result. There are currently over 100 American companies with branches operating in Israel. With the establishment of the free trade area, Winter told the Senate Finance Committee, more will be on the way. And Israel will be on the road to economic independence. But that day still seems far away.

THE AMERICAN LABOR MOVEMENT

It should not come as much of a surprise to visitors at the impressive AFL–CIO headquarters building one block away from the White House that a statue of the late Golda Meir stands in the lobby. The fact is that, with the exception of the American Jewish community, the American labor movement has been the single most consistent source of support for Israel among various groups in the United States over the years. This support has been translated into crucial political action on behalf of Israel. It has also resulted in impressive purchases of Israel Bonds. Al Terestman, who served as the Israel Bonds liaison to the American labor movement, said that such purchases, mostly from affiliates of the AFL–CIO, have been "in excess of $250 million" over the past thirty years. At one point, he told me, the Teamsters, who do not belong to the AFL–CIO, were "the largest single institutional holder of Israel Bonds in the world, holding between $35 and $40 million worth."

Support for Israel in the labor movement preceded Israel's independence in 1948 by more than thirty years. Thus, in 1917, the old American Federation of Labor, meeting in Buffalo, went on record declaring support for "the legitimate claims of the Jewish people for the establishment of a national homeland in Palestine on a basis of self-government." AFL–CIO Secretary–Treasurer Thomas R. Donahue told a group in October 1982 that the 1917 convention had adopted a resolution calling on President Woodrow Wilson to advance articles of peace, when the time came to negotiate the end of the Great War, that would honor the right of the Jewish people to their own homeland. "As it turned out," Donahue said, "it wasn't easy. But over the decades of blood, sweat, and tears that went into the creation of Israel, the support of the American labor movement never wavered. We were, and are, immensely proud that the creation and defense of Israel were carried on by people like ourselves, unionists— members of Histadrut—who built a democratic national trade union movement like our own, and who then succeeded in building a nation on the solid foundations of the democratic social philosophy they learned and shared in the union hall."

There has been, of course, an almost natural affinity and alliance between the American labor organizations and the Histadrut, Israel's national trade union federation. But the late George Meany, longtime president of the AFL–CIO, made it clear with the election of the Likud's Menachem Begin as prime minister of Israel in 1977 that American labor's support for Israel went beyond its links to the Histadrut and the Israeli Labor Alignment. At the 1977 AFL–CIO convention in Los Angeles, a resolution was adopted which said: "Our support of Israel is not a function of which party is in power at a particular moment, but rather is rooted in a deep respect for the extraordinary achievements of that small country, working through the democratic process, and in our conviction that the democratic road offers the best hope of progress and peace for all the countries of that region."

When Israel's President Yitzhak Navon visited Washington in early January 1983, he did what almost all other important Israeli personalities do when they come to the U.S. capital: he asked to meet with AFL–CIO President Lane Kirkland, a real power in Washington who is fiercely pro-Israel. They met for breakfast at the Sheraton Washington Hotel, where the Israeli president was staying. Kirkland was accompanied by Donahue and Tom Kahn, an assistant to the AFL–CIO president. Joining Navon were Israeli Ambassador Moshe Arens and Embassy Labor Counselor Danny Bloch. They spoke for more than an hour, reviewing all sorts of issues, political as well as labor-related. Navon was curious about unemployment problems in the United States. Kirkland wanted to know about the split in the opposition Labor party in Israel between Yitzhak Rabin and Shimon Peres. The meeting was part of that continuing consolidation of ties between Israel and the AFL–CIO.

Those ties, of course, were strained slightly in 1982 as a result of developments in Lebanon. The top leadership of the AFL–CIO was solidly behind Israel's Operation Peace for Galilee. But within the ranks, there were some voices expressing criticism, especially following the Sabra and

Shatila massacres. "I don't think there has been any erosion of support for Israel, although some may have disagreed with the move into West Beirut, along the lines of some people in Israel itself," said Irving Brown, the AFL–CIO international affairs director. Brown, during an interview with me, made it clear that the AFL–CIO had supported Israel's initial move into Lebanon on June 6. Indeed, on June 14, Kirkland had issued a statement which said: "Israel's military action in Lebanon is entirely justified. No nation is required to suffer daily terrorist attacks on its population without striking back at the source of those attacks." He went on to urge the Reagan administration to support Israel's move. Israel, he declared, "deserves the sympathetic support, not the carping and scolding, of the Reagan administration."

On July 20, 1982, a three-man delegation from the AFL–CIO went on a fact-finding tour of Israel and Lebanon. It included Donahue, Kahn, and John Sweeney, president of the Service Employees International Union. Their conclusions were seen as instrumental in setting the stage for a very pro-Israeli plank adopted at the AFL–CIO executive council meeting in New York on August 5. "In the conflict between Israel on the one hand, and the PLO and Syria on the other, the AFL–CIO is not neutral," it said. "We support Israel. The world should demand that the PLO and Syria leave Lebanon now and allow the Lebanese to proceed with the task of reconstruction and the creation of an independent central government." The statement went on to note: "In destroying the PLO's military infrastructure, Israel has not only created the possibility of a free Lebanon; it has dealt a blow to international terrorism and set back Soviet influence in the Middle East—and thus advanced the interests of the western democracies."

Before adopting that declaration, two important leaders in the AFL–CIO had asked for some modifications which slightly watered down its pro-Israeli character. William W. Winpisinger of the Machinists and Donald Fraser of the United Auto Workers were clearly upset by the Israeli aerial bombardment of PLO strongholds in West Beirut in early August. "In the discussions, they raised some questions," said Brown. "They wanted certain phrases changed. It was not that they questioned our support for Israel. They were critical of certain actions of the Sharon operation." In the end, the resolution, which was still quite supportive of the entire Israeli campaign, was adoped unanimously. By the middle of August, Winpisinger had delivered a speech at an Israel Bonds dinner in St. Louis which was extremely pro-Israel.

In explaining the AFL–CIO resolution, Kirkland told a news conference on August 5: "We regret the loss of those lives in the present conflict. And we note that a great share of that is attributable to the fact that the PLO has systematically placed its forces and its arms and storage of weapons in schools, hospitals, and other public facilities, and in civilian areas, and that it is, in effect, holding the civilian population in West Beirut hostage." Kirkland added: "We would also point out that in the absence of any action by Israel in moving into Lebanon, there was wholesale slaughter taking place for the last seven years in Lebanon at the hands of the Syrians and the PLO without arousing any world outcry or even attracting that much attention from the United Nations. That slaughter and damage dwarfs anybody's estimate of civilian casualties since this even began."

Even after Sabra and Shatila, the AFL–CIO remained solid in its defense of Israel. On September 24, Kirkland condemned the massacre. "It is another gruesome chapter in the continuing tragedy of civil strife which has claimed 100,000 lives in Lebanon over the past decade," he said. "The worldwide revulsion it has evoked must be turned against the vicious terrorism that has been the special hallmark of the conflict in the Middle East and that has been openly espoused as an appropriate political tactic by the PLO and its supporters."

After calling for "an objective and impartial investigation" of the massacre, Kirkland added that "what is more important, if such tragedies are not to recur, is rapid progress toward the reconstruction of Lebanon and the creation there of an independent and stable central government capable of maintaining order and public safety."

On October 10, Kirkland was the guest on CBS's *Face the Nation*. He was asked whether the massacre had changed his position on Israel's entry into Lebanon. "No," Kirkland replied, "not insofar as the invasion—the incursion into Lebanon itself is concerned. We believe it was justified. Lebanon was being taken over by the PLO and the Syrians and was being used as a staging ground for attacks upon Israel, so they were quite justified both in international law and in terms of the realities of the necessities of their self-defense."

That solidarity with Israel has been important in other areas over the years. The American labor movement has many friends in the U.S. Senate and House of Representatives. Traditionally, they have supported economic and military assistance to Israel. During the 1978 debate over the Carter administration's "package" sale of F-15 fighters to Saudi Arabia, the AFL–CIO executive council flatly came out against the deal. "Aside from the issue of U.S. credibility," it said, "the arms package raises the additional questions of the wisdom of the U.S. policy. . . . Unfortunately, our credibility as a mediator is not enhanced by demanding one-sided concessions from Israel, by breaking promises made to Israel, or by offering arms to Israel's enemies as an incentive for peace. Our present policy is likely to increase Arab intransigence, as well as Israeli doubts about U.S. intentions and reliability."

The AFL–CIO later come out against the Reagan administration's 1981 sale of AWACS surveillance aircraft and other weapons to Saudi Arabia. Indeed, J. C. Turner, president of the Operating Engineers was quite active and effective in arousing opposition to the sale, even though it was eventually passed fifty-two to forty-eight in the Senate.

Danny Bloch, the former political correspondent of the Histadrut-owned *Davar* daily, who served as the Israeli embassy's labor counselor in Washington, also cited the other critical work the American labor movement has done for Israel. In an interview with me, he referred to the strenuous efforts to help ensure Israel's standing in the International Labor Organization and other international groups. At the 1982 gathering of the International Secretariat of Textile Workers in Japan, he pointed out, some delegates moved to transfer the scheduled 1984 meeting in Israel to a country in Western Europe. They expressed fear that holding the meeting in Israel could be interpreted as support for the Israeli government of Prime Minister Begin. Sol Chaikin, president of the International Ladies Garment Workers Union, which is affiliated with the AFL–CIO, strongly resisted that effort, and in a six-to-five vote, he won.

In recent years, there have been intensified efforts by Arab and pro-Arab groups to weaken American labor's support for Israel. For the most part, they clearly have not been very successful. The one exception is with the United Auto Workers, basically because of the large number of members in the Detroit area who are of Arab ancestry. In Canada, the Arabs have met with some greater success. The Ontario Federation of Labor adopted a resolution in 1982 calling the PLO the legitimate representative of the Palestinian people. But, within a matter of days, the parent Canadian Labor Congress overruled it.

According to Israeli officials and their supporters in American labor organizations, pressures are indeed mounting to distance the United States from Israel—pressures from the rank and file. There were some serious strains, for example, during the debate over the free trade area, which the unions opposed. They feared the loss of U.S. jobs. The consequences of any real erosion of support for Israel in the AFL–CIO and other important U.S. labor unions could be disastrous for Israel's standing in the United States, according to Israeli embassy officials.

As Golda Meir recalled shortly before her death, it was George Meany, among others, to whom she turned for help when Israel was in deep trouble in 1973 after Syrian and Egyptian armies crossed into Sinai and the Golan Heights. "I don't think he knows, because I don't know how to say it, what it meant to me just to hear his voice. What it meant to me, knowing what is happening down south, knowing, believing, having faith that we will come out all right, but in the meantime, boys are losing their lives for no reason." And of course, Meany, like his predecessors and successor, heard the plea and immediately responded.

BLACKS

There is both good and bad news regarding the current state of relations between the Jewish and the black communities in the United States. The bad news, highly publicized during Jesse Jackson's unsuccessful bid for the Democratic presidential nomination, is that clear strains remain over a whole gamut of issues—the Middle East, affirmative action, Israeli ties with South Africa, and other matters. The good news is that responsible leaders on both sides, especially elected government officials, are discussing these very real problems in a serious and sober manner, with the hope of reviving the historically solid alliance between the two communities.

There is no doubt that many obstacles remain on the road toward re- solving all the differences and hard feelings generated in recent years. But there does appear to be a genuine desire to do something about them before they get out of control.

In his address before the 1984 Democratic National Convention in San Francisco, Jackson, for his part, clearly sought to patch up the rift with the Jewish community. "Feelings have been hurt on both sides," he de- clared. "There is a crisis in communications. Confusion is in the air. But we cannot afford to lose our way. We may agree to agree, or agree to disagree on issues, but we must bring back civility to the tensions."

"If in my low moments," he said, "in word, deed, or attitude, through some error of temper or tone, I have caused discomfort, created pain, or revived someone's fears, that was not my intention."

Jackson referred to the historic ties between blacks and Jews, especially in the civil rights movement. "We are copartners in a long and rich religious history—the Judeo-Christian traditions. Many blacks and Jews have a shared passion for social justice at home and peace abroad. We must seek a revival of the spirit, inspired by a new vision and new possibilities. We must return to higher ground."

The black leader added: "We are bound by Dr. Martin Luther King, Jr., and Rabbi Abraham Heschel, crying out from their graves for us to reach common ground. We are bound by shared blood and shared sacri- fices. We are much too intelligent; much too bound by our Judeo-Christian heritage; much too victimized by racism, sexism, militarism, and anti-

Semitism; much too threatened as historical scapegoats to go on divided one from another.

"We must turn from finger pointing to clasped hands. We must share our burdens and our joys with each other once again. We must turn to each other and not on each other."

But even as Jackson sought to ease the tensions, others in the black community, led by Black Muslim leader Louis Farrakhan, continued to make things worse. Farrakhan appeared on July 30, 1984, before the National Press Club in Washington and repeated his anti-Semitic assertions, which Jackson earlier had pointedly delayed in condemning. Farrakhan, at the press club, said Israel had had no peace in "40 years and she will never have any peace because there can be no peace structured on injustice, lying, thievery, and deceit using God's name to shield your dirty religion or practices under His Holy and Righteous Name." Earlier, of course, Farrakhan had referred to Judaism as a "gutter religion" and had called the creation of Israel an "outlaw act."

Democratic Congressman Henry Waxman of California recognized the continuing tensions in the black–Jewish relationship, especially as they surfaced during the drafting of the Democratic Party platform. "I do not want to be a Pollyanna," he said. "Among some blacks there is quite overt hostility, not only toward Israel but also toward American Jews."

Writing in the *B'nai B'rith Messenger* in Los Angeles, Waxman said the unwillingness of many blacks to denounce Farrakhan was symbolic of this hostility. "Imagine the response that would have come had anyone associated with a major white politician referred to Christianity as a 'dirty religion' or 'gutter religion.' "

But Waxman, like many Jewish members of Congress who have traditionally maintained a very strong alliance with their black colleagues, was quick to point to many areas where Jews and blacks share the same basic interests. Other Jewish Democratic congressmen, including Barney Frank of Massachusetts and Howard Wolpe of Michigan, made the same point. "Blacks and Jews must stand together because we recognize what it means to stand alone," said Wolpe, the chairman of the House Foreign Affairs Subcommittee on Africa and an outspoken opponent of the apartheid regime in South Africa. "Blacks and Jews, because of our common experience with overcoming the social barriers of prejudice and exclusion, are in a unique position to impact in a human and positive way on decisions that affect us all on the local, national, and international levels."

Frank sought to dispel the notion that the black and Jewish communities have become each other's opponents. "Black support in Congress for an American policy supportive of the state of Israel has been and remains high," he said. "Jewish opposition to the oppression in South Africa remains equally strong, as does the support of most Jewish members for firm action against the racial discrimination that still plagues our nation. Blacks and Jews in the House share a commitment to the protection of pluralism so important to minority groups."

The close ties between blacks and Jews in the House of Representatives was underlined by the fact that Wolpe spoke at a Philadelphia Board of Rabbis meeting honoring Democratic Congressman Bill Gray, a black and a longtime supporter of Israel. In the House, Gray, among blacks, is not alone. His Democratic colleague from Texas, Mickey Leland, for example, sponsors an annual summer program bringing black youths from Houston to Israel to work on kibbutzim.

Wolpe, in his speech, laid some of the blame for current black–Jewish tensions on the Jewish community. "I emphasize the importance of Jews coming to terms with our own racism this evening because I believe it is this that lies at the core of contemporary tensions between the black and Jewish communities," he said. "What we Jews often ignore, but what blacks can never forget, is that we are also white and have historically been as much a part of the problem as a part of the solution. . . . My point this evening is not to denigrate the significant contributions Jewish Americans have made to the civil rights struggle in the United States, but rather to suggest that if we are to eradicate the growing tensions between blacks and Jews we must probe our own racism."

Wolpe, at the same time, went on to urge the black community "to recognize and confront the irrationality and destructiveness of their anti-Semitism. At the core of that confrontation must be the realization that just as certain catch words and behaviors are signals to blacks of an anti-black attitude, the same thing applies in regard to Jewish sensibilities."

Public opinion polls show that blacks and Jews do agree on many critically important issues. Addressing a 1984 meeting of the B'nai B'rith Anti-Defamation League, pollster Louis Harris said there was even substantial agreement between blacks and Jews that Jackson was "dead wrong when he made his Hymie remark," a reference to Jackson's highly publicized slur against Jews in 1984. According to Harris, 76 percent of Jews condemned the statement, as opposed to 58 percent of the blacks.

Harris also said that Jews are "more sympathetic than most other non-black Americans with the aspirations of blacks to achieve equality." But he added: "Where Jews and blacks really part company is in their overall positive/negative assessment of Jesse Jackson. What worries Jews most about Jesse Jackson is their concern that he has made remarks that appear to them to reflect anti-Semitism. . . . The challenge is not to paper over the events and statements, but to face them squarely and to find ways to mitigate against their implications."

Vernon E. Jordan, Jr., the former president of the National Urban League, agreed. Addressing the American Jewish Committee, he offered a prescription for easing the strains. "Instead of despairing about the deterioration of black–Jewish relations or the unfairness of the perceptions many Jews and blacks have of each other," he said, "we should see the current situation as an opportunity to rebuild a relationship free of the romanticism and paternalism of the past—a healthy, equal partnership based on mutual respect and understanding."

Jordan recognized that the two communities were going to disagree on affirmative action. But he urged Jews to reconsider, especially the organizational leadership. "How does it benefit the Jewish community to have its organizations act as the point men on an issue on which Jews themselves differ?" he asked. "What conceivable benefit is there for the American Jewish Committee, for example, to sponsor and to be identified with *Commentary*, an organ of extreme conservatism that does not reflect the viewpoints of the AJC or of its members, much less of the Jewish community at large?"

Regarding Israel, the black leader also urged the Jewish community to be more tolerant of criticism. "I have been consistent in support of Israel and in opposition to the terrorists who would overthrow Israel, whether they are thugs like the PLO or brutal dictators such as are to be found in Libya, Syria, Iran, and similar places. But what is at issue is the degree to which unswerving support for current Israeli government policies is seen as the litmus test for black–Jewish reconciliation. And I would argue that the litmus test has to be broader. If blacks are willing to overlook enmity to affirmative action in rebuilding our coalition, Jews should be willing to accept a broader range of opinions on Israel as well."

Jordan's most important message was that blacks and Jews "must guard against judging each other as groups on the basis of statements made by individuals. It is morally objectionable to say that Jews are against blacks because some Jews oppose affirmative action. It is just as morally objectionable to say that blacks are anti-Semitic because some blacks may have made an anti-Jewish or an anti-Israel statement."

Reflecting the opinion of many liberal Jews, Howard Friedman, president of the American Jewish Committee, said that "the state of black–Jewish relations in this country is far healthier, notwithstanding some differences of opinion, than the popular perception suggests." He blamed the media for reinforcing the notion of tension between the communities. "The forces which bind us together are far greater than those that separate us," he said. "We owe it to our common sense of shared values and shared experiences not to allow the divisive forces to overwhelm the unifying forces."

This position was also shared by Rabbi Alexander Schindler, president of the Union of American Hebrew Congregations (Reform), who delivered a moving address marking the twentieth anniversary of the murder of three civil rights workers in Mississippi. Two of the three, Michael Schwerner and Andrew Goodman, were Jewish. The third, James Chaney, was black. "They were young, of different color, but they were bound together by the bonds of a common conscience," Schindler said. "They were of differing and divergent creeds, but they shared the same fierce determination to resist repression and to extend the range of freedom. This is why the killers drew no distinction between them and murdered them all."

Many elected black leaders, including mayors Tom Bradley of Los Angles, Coleman Young of Detroit, Harold Washington of Chicago, and Wilson Goode of Philadelphia, have been in the forefront in reminding others of this unique black–Jewish link. Their campaigns over the years have been significantly assisted by Jewish constituents. Behind the scenes, they have actively sought to ease the rift generated during the Jackson candidacy. They have been aided by Democratic Congressman Charles Rangel of New York.

But other black leaders continue to upset the Jewish community, especially because of their positions regarding Israel. In this category are Mayor Richard Hatcher of Gary, Indiana; District of Columbia delegate to the House of Representatives Walter Fauntroy; and Democratic congressmen George Crockett and John Conyers of Michigan, and Mervyn Dymally of California.

It was no mere coincidence that the winter 1981 issue of the *Journal of Palestine Studies*, the quarterly published jointly by the Institute for Palestine Studies in Beirut and Kuwait University, was devoted exclusively to an examination of "American Blacks on Palestine." In recent years, and especially following UN Ambassador Andrew Young's forced resignation, which resulted from his unauthorized meeting with the PLO in New York, the Arab states and their supporters have undertaken a major effort to attract black followers in the United States. At the same time, they have tried to drive a wedge between blacks and Jews in America.

Writing the lead article in the quarterly, Professor Ronald W. Walters of Howard University in Washington echoed the familiar theme sounded at the time of Young's resignation by Jesse Jackson, Walter Fauntroy and Rev. Joseph Lowery of the Southern Christian Leadership Conference. Specifically, Walters complained that the large sums of U.S. financial assistance to the Middle East were "black tax dollars." He said that blacks have a major stake in the Middle East because "at the same time, domestic spending programs such as funds for 150,000 CETA jobs are being curtailed for lack of sufficient funds."

Just as many members of Congress were receiving that issue of the journal, the Palestine Congress of North America was inviting members of the House and Senate to an all-afternoon conference on the "Domestic Implications of the Mideast Crisis and U.S. Policy." The letter of invitation had this warning: "From energy prices to the threat of military conflict— and the prospect of American troops once more fighting a foreign war— to the massive arms and aid programs that drain a budget already insufficiently geared to the pressing needs of black communities, the Middle East crisis impacts disastrously on our everyday reality."

Fauntroy, who met with the PLO's Yasser Arafat during the SCLC's visit to Beirut shortly after the Young resignation, signed an accompanying letter urging "all invited who are committed to world peace through nonviolence to attend" the meeting in the Rayburn House Office Building. He said the roundtable discussion would "focus its attention on strategies to lessen tension in the troubled Middle East and the domestic implications of U.S. decision-making on foreign policy development." Fauntroy's endorsement seemed to have some added significance since he was then head of the Congressional Black Caucus.

Fauntroy, Thatcher, and Lowery, meanwhile, were among those who signed an angry telegram to Israeli Ambassador Ephraim Evron in February 1981, calling on Israel to readmit the two West Bank mayors, Muhammad Milhem of Halhul and Fahd Qawasmeh of Hebron, who had been expelled. Dr. James Zogby, national chairman of the Washington-based Palestine Human Rights Campaign, organized the telegram. Other singers included Representative Conyers of Michigan and Rev. Ralph Abernathy. The familiar list of pro-PLO spokesmen in Washington, including former South Dakota Senator James Abourezk and Republican Representative Paul Findley of Illinois, was also represented on the telegram. "We Americans concerned with human rights and peace cannot remain silent in the face of this powerful challenge," they warned.

Yet, despite these incidents, efforts to split the traditional liberal coalition between blacks and Jews on Capitol Hill have met with only mixed results. Relations between most black and Jewish members in the House of Representatives remain strong.

"For all of the tensions which may have developed between Jews and blacks in the country as a whole, there is a very strong and mutually supportive relationship on a wide variety of issues between Jews and blacks in Congress," commented Democratic Representative Steve Solarz of New York during an interview with me. "By and large, the blacks strongly support Israel, and the Jews strongly support the black position on Africa."

Solarz spoke with some authority on the subject, since he had once served as chairman of the House Foreign Affairs Subcommittee on Africa.

Among the Jewish members, he takes a very high profile on issues of Jewish concern, especially Israel. The black members know very well that he is Jewish. "One of the things I tried to demonstrate while I was chairman of the subcommittee," he said, "was that you don't have to be black to support racial justice in Africa, and you don't have to be Jewish to support the security of the state of Israel."

Blacks in Congress are not really making much of an issue out of the Middle East. Their priorities are elsewhere, just like their constituents. Recent public opinion polls have demonstrated that the Arab–Israeli conflict is not a very serious issue for American blacks; they are more concerned with domestic programs for health, education, and social justice. The Palestinian supporters in Washington, for the most part, have failed in their intensive efforts to convince black lawmakers to get more involved in taking anti-Israel positions. The direct connection between U.S. support for Israel and the economic condition of blacks in America has not hit home for most blacks.

Even the drive to bring in other marginally related issues, such as the treatment of the so-called Black Hebrews in Israel or Israel's trade relationship with South Africa, has not been very successful. The organized American Jewish leadership, together with many blacks who have supported Israel in the past, have taken concerted steps to combat these efforts. Bayard Rustin of the A. Phillip Randolph Institute and Ron Brown of the AFL–CIO led a delegation of prominent blacks to Israel shortly following the Lowery–Fauntroy mission to the Middle East. And on February 24, 1981, Prime Minister Begin issued a "top priority" order to prevent the recurrence of any harassment of incoming black visitors to Israel. Earlier, some blacks, suspected of planning to join the Black Hebrews in Dimona, had undergone some less than dignified treatment by border control officers at Ben Gurion Airport.

Responsible black leaders in Washington recognize that any serious confrontation with the Jewish community over Israel clearly would not be in their overall best interest. And even at the time of the Andrew Young affair, most blacks made a concerted decision to play it cool, to avoid a collision course.

Over the years, the Jewish leadership has devoted a considerable amount of its efforts to establishing some credibility with its black counterpart. In Washington, representatives of the major Jewish organizations, including Rabbi David Saperstein of the Union of American Hebrew Congregations, Hyman Bookbinder of the American Jewish Committee, David Brody of the B'nai B'rith Anti-Defamation League, Warren Eisenberg of B'nai B'rith's International Council, and Sara Ehrman of AIPAC, have worked hard to establish smooth relations with the Congressional Black Caucus.

It was also no surprise that the Committee for the Dr. Martin Luther King, Jr., Memorial Forest in Israel has planted over 10,000 trees on a hillside in the Galilee. The committee has among its sponsors every black and Jewish member in the House. It is cochaired by Democratic representatives Cardiss Collins and Sidney Yates of Illinois. Jerusalem Mayor Teddy Kollek sends a message in honor of Dr. King to Washington Mayor Marion Barry annually. "With the observance of Dr. Martin Luther King, Jr., Day," Kollek wrote in 1980, "the people of Jerusalem, along with fighters for human freedom and dignity everywhere, once again pay homage to a giant among men." It was recalled that only ten days before his assassination, Dr. King had declared: "Israel is one of the great outposts of democracy in the world, and a marvelous example of what can be done, how desert land can be transformed into an oasis of brotherhood and democracy."

Jewish leaders, by the way, recognize that they must also forge alliances with the Hispanic caucus. Representative Robert Garcia, a Democrat from the Bronx, is pro-Israel. Several of his colleagues, including Democrats Henry B. Gonzales of Texas and Edward Roybal of California, are also friends of Israel.

Israel's best friends in the American Jewish community and on Capitol Hill have always played an active role in trying to promote Israel's global diplomatic interests. This was apparent in 1983 in the determined Israeli effort to establish diplomatic relations with the new socialist government of Spain. Spain was then the only country in Western Europe that had steadfastly refused to recognize Israel. Even Greece and Turkey had formal diplomatic ties with Israel, although not at the ambassadorial level. Spain's western neighbor, Portugal, also had full relations with Israel. There was pressure on Spain from Capitol Hill, from people including Garcia and the ten members of the Hispanic caucus. They presented Spain's prime minister with a letter.

"Your recent election signifies a positive change for the people and government of Spain," the letter said. "It serves to emphasize the total emergence of Spain as a full, democratic partner in the community of European nations.

"As such, the political and diplomatic role of Spain has become increasingly important. We, therefore, request that your government review its present diplomatic situation with regard to Israel. Since Spain maintains open relations with many nations regardless of their political perspectives, it does not seem unreasonable to hope that your government will seriously consider having formal diplomatic relations with Israel.

"The special relationship between Israel and the United States is well known, and the world is also becoming more aware of the growing influence of Spain in world affairs. Also, your country's unique cultural heritage and geographical location put it in a position to act as a conduit between the Arab world and Israel. Any lessening of tension between these nations would be in the interests of not only the nations involved and the United States, but of all nations dedicated to seeking a lasting peace in the Middle East. We hope that you will give this request all due consideration.''

CHRISTIANS

Shortly after President Ronald Reagan took office, he received a telegram from some prominent leaders of the Christian right urging him to maintain his campaign commitments toward Israel. "We are concerned,'' they said, "about morality and reaffirmation of principles of faith, not only on the domestic American scene but also in terms of our international affairs. From our religious, moral, and strategic perspective, Israel supremely represents our values and hopes for security and peace in the Middle East.''

Many Israelis, Prime Minister Begin among them, as well as many American Jews, were delighted when the text of the telegram was made public. Here was some concrete evidence that a new source of political clout for Israel in the United States was emerging. Among those signing the telegram was Rev. Jerry Falwell, president of the Moral Majority. In recent years, Falwell has been a frequent visitor to Israel and has expressed virtually down-the-line support. He often sounds more pro-Israel than many Jews in the United States. "There is no question that Judea and Samaria should be part of Israel,'' he said. What about the Golan Heights? "I believe that the Golan Heights should be annexed as an integral part of the state of Israel.'' When he was asked about the Knesset bill reaffirming Jerusalem as Israel's capital, he said, "Yes, I believe that Jerusalem should be the unified capital of Israel, and I was in favor of the bill.'' Falwell received a personal telephone call from Begin following the June 1981 Israeli aerial strike against the Iraqi nuclear reactor. The premier wanted Falwell's assistance in generating some public support for the Israeli action, which was "condemned'' by the Reagan administration.

Eight months earlier, Begin had made certain that Falwell was included among those friends of Israel receiving a medal during a dinner in New York marking the hundredth anniversary of the birth of Zev Jabotinsky, Begin's political mentor during the struggle leading to the establishment of Israel.

Even before Begin took office in 1977, ties between Israel and the Christian right had grown. But they really expanded and even started to flourish under the Likud-led coalition. Many Israelis earlier had become disillusioned with some of the liberal, largely Protestant church organizations in the United States, especially the National Council of Churches and the Quakers, which had repeatedly flirted with the PLO.

The political right in Israel and the United States also shared some basic ideological positions, namely strong opposition to the Soviet Union and support for a free market economy. The Begin government, immediately after taking office, did depart dramatically from the labor Zionism of Israel's founding fathers. Begin very often tried to ridicule the opposition Labor party by calling it "the Socialist Party." He clearly scored some popularity points in the June 1981 Knesset elections by doing so.

But beyond these underlying attitudes, there was also a personal touch. Probably the single most important reason for the development of a close, personal relationship between Begin and Falwell concerned Gerald S. Strober, a New York Jewish leader with close ties to Falwell and other evangelical leaders. Strober has written biographies of both Falwell and Rev. Billy Graham. "As far back as 1970," Strober said in an interview with me, "major evangelical leaders gave tangible expression to their pro-Israel sentiment."

In that year, Billy Graham released a documentary film called *His Land*, which vividly demonstrated Graham's warm support for Israel. "From then on, the relationship took off." Strober added, "Jerry Falwell's support for Israel is the most significant manifestation yet of evangelical concern for Israel's security in that it brings together positive theological elements and considerable political muscle."

In Israel, the budding connection between the Israeli political establishment and the fundamentalist Christian movement was vividly demonstrated after the Knesset decision to formally proclaim Jerusalem as Israel's capital. More than a dozen countries that maintained their embassies in Jerusalem quickly moved them to Tel Aviv. In response, a Dutch Christian minister, Jan Van der Hoeven, opened the International Christian Embassy in Jerusalem to underline his support for the Knesset action. Speaking in 1982 in Philadelphia, he explained his motivation. "Of course we are happy and blessed in what God has shown us to do," he said. "But I think that after all that Christianity has *not* done, there comes a time that it is sinful to be silent."

Van der Hoeven and his movement have struck a responsive chord among many evangelical Christians around the world who view the return of the Jewish people to Israel as a basic requirement for the eventual return of the Messiah. "So the return of the Jews to their land was an absolute necessity for all that we as Catholics and Protestants value beyond every value," he said. "Peace will come from Jerusalem," he continued. "And because I believe it, I have said in the name of Christian Zionists to [Jerusalem Mayor] Teddy Kollek and to [former Israeli] President [Yitzhak] Navon that we are not supporters of Israel just because we are well-wishers that clap them on the shoulders and say, 'Well, we feel guilty, we'll pray for you.' It's far deeper than this. I believe that to be for Israel is to be for the world."

Thus, despite the clear uneasiness many Israelis and American Jews originally felt about forging a political alliance with the Christian right, there seemed to be evolving a sort of across-the-board consensus that Israel did not have the luxury of selecting its friends. The traditionally liberal Jewish community might feel uncomfortable about the "pro-family" positions of the Christian right, but many of the most important Jewish leaders in the country were willing to accept support for Israel from any quarter. Even Rabbi Alexander Schindler, president of the Union of American Hebrew Congregations and one of the most outspoken critics of the Moral Majority and other New Right groups, met in 1981 with Falwell to see if they could agree to disagree on everything—but Israel.

Schindler had written an article a few months earlier warning that "that Moral Majority and those other religious and political organizations with which they are in coalition reveal themselves to be a threat to American democracy, to America's Jews, and, therefore, also to Israel." He said that he did not consider Falwell an anti-Semite, but that in "his exclusivist emphasis on a Christian America and the tools he chooses to build it, he and his associates are creating a climate of opinion which is hostile to religious tolerance. Such a climate, in my judgment, is bad for civil liberties, human rights, social justice, interfaith understanding, and mutual respect among Americans. Therefore, it is bad for Jews." Thus, the fact that Schindler was even willing to sit down together with Falwell was in itself significant.

But more than a year into the Reagan administration, those Israelis and American Jews who had counted on the Christian right as an important pillar of strength for Israel in the United States were in for a rude awakening. This was largely the result of conservative, right-wing behavior during the Saudi AWACS debate. On an issue of critical importance to Israel, the New Right let Israel down badly.

In 1981, political analysts in Washington identified twenty-eight Republican senators as fundamentally in line with the New Right or the Moral Majority on a wide range of domestic and foreign policy issues. When the final roll call was over on the AWACS sale, twenty-six of them had voted in favor of it. The only two exceptions were Republicans Alfonse D'Amato of New York and Paula Hawkins of Florida. Both represented states with sizable and influential Jewish communities. The lesson for Israel and American Jews: the New Right may make some nice statements about Israel now and then, but when it comes down to the crunch, an actual roll call on an issue of great importance to Israel, their support crumbles.

Falwell himself did sign a full-page advertisement in *The Washington Post* against the sale—along with two dozen other Christian leaders from around the country, including Jesuit Priest Robert Drinan, the former liberal congressman from Massachusetts and himself a bitter opponent of the Moral Majority. But Falwell did very little to generate opposition to the sale among his followers in the Senate. If he did place any telephone calls to wavering senators urging opposition to the sale, they were among the best-kept secrets in Washington. Indeed, reliable administration sources have made the point that Falwell was warned early by "important people" in the White House that any active lobbying against the sale could adversely affect his push for those social issues of greater concern to the Moral Majority—the Equal Rights Amendment, abortion, and prayer in schools. For Falwell, the sale of AWACS to Saudi Arabia never did become a big issue, even though his friend, Prime Minister Begin, was dead set against it.

Schindler was quick to point to this fact. "The Moral Majority did not do nearly so well by us," he told 4000 delegates attending the biennial assembly of the Union of American Hebrew Congregations in Boston in 1981. "Its leader, Jerry Falwell, did sign an anti-AWACS advertisement, but that was all—no mail, no telephone calls, no sermons to support his position. In fact, the higher the Moral Majority rating of a legislator, the more likely he was to approve the arms sale to Saudi Arabia." Democratic Senator Edward Kennedy of Massachusetts told the same gathering: "Israel has no need of fair-weather friends. Neither Israel nor the United States will be served by politicians who profess one thing and do another. And none of us can rely on New Right conservatives proclaiming a biblical allegiance to Israel who can be turned around in a single White House meeting."

Many of Falwell's most effective ideological supporters in the New Right, despite their pro-Israeli rhetoric of the past, actually went on to lobby *for* the sale. Richard Sellers was director of congressional relations for the right-wing American Security Council and Washington director of the Coalition for Peace Through Strength, a conservative defense group. Sellers, according to *The Washington Post*, spearheaded the effort by thirty-four conservative groups to lobby their friends in the Senate for the sale. They clearly were effective in turning around Republican Senator William Armstrong of Colorado, as well as Roger Jepsen and Charles Grassley, both from Iowa.

Others simply sat on their hands during the months-long debate. Paul Weyrich, who heads the Committee for the Survival of a Free Congress, said that he had not supported the sale because he had felt it represented a violation of Reagan's campaign commitments. Curiously, Weyrich, who had cosigned the original telegram to Reagan early in the administration warning against any slippage in support for Israel, was reported by *The Washington Post* to be a supporter of the AWACS sale. "The Stanton Group, part of the network of conservative organizations run by Paul Weyrich, . . . pressed for the sale among its sympathizers, particularly junior Republicans who have strong ties to the right wing," said *The Washington Post*. With hindsight, Weyrich said he should have written a letter to the newspaper "correcting the record." The fact that he did not bother appeared to indicate that he was not all that concerned about the mistake— or the AWACS sale.

Rabbi David Saperstein, director of the Religious Action Center of Reform Judaism in Washington, was one of the early skeptics about the depth of the Christian right's support for Israel. In straightforward political terms, he explained his reservations, noting, for example, that very few of the fundamentalist leaders in the U.S. House or Senate vote for the annual foreign aid bill, of which Israel is the largest individual recipient. "I have as yet to see them make any statement in favor of the Israeli aid package," he said. Referring to the 1980 congressional "Report Card" circulated by the Christian Voice in numerous congressional races, Saperstein pointed out that Israel was not included in the list of sixteen "key moral issues" during the 96th Congress. Among the "moral" issues were the Taiwan Security Bill, aid to Nicaragua, and SALT II ratification. The Los Angeles-based Christian Voice is said to have the support of 37,000 clergy and some 140,000 members.

What was especially disconcerting to Saperstein and other Jewish political activists was the fact that the New Right has often targeted so many strong friends of Israel for defeat. If the conservative right's support for Israel were really strong, they would not have placed such pro-Israeli champions as Henry Jackson of Washington and Edward Kennedy of Massachusetts on their "hit list" in 1982. "How friendly can they be if they vote against foreign aid to Israel and work to defeat our friends in Congress?" asked Saperstein.

In the House of Representatives, where the AWACS sale was rejected by a vote of 301 to 111, sixteen of the seventeen black members, all Democrats, and all five Hispanic members, also Democrats, voted against the sale. The only black who did not go along with his colleagues was Democrat Gus Savage of Illinois, who was recorded as "not voting."

Many Jews also have expressed concern over the basic theological justification offered by the Christian right in support of Israel. Rabbi Ira S. Youdovin, former executive director of the Association of Reform Zionists of America, which is affiliated with Schindler's Union of American Hebrew

Congregations, acknowledged that the Christian fundamentalists "have long been among Israel's staunchest supporters." But he maintained that the Jewish community should examine the motives behind the support. Pointing to the religious impetus, he said the return of the Jewish people to their biblical homeland is seen as a "precondition for the Second Coming of Jesus." But Youdovin said that this should not be confused with Zionism. "The ingathering of Jews in Israel is the penultimate step in God's plan," he said. "Once there, the Jews are expected to participate in a massive conversion to Christianity. If they do not, they will be repeating the transgression of their first-century forebearers who resisted Jesus."

Falwell himself has avoided discussing that theological aspect of his support for Israel. Instead, he refers to God's promise to Abraham 4000 years ago: "I will bless them that bless thee and curse him that curseth thee." Thus, Falwell says, "from the theological perspective, I think America should be, without hesitation, giving total financial and military support to the state of Israel."

But Falwell's pro-Israeli statements have not reassured his critics in the American Jewish community, especially those affiliated with the Reform leadership. Albert Vorspan, director of the Commission on Social Action of Reform Judaism, maintained that the "evangelical vision of America ought to arouse alarm on the part of concerned persons, including Jews, whether liberal or conservative. . . . And, in their fanatical zeal to recapture America as a 'Christian country,' there can be little doubt whom they conceive to be among their enemies."

In questioning the religious motivations of the Christian right, Jewish opponents have been able to point to several statements by Rev. Bailey Smith, while serving as president of the Southern Baptist Convention, that God "doesn't hear the prayer of the Jew." Later, Smith, under pressure, expressed "deep regret" for having made that statement. Smith subsequently undertook a highly publicized visit to Israel organized by the B'nai B'rith Anti-Defamation League.

Falwell assured Rabbi Marc H. Tanenbaum of the American Jewish Committee, during a meeting on October 10, 1980, that he opposes the view that "God does not hear the prayer of the Jew," adding that he was committed to religious pluralism. "My position," Falwell said, "is that God is a respecter of all persons. He loves everyone alike. He hears the cry of any sincere person who calls on him."

Falwell, who said that "a very healthy relationship has been developing between bible-believing Christians in America and the Jewish community during the past two decades," promised to try to promote this dialogue. "This relationship transcends any political campaign. . . . We may have differing theological positions, but we must never allow this to separate us as Americans who love and respect each other as united people."

Rabbi Tanenbaum, who has maintained contacts with fundamentalist Christians since 1965, welcomed the Falwell statement, saying it was "necessary and timely." Tanenbaum added: "During our frank and cordial dialogue, Rev. Falwell assured me that he is opposed to the conception of America as a 'Christian Republic,' and that he is deeply committed to the American Constitution's prohibition of a religious test as the basis for the election of political candidates. While he acknowledged that there have been some persons in the conservative evangelical community who have advocated such views, these do not represent his thinking, and he will continue to oppose these positions which contradict the principles of democratic pluralism."

But the uproar that followed Smith's assertion about God, prayers, and Jews, while subsiding in the wake of Falwell's disclaimer, was revived early in 1981 by remarks made by the chairman of New York State's Moral Majority, Rev. Daniel C. Fore. "Jews have a God-given, almost supernatural ability to make money," Fore said, adding that Jews "control the media and this city," meaning New York. Fore, the Texas-born pastor of Brooklyn's Metropolitan Baptist Church, was quickly attacked by Jews and non-Jews alike. Vorspan, for instance, wrote to *The New York Times*: "Mr. Fore's melange of old-fashioned anti-Semitic stereotyping and Christian triumphalism tells us more about the Moral Majority than all of its pietistic and arrogant propaganda, which has the chutzpah to claim a lock on God and morality."

As the spread of the Christian right grows in America and as the news media continue to focus public attention on this development, it becomes increasingly more apparent that there are a variety of views under its spectrum. This is no monolith, as underscored by the fact that Rev. Billy Graham, the dean of evangelical leaders in this country, has taken public issue with Falwell. "It would be unfortunate if people got the impression all evangelists belong to that group," Graham told *Parade* magazine in 1981. "I don't wish to be identified with them."

"I'm for morality," Graham said. "But morality goes beyond sex to human freedom and social justice. We, as clergy, know so very little to speak out with such authority on the Panama Canal or superiority of armaments. Evangelists can't be closely identified with any particular party or person. We have to stand in the middle in order to preach to all people, right and left. I haven't been faithful to my own advice in the past. I will be in the future."

Tanenbaum suggested that the American Jewish community decide pragmatically how to deal with Falwell and the new Christian fundamentalists. "I think we can come to terms with them," he said. "I certainly hope we can."

But there is no shortage of obstacles standing in the way of a healthy dialogue. Among the most serious is the widespread fear in the Jewish community that the fundamentalists' ultimate objective is merely to convert Jews to Christianity. Falwell's position on this tricky issue, like many of his colleagues, is not totally clear. While he insists that he has a strong "commitment to protect the sanctity, the existence, and the perpetuity of Judaism as it now exists in this country," he also maintains the right to "teach, preach, and evangelize." If Jews wanted to do the same, or if other Christian denominations wanted to try to convert fundamentalists, Falwell says he would have no objection. Let there by an open marketplace of religious ideas, and let the best one win out. That's roughly what he says. Falwell denies that he wants to "Christianize" America. "It is as ridiculous to assume that America can be Christianized as to think it can be Judaized. The distinctiveness of America is that we are a melting pot for peoples of the world." Like Rabbi Tanenbaum, Falwell wants Jews and fundamentalists to talk to each other. "I think the answer . . . is that we need to immediately develop a healthy dialogue with the Jewish leadership of this country," he said.

The missionary efforts of the evangelists, especially in Israel, have been the source of considerable concern in Israel. According to the spring 1981 issue of *Evangelical Review*, conversions to Christianity have recently increased in Israel. J. D. Hughey, a Baptist missionary in Israel, is quoted as saying that "professions of faith and baptisms both have increased dramatically during 1980 in Israel." Hughey, a Foreign Mission Board official of the Southern Baptist Convention, added, "I don't think I have seen anything like this during the time I have been area director for Europe and the Middle East."

This fixation with missionary efforts cuts across the board of almost all fundamentalist groups. Falwell points out that Islamic fundamentalism "is the most dangerous movement on the face of the earth." He recently explained that "any Christian missionary in any Moslem land can tell you that it is true. It is very difficult to exist even physically as a Christian missionary in a strongly fundamentalist Moslem country. That is not true in the state of Israel. We have many Christian leaders and workers in Israel who are allowed freedoms and liberties just as Jewish leaders and Christian leaders are in this country."

Falwell goes out of his way to insist that the Moral Majority is not a strictly Christian organization. "We have Jewish members, we have Roman Catholic members, we have Mormons, Protestants, and fundamentalists who are members. All that is required is American citizenship and a commitment to these shared moral values." Indeed, Falwell expressed hope that in the 1980s the Moral Majority will "attract a very large constituency of Jewish people." He said that "bible-believing conservative Christians" and "conservative Jews" are going to "stand or fall together."

In coming up with a proper response, the Jewish community, as represented by its national organizations, has had to carefully assess long-term interests. Certainly, attitudes toward Israel will play a critical role in determining where the Jewish leadership will eventually stand, if indeed a consensus position can be found. The first step involves a strong and healthy dialogue with all religious groups in America. Establishing direct, personal contacts is essential if eventual success is to emerge from these discussions.

10

Henry Kissinger and Israel

Secretary of State Henry Kissinger laughed hysterically as comedian Danny Kaye told stories in his unique French, British, and Russian accents. The secretary, well tanned following a ten day vacation in Jamaica, removed his glasses and wiped tears of laughter from his eyes. As Kaye wound up his remarks, he raised his glass, proposing a double toast in honor of Kissinger and Israel's visiting foreign minister, Yigal Allon. *"L'Chaim,"* Kaye declared. The more than 100 guests at the black-tie State Department dinner, including leading congressmen, administration officials, journalists, American Jewish leaders, and their guests, replied, *"L'Chaim."* They sipped their champagne and applauded. Allon, who appeared to be in an unusually good mood, arose to say, "Tonight we have two K's with us." There was more laughter as Kaye returned to his seat.

But while Kissinger—for once the other K—began to introduce the evening's guest violinist, Danny Kaye, always the showman and aware that he had a captive audience, once again began his act. "Israel Bonds," he declared, "that's the real reason you have been assembled here." As Kaye started a standard fund-raising pitch, there was more laughter. Kissinger took out his handkerchief and began wiping his eyes.

The guests were in a good mood on that January 1976 evening. Nancy Kissinger was a charming hostess as she welcomed her many friends. Kissinger, in his toast honoring Allon, recalled his own personal introduction to American–Israeli affairs. It was 1961, he said, and the then relatively unknown Harvard University professor of government was Allon's guest at Kibbutz Ginnosar on the Sea of Galilee. "I saw the fishermen on the lake," Kissinger said, "right under the Golan Heights. I will never forget their courage." The secretary, continuing his toast, went on to make a very warm and moving statement applauding the traditional American–Israeli friendship.

Allon, for his part, recalled his early friendship with Kissinger and "that exciting seminar" he took with Kissinger in 1957 at Harvard. During the course of that summer, Allon said, he once drove with Kissinger from Boston to New York, about a four-hour trip. They discussed Israel's two previous wars, in 1948–49 and 1956. Allon complained that Israel had been forced by U.S. secretaries of state to retreat from Sinai twice, but not in exchange for peace. Kissinger, the Harvard professor, told Allon that if Israel should ever again take the Sinai, it should not withdraw unless it won peace in exchange. "Henry," Allon said nearly twenty years later, "this was one of the lessons I learned from you, and you are going to pay for it now." Again Kissinger and the guests laughed.

To the casual observer, the dinner party seemed to indicate that everything was just fine in American–Israeli affairs. But there were serious problems in the Middle East that could not be ignored. Despite the 1975 Sinai interim agreement and the much hoped for respite in Middle East tension, further progress was proving to be difficult. The radical Arab camp, led by Syria and the PLO and backed by the Soviets, had adopted a more aggressive posture. The United States was desperately trying to avoid another war in the Middle East, a war that it felt would become inevitable unless some semblance of "diplomatic movement" could be maintained. But all avenues were blocked, and no one in Washington was really sure how best to unplug them. Syrian President Hafez Assad, whom American officials then considered a relative moderate and quite realistic, certainly in Syrian terms, may have been prepared to consider an Israeli withdrawal offer on the Golan front if one had been made immediately following the Sinai accord. But the moment was allowed to pass; Israel offered only cosmetic changes, and Assad raised his demands. Some Americans later expressed a belief that Assad had boxed himself in with the PLO and could not budge without simultaneous Israeli movement on the Palestinian issue.

King Hussein of Jordan was also in a bind. He probably would have liked to consider an Israeli proposal for a disengagement agreement along the Jordan River, but American officials understood that Israel would have to hold its own elections before withdrawing from any part of the West Bank; Prime Minister Rabin was not seen as ready to hold elections. Hussein feared the outbreak of another war, knowing that he would come under tremendous pressure to participate in any new battle against Israel. His Arab allies would not be likely to accept his excuses this time as they had in 1973. Yet the monarch feared that his army would be quickly crushed by Israel, as it had been in 1967.

Egyptian President Anwar Sadat was counted on in 1976 to remain quiet and to implement the Sinai interim accord without major hitches. The American hope was that Saudi Arabia would cooperate over the next months. The Soviet Union, as always, was a question mark. Kremlin leaders did not want in any way to anger the Syrians, the Iraqis, the Libyans, or the PLO. Their policy since 1967 has been consistent: keep the pot simmering because doing so creates opportunities for expanding their influence. But, simultaneously, having learned from history, the Soviets wanted to avoid seeing that pot boil over and seeing their clients lose against a militarily superior Israel.

There was no apparent solution to the knotty problem of PLO participation in negotiations, a precondition demanded by the Arabs and the Soviet Union. But as long as the PLO refused to accept Israel's existence and UN Resolutions 242 and 338, neither Washington nor Jerusalem would recognize the PLO as the legitimate representative of the Palestinians. Kissinger made this abundantly clear to Israeli officials. And there was not much realistic hope in Washington that the PLO would modify its public stance regarding the legitimacy of the state of Israel.

Kissinger and Allon, who had probably never dreamed while they were together at Harvard that they would one day be negotiating with each other, were trying to coordinate their countries' positions in a way that would satisfy the national interests of each, without overly antagonizing the other. The talks were tough; no one denied that. Kissinger's robust laughter, Allon's cute stories, and Danny Kaye's jokes aside, Middle East prospects did not seem very good the night of the State Department dinner.

This was how Kissinger's last year as secretary of state began. It eventually proved to be a rather quiet year for the Middle East. One reason, of course, was the U.S. presidential election held that November. The Arabs and their allies had come to expect that no diplomatic initiatives tilting toward their position would likely be attempted during a presidential campaign.

That July, for example, Israeli diplomats and their American supporters were delighted by the Middle East plank in the Republican Party platform, more pro-Israeli than any earlier one adopted by the GOP. Arab diplomats, on the other hand, did not hide their disappointment. The Arabs had expected the Democratic platform adopted in June to include a strong statement of support for Israel, which it did. But they had hoped that the Republicans who were then still in the White House would show more "balance" in drafting their statement, taking Arab interests into consideration. The State Department braced for some stiff reactions in the Arab world.

White House officials, eager to attract the Jewish support that could tip the declared vote in many large states, had made a decision that the party platform should be decidedly pro-Israeli, despite State Department misgivings about possible ramifications in the Arab world. A group of American Jewish Republicans, led by Max Fisher of Detroit, met with White House Chief of Staff Richard Cheney to discuss the proposed plank, and Cheney agreed in principle to work for a strongly worded statement, even if it meant going slightly beyond existing administration policy. The platform committee drafted the Middle East plank. It was no accident that there was no mention of "stalemate" or "stagnation" in Middle East diplomacy, code words that both Ford and Kissinger had used publicly on numerous previous occasions to nudge Israel into accepting more concessions. Except for a brief statement on Lebanon, there was only one reference to America's relations with the Arab states: "Republican administrations have succeeded in reestablishing communication with the Arab countries and have made extensive progress in our diplomatic and commercial relations with the more moderate Arab nations."

Most of the original Middle East plank dealt only with Israel and America's commitment to the Jewish state. And then, as if to add insult to injury to the Arabs, the Republicans actually strengthened the draft statement. The first draft called for a "just and durable peace for all parties in that complex region." When someone pointed out that the word *parties* could be interpreted to include the PLO, the committee quickly voted to change it to *nations*. Similarly, in the section calling for "face-to-face, direct negotiations," the committee substituted *states* for *parties*. They were not leaving a loophole the Democrats might later try to exploit. The secretary of state gave his approval to the politicians' efforts to win support among Israel's friends.

More than any other American, Henry Kissinger has shaped the nature of U.S. policy toward Israel and the Middle East in the years since the 1973 Yom Kippur War. His imprint, of course, was evident during the Nixon and Ford administrations. But it also has had a lasting impression on policy through the Carter and Reagan administrations, which followed his departure from government.

To this very day, Kissinger's opinions on the Middle East are actively sought. His briefings for Secretary of State George Shultz during the summer of 1982, shortly after Shultz succeeded Alexander Haig, were widely recognized as instrumental in setting the tone for President Reagan's September 1, 1982, Arab–Israeli peace initiative. A close reading of that proposal and related side documents, especially the concept of a West Bank associated with Jordan, demonstrates a pure Kissingerian approach. "His fingerprints were all over the place," an authoritative American official commented.

Kissinger, while secretary of state, set in motion several other trends in U.S. policy that also remained very much in effect ten years later. He promoted, for example, the concept of a step-by-step peace process whereby partial agreements dealing with relatively easier matters would be sought rather than the all-or-nothing comprehensive approach. His incremental style was based on the assumption that with more modest agreements in effect the confidence of both sides might increase and that concessions on the more sensitive issues that at first might seem unrealistic would, over time, become more acceptable. It was this approach that led to the two Israeli disengagement-of-forces agreements with Egypt and Syria after the 1973 war, the Sinai II accord in 1975, the Camp David framework agreements in 1978, and the Israeli–Egyptian Peace Treaty in 1979.

The former secretary's efforts to reduce Soviet prestige and influence in the region have also remained as general U.S. policy, although Carter did deviate from this objective by fostering the October 1, 1977, American–Soviet joint communiqué on reviving the Geneva Middle East Peace conference, where all of the issues theoretically would be resolved in one fell swoop. Egyptian President Anwar Sadat feared, however, that a new agenda was about to be introduced and that progress on resolving old issues would be threatened by Syrian President Assad's rejectionism strengthened now by the Soviet presence at the negotiating table. So Sadat, a month later, effectively killed the Geneva option by going to Jerusalem. Kissinger's step-by-step program was revived.

Kissinger also established the pattern of providing Israel with extensive economic and military assistance in exchange for Israeli political concessions in negotiations with neighboring Arab states. The $2-billion-a-year foreign aid allocations for Israel began with Kissinger, although, of course, they had the backing of President Richard Nixon and a large bipartisan and influential group of senators and representatives. At that time, the big aid package was supposed to be a one-shot deal. But the massive sums have continued ever since. Today, most Washington observers have come to take those large amounts of economic and military aid for Israel almost as a given.

The former secretary also established the formula of not dealing with the PLO until it accepted two important conditions: Israel's right to exist and UN Security Council Resolutions 242 and 338. Those conditions were formally codified in the September 1, 1975, American–Israeli Memorandum of Agreement that accompanied the signing of the Sinai II accord. Kissinger and Allon signed that historic memorandum which the Carter and Reagan administrations later continued to honor, very often to the irritation of many U.S. officials who have been eager to open formal contacts with Yasser Arafat and the PLO. A U.S. backing away from that pledge would have raised the most serious questions in Jerusalem about America's willingness to honor its word and would have seriously undermined Israeli confidence in Washington. Thus, a very reluctant Jimmy Carter was left with little choice but to maintain the agreement despite strong urgings to the contrary from some of his closest associates.

With the more recent disarray in the PLO and Yasser Arafat's decline, coupled with the ascendancy of Syria as a dominant force in shaping various elements of the PLO, the U.S. commitment to the Kissinger pledge has become less a source of tension. But, from Israel's point of view, there is no doubt that the Kissinger pledge was the single most important reason why the United States has not formally opened contacts with the PLO over the years.

Today, Kissinger may no longer be in government, but his behind-the-scenes role in shaping U.S. policy toward the Middle East is considered by well-placed U.S., Israeli, and Arab experts as quite impressive. This was apparent in the immediate aftermath of the October 24, 1983, truck bombing of the U.S. Marine headquarters in Beirut. Kissinger's public and private advice quickly became dominant thinking within the Reagan administration, as underlined during the November visit to Washington by Prime Minister Yitzhak Shamir and Defense Minister Moshe Arens. The Israelis received from Reagan, Shultz, and other U.S. policymakers a strengthened commitment for closer strategic, military, economic, and political ties. At the end of October, Reagan authorized a new course of action toward Israel, as recommended by Kissinger a week earlier on ABC's *This Week with David Brinkley*. "I must point out it is an amazing phenomenon that the Israeli army is sitting 2 kilometers from where Americans are being killed and that there seems to be no coordination between our policies at all," Kissinger had said. He urged the United States to take specific steps, in conjunction with Israel, to change the balance of power in the region, which by then had tilted in Syria's favor. It was clear to Kissinger that the Syrians were not about to demonstrate any flexibility in negotiations to remove their troops from Lebanon until they had some real incentive to do so, and that could come only from their fear of Israel's military machine. Reagan and Shultz came to agree, and much of the talk of enhanced strategic cooperation with Israel today is the result.

There is also the fact that two of Kissinger's closest former aides were instrumental in advancing this concept of closer cooperation with Israel during the internal deliberations of the Reagan administration. Under Secretary of State for Political Affairs Lawrence Eagleburger was once considered Kissinger's right-hand man at State. Later, he won Shultz's deep confidence. Peter Rodman of the Policy Planning Staff at the State Department served on Kissinger's personal staff from 1969 until 1983.

He learned about the Middle East while working for Kissinger.

But it would be a mistake to conclude that all of the actions that Kissinger had set in motion and which remain very much operational today were necessarily beneficial for Israel. Most Israeli officials and American Jewish political activists give the Kissinger legacy somewhat mixed reviews.

Many were irritated, for example, by Kissinger's failure to identify the PLO as terrorists. In the first volume of his memoirs, *White House Years*, he never refers to members of the PLO as terrorists, not once in the four chapters or 138 pages dealing with the Middle East. Even when Kissinger discussed various Palestinian murders, hijackings, and other atrocities, he carefully avoided this pejorative description. Instead, he chose from among the more neutral or even complimentary *commando*, *guerrilla*, or *fedayeen*, the last word loosely translated from the Arabic as "religious martyrs" or "those willing to sacrifice their lives heroically for a just cause." This conforms to the standard description of the PLO in the Arab world. Kissinger's omission of the word *terrorist* was most conspicuous when he recalled the events surrounding the Palestinian hijacking to Jordan in September 1970 of American, Swiss, and British commercial airliners carrying several hundred passengers. "On September 7, the PFLP [Popular Front for the Liberation of Palestine] offered to release all passengers except Israelis and dual-nationals in return for the release of all fedayeen held in Swiss, German, and British jails," Kissinger wrote. "Israeli and dual-national passengers were to be held in return for guerrillas in Israeli jails." A page earlier, Kissinger noted that "the extremists among the fedayeen" had as their "goal not peace with Israel but its destruction." The only time the word *terrorist* appeared was when Kissinger pointed out that the PLO were regarded as "terrorist criminals by Israel."

For cognoscenti of the Arab–Israeli conflict, Kissinger's choice of words could not be seen as accidental. There must have been a deliberate decision made not to offend the Palestinians and the rest of the Arab world. After this criticism was leveled Kissinger did occasionally refer to the PLO as terrorists in his second volume. But it will still clear that Kissinger did not want to burn his bridges to the Arab world after leaving office.

Since January 1977, in fact, Kissinger has been maintaining a delicate balance on the Middle East tightrope. His strategy appears to have been two-pronged: avoid overly upsetting the Arabs, while currying favor simultaneously with Israel and its American Jewish supporters, who could prove to be valuable allies. This combined strategy was foreshadowed before the 1976 elections, when Kissinger started making major appearances before Jewish audiences. Clearly, he was stung by the sharp Israeli and Jewish response to his 1975 six-month "reassessment" of U.S. policy in the Middle East, which followed the initial collapse of his Sinai II mediation effort. While an agreement was eventually signed on September 1, 1975, the "reassessment" marked one of the most acrimonious periods in American–Israeli relations, going back to 1948.

The "reassessment" represented a genuine watershed. The strains that developed still continue to have their impact today. It was during this crisis that Kissinger began his highly publicized sniping at Israel for allegedly standing in the way of an agreement. By legitimizing a policy of pressure against Israel, Kissinger also sought to intimidate American Jews into either abandoning their support of Israel or jeopardizing their reputations as informed and patriotic American leaders. Whenever the secretary of state publicly criticizes Israel, the Arabists in the State Department bureaucracy become emboldened and increase their condemnation of Israel's "intransigence." For instance, public criticism of Israel became politically chic during the "reassessment." Much of the erosion of Israeli support in the news media can be traced back to that period, when Kissinger put forward during his private briefings the intellectual justification for blaming Israel for the lack of progress toward Middle East peace. The phenomenon of a Jewish secretary of state telling non-Jews that one could criticize Israel without worrying about being called an anti-Semite continues to have its effects today.

But, however narrow the goals of Kissinger's sophisticated public relations campaign, and however transient he intended it to be, it later became a central feature of the Carter administration. President Carter followed Kissinger's lead when he candidly told *Time* magazine in August 1977 that he would try to stir public opinion to persuade Israel to accept the U.S. position at a reconvened Geneva peace conference. "I would try and marshall the support of the [Israeli] leader first of all; secondly, the opinion of his people back home, the constituencies that might exist in our country that would have influence around the world, opinion that exists in the European community and the Arab nations as well," Carter said. That approach, which is premised on Israel's sensitivity and vulnerability to American public opinion, was originally taken by Kissinger.

Carter did not go as far as incorporating Kissinger's use of U.S. economic and military assistance to Israel as additional leverage to drive home the point. Many friends of Israel, in their nostalgia for Kissinger, have either forgotten or were never aware of the fact that during the "reassessment" the United States refused to sign any new arms contracts with Israel; the administration, moreover, delayed for over six months the introduction of a new foreign aid bill to Congress. By then, Israel had become highly dependent on America's foreign aid, and the delay squeezed Israel tightly.

In dealing with Israel, Kissinger refined carrot-and-stick diplomacy to an advanced form. Whenever there was some flexibility by Israel, the

United States could reward the Israelis by providing some military assistance. In *White House Years*, Kissinger blamed the State Department for trying to keep Israel on a "short leash," but it seems more likely that he was the principal architect of that policy. (In fairness to Kissinger, however, it should be noted that Israel, under the governments of Golda Meir and Yitzhak Rabin, indirectly encouraged Kissinger to pursue that policy by itself often linking concessions to further arms supplies. This led many Israelis to twist Rabin's stated policy of "a piece of territory for a piece of peace" into "a piece of territory for a piece of military equipment.")

After being forced out of the Ford administration, former Defense Secretary James Schlesinger publicly characterized as unfair this treatment of a supposed friend and ally. Addressing the American Israel Public Affairs Committee in Washington on May 4, 1976, he did not mention Kissinger by name, but his target was nevertheless clear. He condemned a policy of forcing "one-sided" concessions upon Israel. He said it has led "to a condition which one describes as the Vietnamization of Israel." Noting Israel's need for extensive U.S. economic and military aid, he said: "I do not refer to this dependence that puts us in a position in which we can force concessions when I refer to the Vietnamization of Israel. Nor do I refer to the structure and language of communications to Prime Minister Rabin which is similar to the structure and language of communications to General Thieu in earlier times. The point that most concerns me is the undermining of the moral basis of support for the state of Israel. And that, of course, is reflected in parallel tactics that were employed in earlier times by us in our negotiations in Southeast Asia. There has been a tendency to place the blame for non-progress, slow progress of negotiations, on Israel, to assert that stagnation is bad, that momentum and progress are good, and that the failure to achieve momentum is a direct consequence of Israeli intransigence. The finger of blame has been pointed at Israel."

Largely because of the fallout from the "reassessment," especially the organized attacks against Kissinger by Israeli and American Jews, the secretary came to exaggerate the power of the so-called Jewish lobby. He personally resented the letter from seventy-six senators to President Ford during the "reassessment," calling for continued strong support of Israel. After that ordeal, he began to give the impression to Israeli visitors and American Jewish intellectuals that he knew what was best for Israel. In the first volume of his memoirs, Kissinger disclosed that President Nixon, in late 1969, wrote the following in longhand on a memorandum which Kissinger had prepared explaining King Hussein's pessimism in the face of Israel's tough stand: "I am beginning to think we have to consider taking strong steps unilaterally to save Israel from her own destruction." Yet Kissinger later seemed to move toward that same approach. He explained it this way in *White House Years*: "An Israeli cabinet meeting is well-suited to nitpicking peace proposals to death, less adapted to developing a long-range policy. Israel sometimes finds it easier to shift the responsibility for difficult choice to its great ally than to make the decision itself; 'American pressure' can be an excuse for what many Israeli leaders know in their hearts is necessary for Israel anyway."

Nixon disclosed on May 12, 1977, that the United States had to use "godfather" tactics to restrain Israel from destroying Egypt's Third Army during the final days of the 1973 Yom Kippur War. Kissinger was then both secretary of state and national security adviser. In an interview with David Frost, Nixon was asked how the United States had exerted pressure to prevent Israel from wiping out the encircled Third Army, which was then on the eastern bank of the Suez Canal. "We didn't put the Israelis in the spot where we were trying to threaten them, because they won't take it," the former president said. "I mean, they're not . . . they'll never take it. And we wouldn't put them in that spot. What we did was to reason with them, but to reason with them in a way—well, we in effect, if I may paraphrase from *The Godfather*, 'we gave 'em an offer they couldn't refuse.' " The former president said Israel "had insisted on capturing and destroying the Egyptian Third Army." Nixon said he rejected this Israeli demand because it would probably have brought about "a coup or worse as far as Sadat was concerned. Somebody would have come into power in Egypt, probably worse than Nasser—oriented toward the radical point of view. Egypt would have become a total Soviet satellite state, and Israel would have won a Pyrrhic victory."

Saul Bellow captured Kissinger's spirit in an article in *New Yorker* magazine during the summer of 1976. After interviewing Kissinger, Bellow offered these impressions: "He represents himself as a strong defender of Israel whose efforts are not appreciated. . . . The impression he wants to convey is that he has stood between Israel and its enemies in the American government. When he steps down, and he must step down soon, he will be missed by the very people who now assail him. Mr. Kissinger has the deftness of a master manipulator, but I feel his touch, subtle as it is. For what it may be worth, he wants to convince me of its warmth. In this warmth, however, there are icy spots—a scattering of threats which he perhaps has the habit of making when talking to American Jews: they had better understand that in letting themselves be used as lobbyists by Israel's leaders they are helping neither Israel nor themselves; in the disastrous event of Israel's defeat, they too will get it in the neck. So they had better stop making so much noise in Washington and undermining their chief protector, Henry Kissinger."

In analyzing Kissinger's comments on the Arab–Israeli conflict since leaving office, one should not lose sight of the fact that Kissinger apparently has been motivated to a great extent by a desire to erase some of the historic record and to return to the State Department. Seen from this perspective, his spate of very "pro-Israeli" statements (made without overly upsetting the Arabs) takes on a new light.

During his last year in office, Kissinger embarked on a determined drive to improve his image in Israel and in the American Jewish community. He tried to package himself as Israel's great friend. The first public demonstration came on May 9, 1976, when he addressed several hundred Jews at Baltimore's Chizuk Amuno Synagogue. "All of us who are friends of Israel and who are at the same time dedicated to further progress toward peace understand Israel's uncertainties—and at the same time we share her hope," he said. "There will be no imposed solutions; there should be negotiations between the parties that will eventually have to live in peace."

Kissinger's defense reached a new climax on January 11, 1977, after Carter had won the election but before the January 20 inauguration. The occasion was a rather moving if somewhat fulsome tribute to Kissinger by the Conference of Presidents of Major American Jewish Organizations. After being warmly praised by the conference's chairman, Rabbi Alexander Schindler, its immediate past chairman, Rabbi Israel Miller, and Israeli Ambassador Simcha Dinitz, Kissinger spoke of his relationship with Israel and the organized Jewish leadership in the United States. "From my point of view," he said, "probably no criticism has hurt me more than if it came from this community. And probably from your point of view, it was especially painful if disagreements occurred between the Jewish community and the first Jewish secretary of state in American history."

Speaking emotionally, Kissinger continued: "I have never forgotten that thirteen members of my family died in concentration camps, nor could I ever fail to remember what it was like to live in Nazi Germany as a member of a persecuted minority." And in concluding his remarks, he said: "The problems of security and of peace in the Middle East will be with us for as long as we can see. I will remain dedicated as a friend of Israel, and as a friend of this group, for as long as I live. And I want you to know that this meeting has meant a great deal to me. Throughout their history, Jews have been saying to themselves, 'Next year in Jerusalem.' I would like to think that sometime soon, we can say this in its deepest sense, in an Israel that is secure, that is accepted, that is at peace. And it will always mean a great deal to me to have worked with this group, and with my friends in Israel, to achieve this objective."

After leaving office, Kissinger initially adopted a low profile on the Middle East. His public comments were kept to a minimum. Even at a March 10, 1977, black-tie dinner at the Madison Hotel in Washington, when receiving an honorary doctorate from the Weizmann Institute of Science, Kissinger avoided any substantive or controversial comments. It was not until November 13 of that year, only days before Sadat stunned the world by announcing his decision to go to Jerusalem, that Kissinger broke his silence. The occasion was an American Jewish Congress dinner in New York honoring Golda Meir. "Given my own involvement in the conduct of foreign policy over eight years, I have thought it inappropriate since January to participate in a discussion of day-to-day tactics," he said. "But I would like to use this occasion to articulate a few general principles."

Kissinger included an impassioned statement of support for Israel. "No people have suffered more from the absence of peace than the people of Israel, every square mile of whose country is drenched with the blood of its pioneers and whose existence has never been recognized by any of its neighbors." His criticism of the Carter administration's policies, including the October 1, 1977, American–Soviet joint communiqué on the Middle East calling for a reconvened Geneva conference, was tempered and veiled. "My own acquaintance with President Carter, Secretary of State Vance, and their senior advisers convinces me that this administration would not deliberately put Israel's security at risk. But there is always the danger that actions undertaken in good faith may inadvertently produce unforeseen consequences. If such a miscalculation took place, either Israel would become totally isolated or diplomacy would become abruptly deadlocked." Kissinger insisted that the "art of diplomacy is to move events carefully and shape them toward achievable ends so that neither the United States nor Israel ever face such a stark, impossible choice."

At the dinner, Kissinger obliquely challenged the Carter administration's then prevalent "comprehensive" approach toward resolving the Arab–Israeli conflict at a full-scale Geneva conference with Soviet participation. "An overall solution is, of course, the ultimate prize," he said. "But realism forces us to recognize that to achieve it involves issues of enormous complexity and parties with an unequal commitment to peace. It also requires a process that is bound to be protracted. Thus, while striving for an overall settlement, we must take care not to foreclose other opportunities that may arise to ease tensions and to enable the peoples of the area to build confidence. We must not give a veto to the most intransigent elements within the area. We must not permit outside powers to emerge as the advocates for a point of view that penalizes moderation."

In *White House Years*, Kissinger maintained that he "always opposed" comprehensive solutions because he felt they would be rejected by Israel and the Arab states, and would "only serve Soviet ends by either demonstrating our impotence or being turned into a showcase of what could be exacted by Moscow's pressure. My aim was to produce a stalemate until

Moscow urged compromise or until, even better, some moderate Arab regime decided that the route to progress was through Washington." Kissinger pointed out that "America's ace in the hole was that if we played our cards right, we could produce tangible progress in diplomacy while the Soviets could promise only help in war."

Today's conventional wisdom has it that Kissinger would have continued his step-by-step diplomacy in the Middle East if Ford had been reelected in 1976. By earlier having avoided the illusive search for a "comprehensive" agreement, Kissinger had successfully nurtured two partial Israeli accords with Egypt and an Israeli–Syrian disengagement-of-forces agreement on the Golan Heights following the 1973 war. The two agreements with Egypt did indeed represent the precursor of the Israeli–Egyptian Peace Treaty, yet Kissinger would probably also have fallen into the simplistic but intellectually enticing trap of reaching for the entire pot of gold during the first year of a presidential administration, when domestic pressures from the Jewish community are weakest. This was the approach recommended by the Brookings Institution report in December 1975; it was based on the belief that the United States should not waste its leverage on Israel in the search for "only" another "step," but should go for the whole thing.

Thus, throughout much of 1976, Kissinger harped on the theme that peace between Israel and its Arab neighbors was within sight. "Endless conflict will have profound consequences for the peoples involved and profound global consequences, and, therefore, I believe that the parties are now more ready and conditions more ripe for a significant effort for peace than has been the case for a long time," he told a Brussels news conference on December 10, 1976, after Carter had been elected. Two and a half months earlier, on September 29, he told eighteen Arab ambassadors and foreign ministers at a UN luncheon that that "conditions now exist that make comprehensive solutions a useful approach" in the Middle East. He said the United States believes that the search for peace "can be resumed with energy and conviction, and we hope that significant progress can be made in the months ahead." The Middle East, he added, was "closer to the goal of peace than at any time in a generation." Kissinger had said in May: "The Middle East today is at a moment of unprecedented opportunity. We do not underestimate the dilemmas and risks that Israel faces in a negotiation. But they are dwarfed by a continuation of the status quo."

The belief that an all-out push would have come under Kissinger in 1977 was buttressed by the fact that Ford was also talking about "comprehensive" agreements in 1976. In May, he said the United States has "gone about as far as we can in the step-by-step process," and the time has come "to be doing some serious talking about a broader settlement—and that, of course, means peace and recognition of Israel." It seems unlikely that Ford would have made that comment without clearing it with Kissinger.

Kissinger has been consistent in opposing the creation of an independent Palestinian state on the West Bank and Gaza. He has always advocated an Israeli agreement with Jordan as an alternative. "When I was in office and after, I have never believed, and I do not believe now, that the solution to the West Bank problem can be the creation of a Palestinian state," he said on May 7, 1980, at a dinner sponsored by B'nai B'rith's Anti-Defamation League. He said he had signed the September 1, 1975, American–Israeli Memorandum of Agreement, which stipulated that the United States would not recognize or negotiate with the PLO until the PLO accepted UN Security Council Resolutions 242 and 338 and Israel's right to exist, because that represented U.S. policy. "That promise was not made as a favor to Israel; it did not result from an attempt to placate any group in this country. That statement arose from our conviction that the settlement on the West Bank must be one that includes Arabs who want to work for peace and not the most intransigent group that cannot possibly be satisfied—no matter what its proclamations—with what is achievable."

Kissinger also rejected any connection between the Arab–Israeli conflict and the supply of Arab oil to the United States. "I think it is in the American interest to separate the oil problem as much as possible from any political negotiation. I think the more we involve the oil issue or the more we talk ourselves into involving the oil issue in these negotiations, the more—paradoxically—we undermine the position of the moderate elements, even in the Arab world. Because, if we affirm the connection, they cannot resist the linkage. And they will not be able to oppose those radical elements who have always advocated an explicit linkage between oil and a settlement."

But Kissinger was saying the same thing while in office, even as his actions and policies often conveyed different impressions. His willingness to provide vast arms supplies to Saudi Arabia, for instance, immediately following its participation in the Arab oil embargo against the United States, combined with the widely held perception that the United States was pressuring Israel into making concessions because of America's oil interests, merely stoked Arab self-confidence in their oil card and intensified their sense that economic, military, and diplomatic trends were on their side. It must be recalled that the PLO emerged as an important political factor only following the 1973–74 oil embargo. The Rabat Summit Conference declaring the PLO the "sole, legitimate" representative of the Palestinians was in October 1974. A month later, Arafat addressed the UN General Assembly. The PLO was rewarded in November 1975 with "the Saunders document," which had the United States, for the first time, move toward the Arab perception of the Palestinian question. "In many ways, the Palestinian dimension of the Arab–Israel conflict is the heart of that conflict," Deputy Assistant Secretary of State for Near Eastern and South Asian Affairs Harold Saunders told a House Foreign Affairs sub-committee. Saunders was one of Kissinger's most trusted aides; he was moved from the National Security Council to the State Department after Kissinger had made the move himself. Kissinger later informed Ambassador Dinitz that he had only looked briefly at the document, but, according to Saunders, Kissinger had personally edited two initial drafts and cleared the final version. It was the first time that the United States had officially diverged from the concept that the Palestinian problem was largely one involving refugees, as advanced in Security Council Resolution 242.

Still, it is Kissinger's continued ability to influence policy years after he has left office that is truly remarkable. Although one of Nixon's most important advisers, he emerged from Watergate virtually unscathed, and his reputation still remains extremely high today and will no doubt remain so, irrespective of whether there is a Democrat or a Republican presence in the White House.

11

Jimmy Carter
and Camp David

From Thurmont, Maryland, the road uncoils for seven miles up the Catoctin Mountains, through virgin forests, to Camp David, the presidential retreat, sixty miles or a thirty-minute helicopter ride from the White House. There, behind the electronically monitored barbed-wire fences of the heavily guarded 143-acre compound, President Jimmy Carter asked Prime Minister Menachem Begin and President Anwar Sadat to sign the traditional guest book at Aspen Lodge, the main residence. In the lodge perched atop a high peak, the three leaders looked out of a large window to see what earlier guests had described as a breathtaking view of northern Maryland. Sadat was familiar with the panorama and the oak-paneled room with a stone fireplace. He was the only foreign leader to have met earlier with Carter at Camp David; he and his family spent a weekend there as Carter's guests in February 1978.

Since the day of Franklin Roosevelt, presidents have been escaping from Washington to Camp David. At that time, the place was not called Camp David; Roosevelt had dubbed it Shangri-La, more poetic than Hi-Catoctin, its original name when built in 1937. In April 1942, after Roosevelt, seeking a secluded area outside Washington, selected Camp Hi-Catoctin for his retreat, the entire area was declared a security zone, and officials from the Office of Strategic Services (OSS), the predecessor of the CIA, and marines were stationed there. Construction of the main lodge and other work required to support the president were completed that summer.

Harry Truman hardly used the camp, preferring a Key West, Florida, retreat. But Dwight Eisenhower fell in love with it when he visited it shortly

217

after his inauguration in 1953. He quickly renamed it Camp David in honor of his grandson David Eisenhower, who nearly two decades later honeymooned there with his wife, Julie Nixon. She called it a "resort hotel where you are the only guests."

Eisenhower recuperated from his heart attack there late in 1955. After Camp David underwent major renovations in 1957 and 1959, Eisenhower invited several foreign leaders there including British Prime Minister Harold Macmillan, Mexican President Adolfo López Mateos, French President Charles de Gaulle, and Soviet Premier Nikita Khrushchev.

John F. Kennedy did not use Camp David frequently. He was in the process of building a separate retreat in Virginia when he realized that Camp David was there for his exclusive use.

When Lyndon Johnson became president, his ranch in Texas was too far away for regular visits. He resumed the practice of receiving foreign guests at Camp David, entertaining Canadian Prime Minister Lester Pearson in 1965 and Australian Prime Minister Harold Holt in 1967.

Camp David was used even more frequently by Richard Nixon, who drafted many of his speeches there. During the Watergate era, he spent many hours in front of the massive fireplace in his favorite armchair, with legal pad and pencil, trying to devise explanations for the crisis. During his first term, Nixon made nearly 120 trips to Camp David. He refurbished Aspen Lodge. Among his foreign guests were Tito, Pompidou, Brandt, Medici, Echeverria, Heath, Houphouet-Boigny, Ceausescu, and Brezhnev.

Gerald Ford met with only one foreign leader at Camp David: Indonesia's President Suharto. Ford used the site frequently for his personal pleasure, as did Carter.

It was at Camp David ten days before Secretary of State Cyrus Vance went to Egypt and Israel in early August 1978 with Carter's handwritten invitations that the president assembled his top foreign policy aides for a brainstorming session which resulted in the idea for the trilateral summit. Carter often assembled his cabinet and other advisers for meetings in the relaxed Maryland atmosphere.

Physically, the site has many diversions. In the surrounding woods are deer, raccoon, bluejays, snowbirds, and woodpeckers. For relaxation, there is a heated swimming pool, a sauna, two tennis courts, a bowling alley, a trout stream, movie facilities, and so on. There are eleven residence cabins, including Aspen Lodge. The interiors of all the cabins are similar: stone fireplaces, exposed heavy beams, and a generally rustic atmosphere. But make no mistake about it—it is a plush rustic. No one at Camp David has to rough it. The cabins have such sylvan names as Witch Hazel, Birch, Dogwood, and Maple. The dining room is named Laurel, and smaller cabins, used for conferences, are named Hawthorne, Walnut, Sycamore, Linden, Red Oak, and Hemlock.

About 100 Navy personnel and marines are permanently stationed at Camp David, although their number was considerably augmented during the peace conference. Security was extremely tight. Even the main roadway leading to Camp David was blocked off.

The only danger to Carter and his guests was from poison ivy. Vance was its victim during his earlier visit there just before he went off to the Middle East.

The first time the assembled journalists, photographers, and television technicians were allowed into this tightly guarded mountain retreat actually to see Carter, Begin, and Sadat together was on Thursday evening, September 7, at a forty-five-minute sunset U.S. Marine dress parade. The only evidence before then that the three leaders were in fact meeting jointly was the series of official White House photographs released to the press.

At the end of the impressive ceremony—attended by all the members of the three countries' official delegations, the families of some of the marines based at Camp David, and about seventy invited representatives of an increasingly frustrated media starving for some hard news—Sadat, Begin, and Carter were asked to sign a thick red book presented to them by the marine commander.

Carter wrote: "You all made our country proud." Sadat's inscription was: "It was wonderful." And Begin jotted down, in very small writing: "It was a great performance of a great army. In deep appreciation for the famous Marines." Those who pay attention to the little things here pointed out that Sadat used only three words, Carter used six, while Begin used sixteen. Perhaps it was indicative of the different styles of the three leaders. It certainly highlighted Begin's well-known respect for the written word. And it also reflected their approach to the negotiations at the extraordinary summit.

Begin meticulously scrutinized every word under consideration. While both Carter and Sadat also carefully studied the language in early drafts, they were not as intricately fixated on every potential interpretation of each word.

There were many meetings in Camp David, comprising virtually every possible combination of leaders and aides. The informal, relaxed atmosphere was conducive to the development of as much personal contact between the visiting Israeli and Egyptian officials as possible. It enabled them to explore as many options as could be devised during the talks, on the spot, or beforehand, when the three delegations made their preparations for the conference.

Those who were in close contact with Begin during the Camp David summit agreed that he appeared to be in relatively good physical health. And this factor apparently had a positive impact on the course of the summit. The prime minister's state of health was one of the things helping him to rethink some of Israel's earlier positions in the difficult search for peace in the Middle East. The theory was that Begin was more willing to risk political opposition from the right wing of his Likud party when he felt strong and healthy. When he was tired and sick, the prime minister was reluctant to take bold new steps.

At Camp David, Defense Minister Ezer Weizman and Foreign Minister Moshe Dayan were instrumental in convincing Begin to swallow some of the once unacceptable—even unthinkable—code words and catch phrases of the tired diplomacy of the Arab–Israeli conflict so that Egypt might make peace with Israel. If Weizman and Dayan had not participated in the thirteen-day ordeal at President Carter's retreat, there would have been no agreement.

Weizman came to Camp David convinced that Sadat was sincere in his quest for peace. The defense minister, who before Camp David had spent more time with the Egyptian leader than any other Israeli, had felt for some time that Egypt would be prepared to make a deal with Israel if only Israel would offer some "words" to help Sadat deal with the internal pressures of the Arab world. Several top U.S. officials agreed with the defense minister. But Weizman's rosy assessment had been challenged for months by Begin and Dayan, both of whom were much less certain of Sadat's intentions. They called Weizman naive.

But Weizman was far from naive. He correctly understood the implications of Sadat's journey to Jerusalem in November 1977. Sadat had come to make peace with Israel on some reasonable basis, even if he had to do it alone. At the time, Sadat was accused by much of the Arab world of accepting the principle of a separate deal with Israel. He, of course, denied it. The Americans also insisted publicly that Sadat had no such plan; he would only sign a peace treaty with Israel once a comprehensive accord involving all the Arab states as well as the Palestinians had been resolved. The Egyptian assertions were repeated so often that most observers of the Middle East scene began to believe them.

Weizman wanted to finish what Sadat had started when he visited Jerusalem. But Weizman needed a strong ally in the cabinet, someone who could influence the prime minister to grasp Israel's greatest opportunity ever to make peace with an Arab state. Despite the severe strain in their personal relations, the defense minister knew that only Dayan could do that. Dayan would have to be convinced that Sadat was sincere.

This became one of Carter's first objectives at Camp David. He suspected his job of getting Begin to budge would be easier with Dayan's backing. Dayan's influence over Begin had been demonstrated to the Americans in the past; they recalled his decisive role during the October 1977 talks leading to the American–Israeli "working paper" on the Geneva conference. Dayan successfully negotiated the terms of the conference with the Americans and then sold them to Begin.

The best way to win his support at Camp David was to have the Egyptians, including Sadat himself, woo Dayan, to show him that real peace between the two countries was not only possible but actually at hand. Going into the summit, Sadat had declined to agree to meet alone with Dayan, and the foriegn minister, a sensitive man, resented this. Both Weizman and the Americans asked Sadat early during the summit to agree to meet with Dayan in private. Such a session could move Dayan in the right direction, the Egyptian leader was told.

Sadat spent a few days at Camp David mulling it over, and he finally agreed. The initial chat between Dayan and Sadat nine days into the conference was a critical factor in moving the foreign minister closer to the views of Weizman. Dayan later told me this. By the time the final draft of the agreements regarding the framework for an Israeli–Egyptian peace treaty and the framework for achieving peace in the Middle East had been accepted by both sides, Begin had indeed accepted some new "words" which he once considered anathema, words he would not have been likely to accept without the concurrence of Dayan.

The prime minister later tried to deny it, but he had clearly moved from some of his earlier ideological principles. Specifically, Israel recognized "the legitimate rights of the Palestinian people." Israel agreed that the Palestinian problem had to be resolved "in all its aspects." Not later than three years after the creation of the Palestinian "self-governing authority" on the West Bank and Gaza, Israel would have to agree to begin negotiations with Jordan, Egypt, and the Palestinians to "determine the final status" of these areas. (Earlier, Israel had maintained that such discussions could take place only after a five-year transition period.)

The negotiations involving the future of these areas "shall be based on all the provisions and principles of UN Security Council Resolution 242," one clause of which calls for "withdrawal" from territories.

For someone like Begin, who had always believed in the power of words, acceptance was no easy matter. But while Weizman and Dayan differed in many areas, neither was nearly as ideologically oriented as Begin. They were practical men who wanted to know how the meaning of the words would be translated on the ground. What does it mean to recognize "the legitimate rights of the Palestinian people"? They developed the concept that the agreements could incorporate such "unpleasant" language if other clauses clearly defined what would occur. There would have to be built-in constraints on the words. And herein lay the beauty of the truly imaginative language drafted into the documents. While on the one hand it allowed Sadat to assert that he had not forfeited "one inch" of Arab land or sovereignty, it also enabled Begin to declare that Israel had not agreed to withdraw from Judea and Samaria.

Carter and his team of advisers, especially Secretary of State Vance, must be given a large measure of the credit for the strategy that resulted in success at Camp David. Delicate U.S. prodding of both Begin and Sadat never ceased during the summit; but it never went too far either, beyond the point either man could not tolerate. It was always finely balanced, interspersed with just enough ego stroking to encourage tractability.

The Americans had done their homework. In advance of the talks, the president received a lengthy psychological profile of both Sadat and Begin from the CIA. Experts there had been conducting a running study of the men's characters and minds. If the Egyptian and Israeli leaders were to be budged, the Americans felt, it was necessary to understand exactly what made them tick.

Everyone recognized that the first few days would not be easy for anyone. But thanks to Carter's wife, Rosalynn, the talks did get off on the right foot. She had correctly recognized that the three leaders had one common thread running between them: their deeply held religious convictions. Religion played an important role in the lives of all three men, but Sadat was probably the most religious. He was almost mystical in his devotion to God. Recognizing the intensity of the Egyptian leader's religious beliefs, the First Lady suggested to her husband that the three leaders begin the conference with a joint statement, asking for the world's prayers during the coming days as they searched for peace in the Middle East. Carter thought the idea was good.

On Tuesday evening, September 5, just hours after Begin's helicopter touched down near the football field at Camp David, Carter asked him for his reaction to such a joint prayer. Begin loved the idea. The prime minister quickly realized that any joint statement signed by the three leaders, no matter what the subject, had significant political implications. The next morning, Carter sat down with Sadat, who readily agreed. For months, Sadat had been talking of building a mosque, a church, and a synagogue atop Mt. Sinai as a tribute to the three religions. The joint prayer neatly fit into his overall scheme of things.

By the end of the conference the three men had progressed from an agreement to pray together to an agreement to make peace once and for all. There were moments during the ordeal when things looked bleak. Moods of euphoria were followed by severe depression as the wide gaps separating the two sides seemed irreconcilable. Officials referred to the "roller coaster" atmosphere at Camp David, the ups and downs of summit diplomacy.

But there was a happy ending to the drama, only bits and pieces of which were released to the outside world while it was taking place. Everyone in the three delegations had reason to be happy; historians would one day refer to the Camp David experience as one of those watersheds in world history. But the two happiest men were probably Carter and Weizman; they had pushed the hardest for success. They wanted success more than any of the other personalities who had gathered at the summit. For Weizman, the achievement of a peace treaty with Egypt had dominated his actions and thinking ever since he first met Sadat. He did not want Israel to have to go to war ever again; a son had been badly injured along the Suez Canal. Carter was putting his political reputation on the line. If the summit ended badly, he would be accused of recklessly ruining the prestige of the U.S. presidency. His political opponents would jump all over him; his standing in the public opinion polls, already very low, would further plummet. He was determined to win and did not give up until 5:00 P.M. on Sunday, September 17, when his aides' thumbs went up.

Later that evening, when Carter told the world that the achievements at Camp David had exceeded "any expectations," he was not exaggerating. No one really thought that they would see the three leaders sign formal documents heralding a new era of peace in the Middle East. Only the naive "optimists" had expected to see Camp David result in much more than the resolution of a few of the difficult issues followed by a willingness to continue negotiations. "Realists" had predicted it would be a waste of time.

With hindsight, however, maybe we should not have been so surprised. Three years earlier, on September 1, 1975, Egypt similarly signed a separate agreement with Israel, the Sinai II accord. At the time, Sadat was vilified by much of the Arab world as a "traitor." He was accused of "selling out." But Sadat resisted the onslaught. Most of his Arab colleagues eventually came to accept his decision, and this appears to explain, at least partially, why Sadat decided to sign these new "framework" agreements. The Egyptian leader, according to his aides, was confident that the "sensible" Arab leaders, especially in Jordan and Saudi Arabia, would accept the agreements. But first, the United States was going to have to lean on both Amman and Riyadh.

Washington was going to have to tell King Hussein in no uncertain terms that a refusal by Jordan to participate in the talks would severely affect American–Jordanian relations. King Hussein, whose country was dependent on the United States for economic and military support, was going to have to think very hard before saying no to the president of the United States. The same went for the Saudis. They were not about to exit from the American camp. The survival of the Saudi monarchy was a function of the continued protection of America's nuclear umbrella.

There was a coincidence of interests among Israel, Egypt, Jordan, and Saudi Arabia; they each wanted to keep Soviet influence in the Middle East to a minimum. That strategic consideration was important. But so were the more narrow parochial issues of the Arab–Israeli conflict.

During the 1976 presidential campaign, Jimmy Carter had made believers out of many skeptics in the United States, especially within the American Jewish community. Having wrapped up the Democratic presidential nomination several weeks before the party convention in New York, the former Georgia governor began uniting the party around him. People in Washington smelled a winner and were quickly lining up to join the Carter administration. The academics, the Wall Street lawyers, the traditional party hacks, and many others were vying for the good jobs that would open up after the elections. Carter and his aides knew it and were moving cautiously. Attention focused on who would get those key spots.

For Israel, the answer was crucial; 1977 would be a critical year in Middle East diplomacy. The foreign policy team Carter assembled could make a difference, but the people surrounding Carter made the point that the candidate was taking one step at a time, that though names had been gathered and considered no decisions regarding these positions had then been made.

When Carter took office on January 20, 1977, it was impossible to figure out the future direction of U.S. policy in the Middle East. Despite the seemingly fast-moving developments (Secretary of State Vance headed for the region in February, and visits to Washington by Israeli and Arab leaders were to follow), no one in Washington, including top State Department experts on the Middle East, had a very clear impression about how the new president eventually planned to proceed. U.S. officials said they had not received any substantive policy directives on the Middle East from either Carter or Vance. Therefore, the State Department continued to react to Middle East developments as if there had been no change in presidential administrations. Since no specific guidance came down from the top, Middle East experts conducted policy as they had during the Ford–Kissinger era.

Sources in the new administration insisted that there would not be any new guidelines issued until after Vance had a chance to assess the thinking in the region and probably not until after Carter had met personally with visiting Arab and Israeli leaders. American officials denied that the Vance journey and the subsequent Arab and Israeli visits to Washington were designed only to win some time before Israel's May 17 general elections. But they did not deny that there were practical benefits to be gained by a delay in any announced change of direction.

Indeed, many Americans were convinced that significant progress in the negotiations was impossible in advance of the Israeli elections. The Carter administration would nevertheless want to be as ready as possible for real progress shortly after a new Israeli government had been assembled. And prior consultations with the various Middle East parties as well as with other interested parties, such as the Soviet Union, were seen as necessary for laying the groundwork.

A complicating factor for the Carter team had been the unexpected economic and food riots in Egypt, the most violent since the 1952 revolution. President Sadat, expected in Washington early in the spring, had suffered both within Egypt and in the Arab world because of the unrest. American experts did not believe that Sadat's regime was actually in any imminent danger of being overthrown, but the situation remained tense, and the United States was closely monitoring developments.

While Carter sought to convey the impression that he would be changing U.S. policy in many domestic and some foreign areas, he left the initial impression of continuity of U.S. policy vis-à-vis the Middle East. The transition of power in Washington resulted in a new top leadership, but when it came to the Middle East most of the second-line positions remained in the same hands.

Did Carter revive the Rogers Plan at his March 8, 1977, news conference and his March 16 town meeting at Clinton, Massachusetts, during which he spelled out in considerable detail his views on the Arab–Israeli settlement? The president's plan closely resembled the December 1975 Brookings Institution blueprint "Towards Peace in the Middle East," but there were conflicting assessments of whether or not Carter brought back to life elements of the Rogers Plan, a plan, it should be recalled, that had been rejected by both Israel and the Arab states. There were those who insisted that Carter's views did not represent much of a departure from the Rogers Plan, though a careful rereading of the two proposals demonstrates that there were some differences.

What came to be known as the Rogers Plan had been born on December 9, 1969, less than one year after President Richard Nixon took office, when Secretary of State William P. Rogers delivered a public adress under the title "A Lasting Peace in the Middle East: An American View." Rogers began by stressing that a peace settlement in the Middle East was crucial: "There is no area of the world today that is more important, because it could easily again be the source of another serious conflagration." Later, Carter would go a step further, warning that the Middle East is "such a crucial area of the world" that a new war there "would quickly spread to all the other nations of the world—very possibly it could be that."

Rogers insisted that only the parties themselves could negotiate a durable peace settlement. "The efforts of major powers can help, they can provide a catalyst, they can stimulate the parties to talk, they can encourage, they can help define a realistic framework for agreement—but an agreement among other powers cannot be a substitute for agreement among the parties themselves." Carter said more than seven years later that only the Arab states and Israel could work out an overall solution. "I want to emphasize one more time—we offer our good offices. . . . We'll have to act as a kind of catalyst to bring about their ability to negotiate successfully with one another."

The former secretary of state, again foreshadowing the Carter aproach taken a few years later, pointed out that the Arabs would have to agree to peace with Israel, and Israel would have to withdraw roughly to the pre-1967 lines. But Carter went considerably beyond any previous U.S. statesman in accepting Israel's definition of peace as more than a simple cessation of armed conflict. Carter said that there would have to be agreement on "the right of Israel to exist in peace—the opening up of borders with free trade, tourist travel, cultural exchange between Israel and her neighbors"—in other words, a stabilization of the situation in the Middle East without a constant threat to Israel's existence.

While Rogers had not gone that far in his speech, his plan did portend a U.S. insistence on an expanded definition of peace. "Our policy is to encourage the Arabs to accept a permanent peace based on a binding agreement. . . . We believe the conditions and obligations of peace must be defined in specific terms. For example, navigation rights in the Suez Canal and in the Strait of Tiran should be spelled out. Respect for sovereignty and obligations of the parties to each other must be made specific." Rogers continued: "But peace, of course, involves much more than this. It is also a matter of the attitudes and intentions of the parties. Are they ready to coexist with one another? Can a live-and-let-live attitude replace suspicion, mistrust, and hate? A peace agreement between the parties must be based on clear and stated intentions and a willingness to bring about basic changes in the attitudes and conditions which are characteristic of the Middle East today."

Another difference between the Rogers Plan and the Carter proposal centered around Carter's recognition of the need for Israeli defense lines beyond its legal borders. It is accurate to say that Carter went beyond Rogers in outlining this need. But, as Carter would do later, Rogers did stress the need for Israel to have special security arrangements attached to any overall settlement. "A lasting peace must be sustained by a sense of security on both sides," Rogers said. "To this end, as envisaged in the Security Council resolution [242], there should be demilitarized zones and related security arrangements more reliable than those which existed in the area in the past. The parties themselves . . . are in the best position to work out the nature and details of such security arrangements. It is, after all, their interests which are at stake and their territory which is involved. They must live with the results."

The similarity between the two plans that was the most objectionable from Israel's point of view was that both presumed that Israel withdraw roughly to the 1967 lines. Carter conceded that there should be only "some minor adjustments" in those borders. Rogers said that any changes "should be confined to insubstantial alterations required for mutual security."

So, if there were so many similarities, where were the differences? Perhaps the major change in U.S. thinking that took place over that seven-year period between the proposal of each of the plans involved the Palestinian question. When Rogers spoke, he said there were four major issues that had to be resolved: "peace, security, withdrawal, and territory." He relegated the Palestinian question, along with the status of Jerusalem, to a secondary category that would have to be taken up only after these four major items were resolved. "It is our hope that agreement on the key issues of peace, security, withdrawal, and territory will create a climate in which these questions of refugees and of Jerusalem, as well as other aspects of the conflict, can be resolved as part of an overall settlement."

Carter redefined the key issues somewhat. In Clinton and elsewhere, he listed three ultimate requirements for peace: Arab acceptance of Israel, Israeli withdrawal, and a solution to "the Palestinian question." Thus, over the years, the Palestinian question moved up a notch to become one of the key issues.

It was also interesting to note that when Rogers discussed the Palestinian question, it was clear that a solution would have to be worked out between Israel and Jordan; those were in the pre-Rabat Conference days. There was no talk of a Palestinian homeland. It was merely a matter of resolving a refugee problem.

During his first year in the White House, Carter was remarkably consistent in his Middle East policy positions, despite what appeared to have been a rather pro-Israeli tilt during the final weeks of the 1976 presidential campaign. On substantive issues, his positions remained virtually the same, even though they were phrased with different emphases at different times.

Carter had devoted much of his time to learning about the Arab-Israeli conflict once he embarked on his long road to the White House in 1975. And he developed a kind of expertise in the diplomatic nuances of the problem. It was overly simplistic to claim, as some did, that National

Security Adviser Zbigniew Brzezinski or any others were responsible for Carter's positions.

Carter believed that the formulations he came up with—including the need for full peace, a resolution of the Palestinian problem, and an Israeli withdrawal from most of the territories captured in 1967—were fair, balanced, and reasonable. He held these views for a long time. In fact, he had entered the White House on January 20, 1977, with his mind pretty well made up on these issues.

Early in the campaign, Carter spoke about the need for Israel "ultimately" to withdraw "toward the 1967 boundaries." On another occasion, early in 1976, he said, "I think, ultimately, a final solution may very well entail a withdrawal of Israel basically to the 1967 boundaries."

On the Palestinian question, his early statements showed this same consistency. His first Middle East position paper stipulated that a final peace settlement will probably involve "the recognition of the Palestinian people as a nation." He said, "The rights of Palestinians must also be recognized as part of any solution." In an interivew with *The New York Times* on April 2, 1976, he said, "I would not recognize the Palestinians as a political entity—nor their leaders—until after those leaders had first recognized Israel's right to exist." He said that if the Palestinians were granted territory by Israel, he would prefer that "it would be on the West Bank of the Jordan, administered by the nation of Jordan."

In January 1976, Carter said: "When we get down to the last stages of solving the Middle Eastern question . . . the recognition of the Palestinians as an entity, with a right to have their own nation, to choose their own government, to exist in a territory possibly on the West Bank and possibly on the East Bank and Jordan, is an integral part of that ultimate settlement." He said Palestinians should have a place they could call home. During the final weeks of the campaign, Carter took his forthright position stressing the need for a full peace.

After taking office, the president retained these same fundamental positions. The Arabs would have to make real peace with Israel, including open borders, full diplomatic relations, commercial ties, communications, tourism, and so on. Carter went beyond any of his predecessors in expanding this definition of peace. Israel would have to withdraw to the pre-1967 borders, with only "minor adjustments" to be negotiated by the parties. And the Palestinians would need some sort of "homeland or entity," which, preferably, would have formal association with Jordan.

In expressing his views publicly on these three core issues, Carter and his aides sought to outline the general framework for a settlement in order to stimulate Israel and the Arabs to abandon what Washington regarded as their worn-our formulas of the past. The president decided to go public because he had been very disappointed in the views expressed by Prime Minister Yitzhak Rabin during his March 1977 visit to Washington. Carter's March 9 press conference statements, which amounted to the first detailed U.S. blueprint for peace in the Middle East since the Rogers Plan of 1969, were made while Rabin was still in Washington but after he had concluded his talks with Carter. The president privately complained that Rabin had only wanted to talk about "history" and had not given him anything to take to the Arabs to get the negotiating process under way.

In subsequent talks with Anwar Sadat of Egypt, King Hussein of Jordan, Hafez Assad of Syria, and Crown Prince Fahd of Saudi Arabia, the president felt that the Arab leaders had gone further in expressing a willingness to negotiate peace with Israel, including acceptance of concrete acts leading toward a normalization of relations, than Rabin had gone in expressing a readiness for territorial withdrawal. Unlike Rabin, the Arabs did not dwell upon history. They told Carter that they merely wanted their territory back and were prepared to live in peace with Israel. To Carter, the Arabs seemed reasonable.

Prime Minister Begin knew that the president's publicly stated "framework" for peace did not merely represent the positions of Carter and his top foreign policy advisers. It also represented the views of the foreign policy elite in the U.S. government. Since the 1967 war, Israel's information and diplomatic campaign was unsuccessful in convincing this elite that Israel had a right to demand more than minor changes in the 1967 line. The Democratic administration of President Lyndon Johnson, immediately after the 1967 war, took the position that Israel would eventually have to withdraw from nearly all of the territories; the Republican administrations of Richard Nixon and Gerald Ford followed suit; the Democratic administration of Jimmy Carter and finally the Republican team of Ronald Reagan did the same. A governmental consensus on borders existed in Washington; the Americans opposed substantial territorial adjustments beyond the 1967 lines. There was no official support for Israel's retaining large chunks of the West Bank, Gaza, or the Golan Heights.

Former Secretary of State Henry Kissinger, who did not publicly talk about the 1967 lines, did not conceal his views in private conversations, even with Israeli leaders. He, too, said that an overall settlement would involve withdrawals from Sinai, the Golan Heights, the Gaza Strip, and the West Bank, virtually to the 1967 lines. That was why he argued for the step-by-step approach; it would temporarily delay the need for Israel to go back to those lines. Rabin understood and appreciated this position when he proposed to Kissinger and Ford in January 1976 that Israel and the Arab states limit their expectations to an agreement calling for something less than real peace, a deal ending only the state of war. The prime minister and his cabinet understood that such a limited deal would naturally preclude returning to the 1967 lines. Kissinger and Ford accepted the idea and tried to sell it to the Arab states. Interestingly, neither Egypt, Jordan, nor Syria rejected the proposal during preliminary consultations in 1976. But then the U.S. election campaign started. Carter won, and the scenario was dropped by the new administration.

After taking office, Carter called only for a comprehensive settlement. The time for step-by-step diplomacy had passed, he said repeatedly. An overall settlement, to be implemented incrementally over several years, was the only viable option. Some of the more skeptical voices in the State Department cautioned that the door to additional partial accords should not be closed completely. But those voices were muted as the new president optimistically spoke about 1977 as the year of peace.

But, by the middle of that first summer in office, even the president, Brzezinski, and other former believers in the comprehensive approach were beginning to have some second thoughts, although they did not express them publicly. With the election of the Likud, the gap in positions between Israel and the Arab states widened. But no one in Washington wanted to see a diplomatic failure, and an effort to find a suitable alternative was under some consideration.

When Prime Minister Begin arrived in Washington in July 1977, he quickly discovered that he and the president each had an important interest in giving the impression that their talks would succeed. Begin was anxious to reassure his Israeli constituency that he could get along with Washington. Similarly, Carter wanted to show American friends of Israel that he was not tilting against Israel in favor of the Arab cause.

The White House was not pleased by the American Jewish reaction to the president's positions on the Middle East. White House aides Robert Lipshutz and Stuart Eizenstat, both of whom were Jewish and served as informal liaisons with the American Jewish leadership, felt that U.S. supporters of Israel had been unfair in their criticism.

Brzezinksi believed that he had been made a "target" because he was supposedly responsible for some of the president's unpopular positions on borders and Palestinians. Sensitive to the accusations being hurled against him in private, much as Kissinger used to feel, Brzezinski went out of his way to try to correct this impression. For example, he made an impassioned statement of support for Israel during a closed-door meeting with some forty-five American Jewish leaders at the White House in early July 1977. "The American commitment to Israel is based on a fundamental moral issue," a participant at the meeting quoted Brzezinski as saying. "To betray Israel would be to betray ourselves." He also said that the United States would not "threaten Israel's security" in order to attain its objectives. "We will not use security leverage even if we disagree with Israel's position."

In seeking to show success in the Begin talks, the president was also interested in having the Arabs perceive that the diplomatic option, as compared to the military option, could continue. So, both Begin and Carter tried to convey the impression of total harmony, at least in public. Privately, there was some tough talk, as confirmed in Carter's memoirs.

The president and his top foreign policy advisers, in advance of the summit, let it be known that they would not be happy to hear only Begin's vague generalities about Israel's readiness to negotiate without preconditions on the basis of UN Security Council Resolutions 242 and 338. Carter wanted to hear Begin state that Israel would in fact make territorial concessions "on all three fronts," meaning Sinai, the Golan Heights, and the West Bank and Gaza Strip. The president felt that he could not go to the Arabs in good faith to press them to make real peace with Israel unless he had such a commitment from Begin in advance. But Begin refused to give Carter this commitment.

So the president asked Begin for an alternative. "How do you propose that we move the negotiations toward peace?" Carter asked. While Begin and Carter talked publicly about their desire to reconvene the Geneva conference later that fall, they each understood the difficulties involved and the dangers of an ill-prepared conference.

Begin was cautioned in advance that Carter did not want to hear him recite Israel's history, its fears and hopes. The Americans had already heard that from Rabin and would not be overly impressed with a repeat performance. An impatient American president, anxious to score a foreign policy victory in the Middle East at a time when his other international initiatives were not going very far, wanted to hear a concrete suggestion on how to achieve diplomatic progress in 1977. During the working sessions, the president, who could be rather blunt, threw back some of the prime minister's own statements, such as the one about the new Israeli government's agreements to honor commitments made by earlier governments. To the Americans, this meant an acceptance of Resolution 242 and a willingness to make withdrawals on all three fronts. The West Bank and the Gaza Strip were open to negotiations, no matter how much historical or religious attachment Begin and others in his new government felt toward these areas, according to Carter. When it came to the biblical rationale for Israel's retaining the West Bank and the Gaza Strip, Begin did not get very far with the president, despite Carter's own religious background.

On security grounds, the Americans, including Carter, understood Israel's reluctance to withdraw from territories. But they convinced themselves that special "security arrangements" could be devised to compensate for such withdrawals. All sorts of ideas were floated. Position papers, briefing books, legal memoranda, and historical analyses were given to the president for his perusal. They were raised with Begin, who was ready to respond to detailed questioning on Israel's evaluation of additional electronic early warning stations, U.S. security guarantees, and even a formal U.S. military presence in Israel. Of course, massive U.S. economic and military assistance to Israel was promised.

But the Americans also told Begin that a restive Congress and public opinion would be unwilling to continue to supply Israel with $1 billion a year in military credits and and almost that much in economic assistance unless "some light can be seen at the end of the tunnel." The American public wanted to see an end to the Arab–Israeli conflict, Carter said. Begin agreed, but he made the point that Israel was not the obstacle preventing a peaceful resolution. The Arabs were not prepared to make peace with Israel, Begin said. He referred to recent statements by Sadat and Assad that under no circumstance would they accept a full normalization of relations with Israel. But Carter disagreed. He perceived a change in the Arab attitude. In any case, the president said Israel need not take anything on good faith alone. There would be ample time for testing during the phased implementation of the agreement. He urged Begin to take risks for peace, because the alternative would almost certainly be war.

It was this question—the Arab willingness to live in peace with Israel—that demonstrated the fundamental gap between U.S. and Israeli perceptions at that time. Israel remained skeptical of Arab peaceful intentions; the Americans were much less so. In fact, the consensus in the White House, the State Department, the National Security Council, the Pentagon, and the CIA was that there was never a group of Arab leaders more "moderate" than Sadat, Assad, Hussein, and Fahd. As Carter was saying all along, the time was ripe for a settlement that year.

Hovering over the talks was the same U.S. fear that had dominated earlier thinking in the Ford–Kissinger era: a diplomatic stalemate in the negotiations might lead to resumed hostilities, another Arab oil embargo, and possibly a superpower confrontation. Since the 1973 war, America's strategic thinking had centered around these fears. It was this concern that led Kissinger to go for partial accords. The appearance of progress could buy valuable time and prevent a war. And it was this fear that later revived step-by-step negotiations, despite the president's seemingly boxed-in desire for a comprehensive deal. But it was Sadat's dramatic journey to Jerusalem in November 1977 that forced a change in Carter's strategy.

Carter's foreign policy inexperience was painfully apparent as he unsuccessfully tried to reconvene the Geneva Middle East peace conference during his first year in the White House. Well intentioned but then still somewhat naive, Carter was saved from a major diplomatic setback by an eleventh-hour stroke of desperation by a less powerful but more experienced world leader—Anwar Sadat. Without Sadat's dramatic coup, Carter's effort to bring the Soviet Union into the peace process would likely have succeeded and resulted in a stalemate. Credit must also be given to Begin for recognizing the desperation of the moment and accepting Sadat's initiative.

When Carter began his second year in office, he tried to capitalize on the new peace breakthrough in the Middle East, bringing his administration more into line with America's new supportive, rather than dominant, role in the talks. The fact that Egypt and Israel were finally involved in direct, face-to-face negotiations allowed Washington to slip back temporarily into the sidelines somewhat. In terms of domestic politics, this new posture made life more comfortable for the administration, but, again, only temporarily. Still, this was important for the White House during 1978, a congressional election year.

The administration had tried to take as much credit as possible for the new hope in the Middle East. National Security Adviser Zbigniew Brzezinski said in early January 1978 that 1977 would be viewed by future historians as the year that saw the first important steps toward a comprehensive settlement.

Sadat and Begin, who recognized that they would have to deal with Carter for at least another three, and possibly even seven years, complimented the president by explaining that the United States had created an atmosphere conducive to the new peace initiative. It did neither Sadat nor Begin any harm to score points with the president, which is something they clearly did by volunteering such comments. But the Israeli and Egyptian leaders did not really believe what they then said. If anything, they managed to break through the worn-out barriers of the past, to avoid the even worse scenario of Soviet codominance with the United States implicit in the Carter administration's policies. Neither was very happy about America's willingness to allow radical Syrian, Soviet, and Palestinian voices to have a veto over their more moderate peace gestures, possibilities made very real in the American–Soviet joint communiqué that was issued on October 1, 1977.

After Sadat's trip to Israel, pollster Louis Harris confirmed what everyone in the United States knew: Sadat's popularity among Americans had risen dramatically. Harris said he had never seen such a remarkable surge upward, virtually overnight. Among Arab leaders, Sadat had always been one of the most popular in the United States, ranking right at the top with Jordan's King Hussein. Harris had his organization conduct a quick poll immediately after the Sadat–Begin talks had ended. More than twice as many Americans believed that Sadat really wanted to achieve peace with

Israel as compared to one year earlier. And this certainly made Sadat happy. Ever since he had decided to move away from the Soviet Union and toward the United States, the Egyptian president had been anxious to win new friends in America. No one could deny that his increased popularity and stature among Americans were very important and tangible rewards for his trip to Israel. Harris said that Israel's popularity also increased as a result of the Sadat mission. But Israel was already very popular; thus, the increase for Israel was considerably more marginal.

If Egypt played its cards correctly, it would have very little difficulty transforming its new popularity in American public opinion into more concrete results. For Egypt, almost as much as for Israel, the United States had become the main address for seeking economic, political, and military assistance. After reestablishing ties with Washington in the wake of the 1973 war, Sadat became increasingly aware of the fact that he would never really stand a chance of winning badly needed aid so long as Egypt was perceived as continuing in its hostile course against Israel. Political scientists have suggested that public opinion is eventually reflected in congressional roll calls. And this was another factor that must have played a part in convincing Sadat that it was worthwhile going to Israel. Sadat, who addressed a joint session of Congress during his visit two months after the 1975 Sinai II agreement was signed, had been wooing senators and representatives very methodically. The State Department was aware of the fact that the Egyptian leader personally received practically every U.S. congressman who visited Egypt after the Yom Kippur War, no matter how junior the legislator. Even though Congress was in recess during the dramatic developments surrounding his trip to Jerusalem, Sadat's support in Congress was strengthened significantly.

The question of increasing U.S. military assistance to Egypt was, of course, another matter. So long as Egypt and Israel remained in a state of war, many legislators in Washington were reluctant to supply offensive hardware to the Egyptians. Egypt already received so-called nonlethal equipment from the United States—C-130 transport planes, pilotless reconnaissance drones, communications equipment, and so on. The administration was also deeply involved in a program whereby the engines of Egypt's Soviet-supplied MiG-21 fighter bombers were being reconditioned in Europe with U.S. technological aid. Sadat knew that his country stood virtually no chance whatsoever of acquiring more advanced weapons from the United States so long as he and his regime remained implacably hostile toward Israel. Therefore, in weighing the success or failure of the Sadat visit to Jerusalem, one could not ignore the American factor. The Egyptian leader may have been condemned in much of the Arab world; he may have been criticized by the Soviet Union; he may not have won as much of a public shift in Israeli policy on key issues as he had hoped for; but there was no doubt that he had scored a remarkable success in America. And this was not to be scoffed at.

Sadat was also pleased to learn that American Jews had started to come around, to a large degree, to accepting his declared desire for peace at face value. For years, the Jewish community in the United States had been skeptical of Sadat's intentions. Hadn't he conspired with Syria to attack Israel on Yom Kippur? Could such a man ever be trusted? There was reason to believe that Sadat's giant step was partially motivated by his wish to see more American Jews accept him as a true man of peace. Just as his image had improved in Israel, so too had his popularity risen among American Jews. For two years before the journey to Jerusalem, Egyptian diplomats in the United States made strong overtures to key Jewish leaders in an effort to enlist their support. Egyptian officials, like many foreign diplomats based in Washington, believe that the American Jewish community is a highly influential factor in American political and economic life.

People were reassessing many of their former convictions. Maybe there really was a golden opportunity for a breakthrough. On the official level, Carter and his senior advisers were insisting that they were pleased by the Sadat initiative and its outcome. They had said that they had been promoting direct negotiations behind the scenes ever since they took office in January and were trying to take some credit for creating the climate for the visit. But the administration was pleased by the fact that Sadat and Begin agreed, at least in public, to continue their efforts to reach a comprehensive settlement at a reconvened Geneva conference. Begin and Sadat said there would be no effort to reach a separate agreement between Egypt and Israel.

At first, the administration said the trip would enhance prospects for reconvening in Geneva. But later it abandoned that course.

It must have been strange for Carter to sit home in November and watch the unbelievable happening in Jerusalem. Here he was, relaxing in the White House with his daughter Amy, watching and listening to Walter Cronkite, Barbara Walters, and John Chancellor. He, and especially some of his foreign policy advisers, must have felt somewhat left out. Apart from rethinking policy after history was made in Jerusalem, officials in Washington hoped that other Arab leaders could be coaxed to follow Sadat's lead. If Sadat could break through the psychological barriers of the past, maybe there was hope that other Arab leaders could do the same. That surely helped motivate Carter at Camp David.

Carter increasingly began to revert to his pro-Israeli rhetorical mode as the 1980 presidential campaign against his Republican challenger, Ronald Reagan, got into full swing.

"I am proud that fully half of the aid that our country has given Israel in the thirty-two years of her existence has come during my administration," Carter told the Democratic convention delegates at Madison Square Garden. "Unlike our Republican predecessors, we have never stopped or slowed that aid. And as long as I am president, we will not do so. Our commitment is clear: security and peace for Israel, peace for all the peoples of the Middle East."

Vice-President Walter Mondale similarly singled out Israel for special treatment. "Let me add a special word about Israel," he declared at the convention. "Israel is our friend, our conscience, our partner. Its well-being is in our moral, political, and strategic interests. I stand before you and say that the people of the United States stand by Israel—in this term, in the next term, and always."

The vice-president's words were carefully considered. They were largely designed to dissuade Israel's friends in the United States from accepting the apparently prevailing fear that a second-term Carter administration, one that would not have to worry about getting reelected, might unleash a heavy barrage of pressure against Israel.

"One of the abiding commitments of my administration is to a strong, secure Israel at peace with its neighbors, living within secure and recognized borders," Carter said. "There is no issue on which I have devoted more of my time and energy than to ensuring lasting peace between Israel and her neighbors. The Camp David accords are a historic step toward this ultimate result. Our policy in the Middle East has been and will continue to be guided by those accords."

Still, Carter was very much convinced of the need to continue the search for progress on the Palestinian front. Indeed, it was exactly this type of thinking, this near fixation on the centrality of the Palestinian question, that became the single most consistent aspect of his Middle East policies. There were dramatic shifts in American tactics during those four years in the White House, especially following Sadat's trip to Jerusalem. But Carter's fundamental objective of achieving a comprehensive settlement and resolving the Palestinian question remained the same. Since leaving office, Carter has continued to underline this approach in his many comments on Arab–Israeli diplomacy, especially in his *The Blood of Abraham*, published in 1985.

The former president has spent a considerable amount of time thinking about the Middle East. He organized a conference at Emory University in Atlanta in late 1983 to explore options for conflict resolution between

Arabs and Israelis. At that time, he said in an interview with me that he had phoned Menachem Begin on September 17, 1983, the fifth anniversary of the Camp David accords. "I called him and told him I was thinking about him that day," Carter said.

He added that he had always valued Israel as a special friend. "We always worked with mutual respect and, I think, recognized the value of that close relationship."

In March 1985, Carter elaborated on the matter of U.S. support for Israel. "It's not just that I and Nixon and Johnson and Ford and Truman have been committed in an official way to the security of Israel and to the prosperity of Israel and obviously to its existence and the hope that Israel can live in peace; that's not the totality of it. The essence of it is that the American people have this feeling," he said in another interview with me. "My neighbors in Plains and people in the Middle West feel that there is a natural, joint relationship between our two countries—a common purpose, a shared religious belief. . . . At the same time, this does not imply for me, as president, or for the American people, an approval of the policies of the Israeli government as they deal with the West Bank and the human rights of the Palestinians, with the invasion of Lebanon, with the tremendous bloodshed, and so forth. There can be sharp differences of opinion about those kinds of things."

12

Ronald Reagan and Israel

Ronald Reagan's relationship with Israel is defined by its contradictions. Despite the fact that during his first term he found himself in more direct conflicts with the Israeli government than had any previous president, there can be little doubt that his gut instincts are extremely pro-Israel. It has been said that Reagan tends to see foreign affairs as an extension of personal relationships rather than as an expression of abstract principles and that he tends to choose sides in conflicts more on the basis of friendship and loyalty than on any attempt at dispassionate appraisal of the conditions of the particular conflict. On this basis, his sympathies in any vital conflict will lie with Israel, for a lifetime of experience has led him to see Jews as part of the "us" group in his us-against-them mind set. For one thing, he has been exposed to many more Jews than Arabs, especially during his Hollywood days, and considers the professional, business, and social success of American Jews as confirmation of the grandeur of the American dream. In 1948, in a little-known incident, he resigned from the Lakeside Country Club in Los Angeles because it refused to admit Jews. Since he probably had no serious political aspirations at that time, the act cannot be dismissed as simply one of pragmatism. It is more consistent with Reagan's character that his resignation represented the act of a person who needed to be seen as someone who could be counted on to stand up for his friends.

Of course, many of Reagan's advisers do not see Middle East conflicts from the same perspective; indeed, some may not at all share Reagan's sense of greater affinity with Jews than with Arabs, for over the past decade many in the business community have come to know Arabs as intimately as Reagan knows Jews. Precisely how much tension is actually created by the clash of Reagan's tendency to formulate Middle East policies on the basis of personal loyalty and that of certain advisers who would prefer to view all foreign relations solely from the perspective of American interests—business as well as strategic—is virtually impossible to measure. But it is clear that Reagan approaches Middle East problems from the clear presumption that he is dealing with the fate of friends, both personal and national.

Still, it would be overly simplistic to cite Reagan's personal inclinations as solely responsible for his special relationship with Israel. Over the years, Reagan has certainly demonstrated a deft understanding of the American political process, and there can be little doubt that he understands the reality of Jewish influence in American political life. There is also a religious aspect to it; the Christian fundamentalism in which the president believes relies heavily on the Old Testament. And finally, from the other side, American Jewish leaders understand that Reagan's attempts to reestablish American military credibility abroad in the face of Soviet expansionism serve well the security needs of Israel.

These factors all came into play during a telephone call the president made on October 18, 1983, to Tom Dine, executive director of AIPAC, to thank the pro-Israeli lobbying organization for having urged members of Congress to support the president's interpretation of the War Powers Act in dispatching forces to Lebanon. "Frankly," Dine said, "we fought very hard because we thought that the United States was being tested. We thought you, as president and commander-in-chief, were being tested by the Syrians. And we felt very strongly that American resolve was appropriate here."

According to a transcript of the conversation made available to me, Reagan replied, "I believe you were right in what you figured out there— on both counts. And I certainly appreciate it. I know how you mobilized the grass-root organizations to generate support."

By his own account, this was an extremely rough period in Reagan's presidency and in his life. Large numbers of American soldiers—sent to Lebanon as peacekeepers—had been killed or maimed. The president confided that speaking with the parents, wives, and other relatives of these young men was the most difficult and painful experience he has had in the White House. Reagan, of course, felt a personal responsibility for having made the decision to send these men off to Lebanon.

During the course of the conversation with Dine, Reagan mentioned that he had spoken with the mother of a marine casualty the night before. "We've got to find a settlement there," the president said. "You know, I turn back to your ancient prophets in the Old Testament and the signs foretelling Armageddon, and I find myself wondering if we're the generation that's going to see that come about. I don't know if you've noted any of those prophecies lately, but, believe me, they certainly describe the times we're going through."

It was not the first time that Reagan had raised the specter of Armageddon in a conversation with a Jew. He had done so on several earlier occasions, including during the campaign in 1980. Early that year, Albert Spiegel of Los Angeles, a Jewish Republican activist of long standing who had established a personal relationship with the former California governor, organized a reception for some fellow Jews to meet Reagan in New York. Reagan addressed the questions most on their minds, beginning with Israel. "Israel is the only stable democracy we can rely on in a spot where Armageddon could come," he said. "The greatest responsibility that the United States has is to preserve peace—and we need an ally in that area."

Reagan, then a presidential candidate, went on to explain another basic reason why he has come to support Israel. "We must prevent the Soviet Union from penetrating the Mideast," he said. "The Nixon administration successfully moved them out; if Israel were not there, the U.S. would have to be there."

This hardline anti-Soviet posture—a constant feature that runs throughout Reagan's entire world view—has certainly been a significant factor in sustaining his support for Israel. Israel is in the American camp; many of the Arab states, led by Syria, are Soviet-backed.

It also helps explain why Reagan was the first president to formally authorize an enhanced strategic cooperation agreement with Israel, aimed at thwarting greater Soviet influence in the Middle East. For many years, there was close American–Israeli intelligence and military collaboration; what Reagan did was bring much, but by no means all, of it out of the closet. In the process, he demonstrated that he was prepared to risk upsetting the Arabs.

This attitude was very much evident when Reagan took the unusual step of writing a personal letter to Prime Minister Shimon Peres on December 12, 1984, to ask that Israel permit the establishment of several radio transmitters designed to overcome Soviet jamming of the Voice of America and the U.S.-funded Radio Liberty and Radio Free Europe. Reagan rarely wrote personal letters to the prime minister of Israel. It was significant that this one dealt with an operation aimed at promoting U.S. propaganda in the Soviet bloc. Israeli officials were forced to pay attention; normally such a matter would not have been raised at the highest level of the U.S. government.

"Dear Mr. Prime Minister," Reagan wrote:

I enjoyed our recent very productive talks here in Washington which I believe form the basis for continued close collaboration between the United States and Israel. I hope that our relationship, which is so important to the prospects for world peace and stability, will continue to broaden and deepen and find new means of expression to the mutual benefit of our peoples.

The president then got to the basic point of his message:

As [U.S.] Ambassador [to Israel Samuel] Lewis has undoubtedly explained, I have made the modernization and expansion of our international broadcasting capabilities one of my administration's highest priorities. As Israel is very well suited geographically to the development of such a capability, I hope that your government will give close and sympathetic consideration to our request for construction of radio relay facilities in Israel. I firmly believe that the western radios provide a priceless form of moral and spiritual support for those who are deprived of full national, civil, cultural, and religious rights in this regard. They serve our common purpose in letting the truth be known and in demonstrating to the peoples of the Soviet Union that we have not forgotten them.

It is fascinating to see how Peres responded. His December 31 reply shed some light on the complicated nature of the American–Israeli relationship.

"Dear Mr. President," Peres wrote. "Ambassador Lewis has handed me your letter of December 12, 1984." After several paragraphs expressing his appreciation of the friendship extended him and his state by the United States in general and President Reagan in particular, he wrote:

I have given careful consideration to your message concerning the importance you attach to the modernization and expansion of the U.S. international broadcasting capability. Indeed, I find myself in complete agreement with your determination to provide those deprived of the right to express a diversity of views with the opportunity to listen to it.

As you probably recall, in the past we have found it difficult to accommodate the request to establish a relay station in Israel. Even though the state of Israel may be geographically suited for that purpose, and we share the appreciation of the need, nevertheless the people of Israel are currently struggling with problems of historical significance that cannot but affect our judgment and freedom of action. Specifically, the fate of the world's third largest Jewish community—the one inside the Soviet Union. This community is deprived of any access to its homeland. Its spiritual existence is threatened as its very peoplehood is constantly oppressed. None of us can be certain that the construction of relay stations in Israel would not lead to further persecution of Jewish activities throughout the Soviet Union.

Yet, upon receipt of your personal approach, we have undertaken to reexamine our position. Based on our observation that the American commitment to the cause of Soviet Jewry and their right to emigrate has been strengthened under your leadership, our concern has somewhat diminished. We trust, Mr. President, that your own firm convictions, as expressed in our conversations, will yield further efforts that may ease the situation so seriously aggravated in recent months.

It is in the wake of these agonizing deliberations that I would propose an early meeting of American and Israeli experts in order to study the various dimensions of the project and the best avenues to further our mutual objectives.

The prime minister signed off: "With warmest season's greetings, sincerely, Shimon Peres." Three months later, Israel officially agreed that the stations could be built.

The president has also come to appreciate Israel because many of its most implacable enemies were also involved, together with the Soviet Union, in attempting to undermine U.S. interests in other parts of the world, especially in Central America. Israel, therefore, could partially thank the involvement of Libya and the PLO in Central America for resulting in a greater Reagan tilt toward Israel. "It's no coincidence that the same forces which are destabilizing the Middle East—the Soviet Union, Libya, the PLO—are also working hand in glove with Cuba to destabilize Central America, and I'd like to urge you to support this nation's efforts to help our friends in Central America," Reagan told the B'nai B'rith Anti-Defamation League in Washington on June 10, 1983.

There is no doubt that Reagan has also been motivated by the legacy of the Holocaust, despite his controversial decision in 1985 to go through with his visit to the Bitburg military cemetery in West Germany. The message has been repeatedly brought back home to him since entering the White House that Israel was established only after 6 million Jews perished during World War II. Every year, for example, he has participated in some ceremony commemorating the Holocaust. He seems genuinely moved, as does his wife Nancy. "The security of your safe havens, here and in Israel, will never be compromised," he promised some 20,000 Holocaust survivors at a ceremony in 1983.

But, while Reagan obviously has very positive feelings toward Israel, he has not been spared conflict with Israeli leaders. Since 1948, after all, every U.S. president has faced a basic dilemma in looking at the Middle East. How, on the one hand, can the United States demonstrate its strong support for Israel's security and well-being, while at the same time reaching out to the Arab world, where the United States also has important strategic, political, and economic interests? Reagan has been no exception.

There had been two previous times in American–Israeli relations when

Democratic administrations handed over responsibility of governing to a Republican president: in 1953, when Dwight Eisenhower succeeded Harry Truman, and in 1969, when Richard Nixon replaced Lyndon Johnson. Those transitions were recalled when Reagan succeeded Carter.

Eisenhower, while personally sympathetic toward Israel, was more concerned with process than with loyalty. When Israel, Britain, and France attacked Egypt in 1956 over the nationalization of the Suez Canal, he put enormous pressure on Israel to pull out of the Gaza Strip and Sinai; it probably represented the low point in American–Israeli relations.

Nixon, during the 1968 campaign against Democratic candidate Hubert H. Humphrey, received only about one-fifth of the Jewish vote. Politics being what it is, it came as no surprise when Nixon's secretary of state, William Rogers, unveiled a peace plan calling on Israel to withdraw from virtually all of the territories captured during the 1967 war.

Perhaps those memories combined to sober Israeli activists in the days following Reagan's election over Democrat Jimmy Carter.

Reagan entered the White House with a strong record of support for Israel, including attending rallies for Israel during the 1967 Six-Day War, when he was governor of California. Albert Spiegel of Los Angeles, in an interview with me, recalled Reagan's participation in one such event at the Hollywood Bowl. Spiegel, a former chairman of the Jewish Coalition for Reagan–Bush, has known Reagan for several years. "Though events moved swiftly so that the rally actually took place the day after the war ended, Governor Reagan got a standing ovation from the 30,000 people inside and outside the Bowl for his courage and friendship in speaking out before the war and for his stirring appeal on behalf of Israel's safety and security," Spiegel said. "I shall remember that speech for still another reason. On the day after the war ended, Governor Reagan already had anticipated problems that would be inherent in the peace process. He warned us then: 'Let us make sure no place is made at the bargaining table for the Russian bear.' "

Spiegel added: "I told Governor Reagan that day that I would not forget and that I would not let my people forget that at the time of our peril and concern he spoke out in our behalf and came to stand with us. More, I promised him that if some day I could help him in turn I would be happy to do so."

There were other actions taken by Reagan in California on behalf of Israel. In 1971, for instance, he was instrumental in getting the state legislature to pass—and he signed into law—a bill authorizing banks and savings institutions to buy and invest in Israel Bonds. "I am told that this was the first such law in the United States and was the model for like laws passed in other states which so dramatically enhanced the sales of Israel Bonds in this country," Spiegel said. Reagan was subsequently honored at an Israel Bonds dinner in Los Angeles.

He may never have actually visited Israel, but Reagan's campaign rhetoric in 1980 suggested to some of his more exuberant backers in the Jewish community that he would indeed emerge as a veritable Theodore Herzl in the White House. "Israel is not only a nation, it is a symbol," Reagan said on September 3, 1980, in an address before B'nai B'rith in Washington. "In defending Israel's right to exist, we defend the very values upon which our nation is built."

But even the purest of intentions do not automatically translate themselves into policy after the ballots are counted. Many presidents have learned this fundamental fact of governance. Reagan has been forced to make decisions and to take actions that he earlier would almost certainly have opposed. He also is not as free a man in the White House as he is on the campaign trail. There are the secretary of state, the secretary of defense, the national security adviser, the director of the CIA and numerous other aides, each of whom significantly shapes final decisions. And all of these advisers, powerful men and women in their own right, know that if their own personal convictions are not given weight in arriving at decisions, then options are no longer as limited as the options of top advisers once were; they can leak material to the press that can create a constituency for their own positions.

As a result, there have been good times and bad times in the Washington–Jerusalem relationship during Reagan's tenure.

Still, according to Michael Gale, a former White House liaison to the Jewish community, "basically the U.S.–Israeli relationship is better today than it was when Ronald Reagan took office, and that while, yes, there have been ups and downs, the fundamental bedrock relationship is better today. You're dealing in a democracy where both in Israel and the United States the press tends to play up the differences. But the two parties—United States and Israel—have found a way under President Reagan to deal with those differences, and to work them out through dialogue and communication, and a willingness to see the other side's views."

These conflicting pressures were obvious from the start of Reagan's presidency. He assumed office on January 20, 1981. By early February, he had agreed to enhance Saudi Arabia's F-15 jet fighters with offensive missiles, missiles specifically denied the Saudis by the Carter administration in 1978 when the F-15 sale was approved. Then, by early April, as he lay recuperating from a bullet wound in his chest at George Washington University Hospital, Reagan signed off on the even more controversial proposal to include sophisticated AWACS aerial surveillance aircraft in the package, thereby setting the stage for one of the most acrimonious periods in American–Israeli relations. The sale was eventually allowed to go through following a fifty-two to forty-eight vote in the Senate, but only after Reagan used an enormous amount of his personal political capital in bringing it about.

There were other decisions taken in 1981 that angered Israel. After Israeli fighter aircraft bombed the Iraqi nuclear reactor at Osirak in June of that year, for example, Reagan slapped a temporary embargo on aircraft shipments to Israel. There were also sanctions after Israeli aerial strikes against PLO targets in Lebanon that year. In December, another aircraft embargo was imposed after Israel formally extended its law to the Golan Heights, captured from Syria during the 1967 war. The two-week-old American–Israeli strategic cooperation agreement was suspended.

On February 15, 1982, less than two months later, the Knesset passed a special resolution by a vote of eighty-eight in favor, three opposed, and seven abstentions. It called on the United States "to refrain—in keeping with the president's declarations and the resolution of Congress—from . . . gravely imperiling Israel's security" by providing advanced military equipment, such as F-16 fighters and improved Hawk anti-aircraft missiles, to Jordan.

The following day, Begin, who loved to correspond with foreign leaders, especially the one in the White House, sent a secret letter to Reagan, a copy of which I have obtained. "This is a rare case in our free, democratic, and rather vociferous Parliament of nonpartisan consensus, and, in fact, a vote of national unity," Begin said. "It demonstrates, as stated in the Knesset resolution, the deep concern of our people and its elected representatives."

The prime minister then went into a personal attack against Secretary of Defense Caspar Weinberger, who had defended a new weapons sale to Jordan during an earlier visit to several Arab countries. "Permit me to say, Mr. President, that I do not understand why it was necessary for the secretary of defense to make his worrying statements, and, indeed, his anti-Israel declarations or, at least, innuendos, whilst he was visiting Arab countries, all of which, but for one, are in a state of war with us and are even preparing for war against us. But of course, if Secretary Weinberger sees fit to make such statements (so negative from our point of view) in such places, it is not for me to ask him to refrain from doing so, at least in the future."

Those earlier sanctions had stunned Israel—and especially Begin, who had such high hopes in Reagan's presidency—but they were mild compared to the tensions that erupted in the relationship during the siege of Beirut by Israeli forces in the summer of 1982. Very angry telephone calls from

Reagan to Begin in early August were important factors in persuading Israel to avoid plans to actually enter West Beirut. There was also extensive opposition within Israel itself to such a move, even from within army and the cabinet.

Later, there was very deep resentment in Begin's government when Reagan issued his September 1, 1982, Arab–Israeli peace initiative; Israelis were angry that Reagan was prepared to exploit Israel's very great dependence on U.S. military support for Israel to force changes in Israeli policy. Reagan lifted the plane embargo only after the signing of the ill-fated Israeli–Lebanese troop withdrawal agreement of May 17, 1983, an agreement that was eventually renounced by Lebanon under Syrian pressure when the marines left Beirut.

That readiness to impose military sanctions against Israel was a departure from the policies of Jimmy Carter, who had taken office in 1977 promising never to impose any "reassessment" of policy toward Israel along the lines of the Ford–Kissinger period. Carter, during the 1976 campaign, had vowed never to force Israel to accept an American position by threatening to cut off military aid. In fact, during an interview with me in 1983, the former president recalled that pledge. "We never deviated, as you probably know, from the record in our commitment to Israel," Carter said. "There were never any threats to Israel of withdrawal of our support, things of that kind, even though obviously on occasion, the policies of Prime Minister Begin and my opinion were quite at odds."

At the 1980 campaign meeting in New York organized by Albert Spiegel, Reagan, according to notes taken by *New York Times* columnist William Safire, said, "If there's one statement I'd like you to remember, it's this: In my administration, there will be no more betrayals of friends and allies by the United States." But the fact is that Reagan did not always fully live up to that commitment. Israel was not always treated like a close ally, as evidenced by both the public scolding and the periodic suspension of arms deliveries. During the AWACS debate, moreover, the president even made some serious indirect allegations against Israel, raising the specter of dual loyalty among American Jews. "American security interests must remain our internal responsibility," he said. "It is not the business of other nations to make American foreign policy."

Still, despite those strains, American–Israeli relations are indeed stronger today than before Reagan took office, by any standard. But, while Reagan is surely committed to Israel, he has clearly demonstrated a readiness to lean heavily on Israel if necessary.

During his first term, Reagan, much like Carter before him, was known to have become frustrated with those governing Israel, especially with its prime minister during much of that period, Menachem Begin. Reagan, according to close associates including Spiegel, sincerely came to believe that Begin had misled him on three separate occasions.

First, during their first White House meeting in September 1981, Reagan was said to have been convinced that he had struck a deal with Begin on the proper Israeli response to the administration's AWACS proposal then being considered by Congress. The president understood that Begin had reserved the right to oppose the sale, but only in a low-key, largely perfunctory fashion. Instead, Begin emerged from the White House to lash out bitterly, pubicly, and repeatedly against the sale during meetings with congressmen and American Jewish leaders, only a day after he left the White House. Privately, Reagan went so far as to accuse Begin of being a liar. White House officials resented Begin's statements; this was reflected in comments made by the chief military officer on the National Security Council, Major General Robert Schweitzer. "It is kind of interesting," he said, referring to the AWACS sale, "that the world leaders who stand for this sale number the president of the United States, Margaret Thatcher of the United Kingdom, and Anwar Sadat. And those opposed to it number Qaddafi, Mr. Begin, and Mr. Brezhnev." Reagan also felt that Begin should have accepted at face value repeated U.S. assurances that the sale would not adversely affect Israel's security, that Israel should have taken the president's word on the subject, given during his private meetings with Begin, as well as in his public statements. "We will make available to Israel the military equipment it requires to protect its land and people," Reagan had written in a letter to U.S. senators aimed at persuading them to support the AWACS transaction. "This proposed sale to Saudi Arabia neither casts doubt on that commitment nor compromises Israel's security."

Second, Reagan honestly believed assurance from Begin that Israel's initial drive into Lebanon in June 1982 was designed to clear out a twenty-five-mile security zone to protect Israel's northern towns and villages from PLO infiltration and rocket attacks. As a result, there was a relatively mild U.S. reaction to the invasion. When, instead, Israel moved its troops all the way to Beirut, the president was once again convinced that Begin could not be trusted. Subsequent Israeli explanations for the deeper incursion were never really accepted by Reagan.

Third, when Israel moved its troops into West Beirut immediately following the assassination of Lebanese President-elect Bashir Gemayel, in September 1982, despite earlier Israeli assurances to Washington, the president once again privately accused Begin and his government of being untrustworthy.

Begin, for his part, had also lost much of his earlier confidence in Reagan. He confided to associates that he had been amazed by the president's lack of sophistication in grasping the complexities of the Middle East. This was especially driven home to the prime minister during what turned out to be his last meeting with Reagan at the White House in June 1982, shortly after Israel went into Lebanon.

Begin, through the Israeli embassy in Washington, had asked for a private one-on-one session with Reagan. The prime minister did not want any aides present. The president, however, was always reluctant to have any such one-on-one meetings, especially in an area as complex as the Middle East. White House and State Department officials also were reluctant to see Reagan go head-to-head against someone as experienced and shrewd as Begin. They feared, for example, that Begin might actually win, or understand that he had won, some commitment from Reagan which would later be hard for the United States to implement. This was indeed what Begin sought. He felt confident that he could use his personal powers of persuasion to move the president closer to Israel's corner. Reagan, he felt, had positive feelings; his advisers were the source of problems for Israel. What the prime minister simply needed was a private opportunity to make Israel's case to the president. Begin felt it was so compelling that Reagan would have no choice but to come around.

But White House advisers were firmly against any such private exchange. In the end, the compromise agreement was to have the U.S. ambassador to Israel, Samuel Lewis, and the Israeli ambassador to the United States, Moshe Arens, sit in during the session in the Oval Office. They would take notes while Reagan and Begin spoke. They would be witnesses if any discrepancies later surfaced regarding what had actually occurred. As subsequently described to me by two of the participants during that meeting, this was how it went.

After the photographers, reporters, and sound crews were escorted out of the room, Reagan took several three-by-five cards out of his inner suit pocket. He then began to read a lengthy prepared statement outlining the U.S. position regarding the war in Lebanon. It was basically a rehash of several earlier public declarations. Begin listened politely until the president stopped reading.

At that point, the prime minister responded in a lengthy, impassioned, and off-the-cuff statement of his own, answering all of the points raised by the president. Begin did not have any notes with him, let alone a prepared statement. After he finished, he assumed Reagan would then react with additional comments, setting the stage for a serious exchange of views with one side perhaps having an impact on the other.

But, as if one cue, as soon as Begin concluded his opening statement, White House Counselor Edwin Meese appeared at the door to announce that the other members of the U.S. and Israeli delegations were already assembled in the Roosevelt Room across the corridor, waiting for the larger, more formal session to begin. The prime minister was stunned. He knew that there was little likelihood of getting the president to change his positions during such an expanded session. The entire visit to Washington would probably turn out to have been a waste of time.

Begin and Arens left the White House very disappointed. They suspected that Reagan's aides simply did not have enough confidence in their own president to let him enter into a free exchange with the visiting Israeli leader. Begin certainly had a warm personal feeling toward Reagan; he thought Reagan charming. But he lost almost all of his earlier respect for him after that incident. "This is the president of the United States of America," he told a close associate. "It's unbelievable."

It was this session at the White House in June, by the way, that in part influenced Begin's sharp rejection of Reagan's September 1 Arab–Israeli peace initiative. For the prime minister, that proposal, which caught Israel by surprise, was simply a refinement of the earlier Rogers Plan, aimed at forcing a nearly total Israeli retreat to the pre-1967 lines.

When Begin stepped down in September 1983, there was a collective sigh of relief in the White House, beginning with Reagan. Begin was a prime minister many American officials had learned to love to hate.

Reagan, for his part, resumed his traditional path of support for Israel. On September 14, 1983, he told reporters at the White House: "I believe, and this is not just our administration, that since 1948, when Israel became a nation, the policy of the U.S. government, under Democratic and Republican presidents and legislatures, has been one of alliance with Israel and assurance of Israel's continuation as a state. I don't think that any American administration would ever forsake Israel."

Today, Reagan finally seems almost comfortable with the language of Arab–Israeli diplomacy. During his years in the White House, he has met with many Israeli and Arab leaders. He has been briefed by top U.S. specialists. While he has spent much more time worrying about the state of the U.S. economy and relations with the Soviet Union, there can be no denying that the Middle East has often moved front and center in consuming his energies, especially during the ill-fated U.S. experience in Lebanon and the events surrounding the June 14, 1985, hijacking of a TWA airliner to Beirut.

Thus, Reagan was more at ease in discussing the Middle East during an interview on February 11, 1985, with reporters from *The New York Times*. He restated support for his 1982 peace initiative and, in response to a question, justified the need for the United States to continue arms sales to Saudi Arabia, and other Arab states. "I feel that we have to make the moderate Arab states recognize that we can be their friend as well as the friend of Israel," he said, summing up his basic approach since taking office. Referring to the Arabs, he said, "They're entitled to some defensive weapons." But he quickly balanced that by adding, "At the same time, we have assured Israel that we will never see them lose their qualitative edge to the point that they're endangered by anything we do." There seems little doubt that Reagan actually believes what he says.

Index